THE CIRCUS ANIMALS

Essays on W. B. Yeats

The Circus Animals

Essays on W. B. Yeats

A. NORMAN JEFFARES

STANFORD UNIVERSITY PRESS
Stanford, California
1970

Stanford University Press
Stanford, California

© 1970 by Felicity Anne Jeffares

Originating publisher: Macmillan and Co. Ltd, London, 1970

Printed in Great Britain

ISBN 0-8047-0754-5
LC 73-130824

TO BO JEFFARES

Contents

Acknowledgements

THIS volume contains essays originally published in various journals as well as the texts of lectures given at the British Academy, the William Andrews Clark Memorial Library, Los Angeles, and Trinity College, Dublin. The author is deeply indebted to Dr T. R. Henn for the suggestion that his copy of the Jack B. Yeats drawing might be used for the cover; the title of the book, drawn from Yeats's poem, was suggested by an ironic phrase about a ringmaster in a review by Mr Terence de Vere White in *The Irish Times*.

The author and publishers wish to thank the following, who have given permission for the use of copyright material:

The British Academy for 'Oliver St John Gogarty', the 1960 Chatterton Lecture, from *Proceedings of the British Academy*, vol. XLVI (1960).

The William Andrews Clark Memorial Library, Los Angeles, for 'Women in Yeats's Poetry' from *Homage to Yeats 1865–1965* (1965).

Poetry, for 'Yeats as public man', which appeared in *Poetry Chicago* (July 1960), as a review of *The Senate Speeches of W. B. Yeats*, ed. Donald Pearce (1960), and The Mercier Press, Professor Denis Donoghue and Radio Telefis Eireann for 'Yeats the public man', a broadcast talk in the Thomas Davis Lectures, which appeared in *The Integrity of Yeats*, ed. Denis Donoghue (1964).

Miss Margaret Willy and the English Association for 'Yeats, Critic', part of which appeared in 'The Criticism of Yeats', *English* (1965).

Miss Anne Butler Yeats for permission to reproduce the drawing by Jack B. Yeats used for the cover of *The Circus Animals*. This is reproduced from *A Broadside* for September 1913, published by E. C. Yeats at the Cuala Press, Churchtown, Dundrum, County Dublin.

Professor R. W. Zandvoort and Swets & Zeitlinger for 'Gyres in Yeats's Poetry', 'Poet's Tower' and 'Yeats's Mask': these essays originally appeared in somewhat different form under the titles 'Gyres in the Poetry of W. B. Yeats', 'Thoor Ballylee', and 'Yeats's Mask' in *English Studies*, June 1946, December 1967 and December 1949 respectively.

Foreword

THESE essays deal with W. B. Yeats; his father, John Butler Yeats; and one of his friends, Oliver St John Gogarty. The three men spent their formative years in Dublin and lived there at different times in their lives, though they felt the pull of the west of Ireland and experienced the pulsations of the further west. They worked intensely while valuing leisurely contemplation; they could match profundity with wit; and they delighted in beauty.

The city that educated them did not always have their love: but it made them – for all three were capable of the lively conversation that city compels – sceptical yet affirmative, creative yet mocking. Here is matter for speculation. It returns us, in their cases, to a contemplation of how their lives and work interacted: how the generalising and occasionally profound if impractical wisdom of John Butler Yeats, the wit, the renaissance exuberance and multiplicity of Oliver St John Gogarty, and the ceaseless work that underlies W. B. Yeats's stature as a poet, playwright and writer of prose, depended upon their upbringing, the effects of their friends' talk, their own reading, and the events of their lives, both public and private.

The dimensions of W. B. Yeats's reading were vast; his capacity to pluck what he needed from that often unorthodox reading is increasingly understood, as scholars find more and more sources for images or ideas in his poetry; and the more that is discovered the more interesting becomes the man who made the poetry. We are fortunate in having many of his manuscripts to examine, diaries to decipher, and letters to read, as well as some – alas increasingly few – of his friends to question, since he put so much of his own life into his poetry. This being so, it would seem perverse not to utilise our knowledge of the man, the currents of whose life swirl purposefully through his poems.

A poem may – and probably should – stand by itself as a work of art. It is probably upon our initial acquaintance with it that our subsequent pleasures and judgements depend: yet in some cases these reactions can be developed, deepened – or altered – as we attempt to find out what was in a poet's mind as he worked at a particular poem. In Yeats's case a poem itself might often alter considerably in the generally long process of composition, as he sought for more precise definition of a thought or an emotion, as he shaped with architectonic skill the organic growth of its lines, as he toiled at his exhausting yet exhilarating trade of matching rhyme and rhythm to image and idea. There are prose drafts, ideas for poems, in his diaries and manuscript books; as well as the many changes he made over the years in different editions of his published work. There are endless pages of unpublished revisions of verse. All these reveal the poet's fastidious mind at work experimenting and rejecting and finally selecting the words which capture what he has – compulsively yet controlledly – to say to himself and to his reader.

The man's own life was sufficiently interesting for him to use it as material: this fact, unpalatable as it may be to Professor Leavis, seems to justify our investigating how he matched the life and the work, for the work itself is the justification.

The complexity of the creative mind behind the poems – which continue to delight an apparently ever-increasing audience, notably of young people, challenges our curiosity, our own desire 'to get it all in order'. A suitable justification for this kind of investigation – into Yeats's attempt to search for what he called unity of being, to struggle to unite his life and art, and in so doing to serve his country and to speak for his generation – was made by Yeats himself on 9 March 1910 when, in a lecture entitled 'Friends of my Youth', he said

> I have no sympathy with the mid-Victorian thought to which Tennyson gave his support, that a poet's life concerns nobody but himself. A poet is by the very nature of things a man who lives with entire sincerity, or rather the better his poetry the more sincere his life; his life is an experiment in living and those that come after have a right to know it. Above all it is necessary that the lyric poet's life should be known that we should understand that his poetry is no rootless flower but the speech of a man.[1]

[1] Quoted by Joseph Rinsley, *Yeats's Autobiography – Life as Symbolic Pattern* (1968) p.

Lédenon, France   A. NORMAN JEFFARES
1969

PART ONE

Yeats's Mask

In his study of Yeats Professor Hough has written that in the period of the prose essay *Per Amica Silentia Lunae*, the three poems 'Ego Dominus Tuus', 'The Phases of the Moon', and 'The Double Vision of Michael Robartes', and *A Vision*, the poet's mind

> was much occupied at this time with what might be called the doctrine of the Mask. Many of his ideas seem to come to him initially as purely verbal suggestions, and we can perhaps discern its origin in the much earlier poem 'Put off That Mask of Burning Gold', a dialogue between lover and his mistress, in which she tries to discover whether it is his real self or his assumed mask that attracted her. Perhaps too we can see traces of it in Yeats's concern with the use of masks and the exclusion of individual character in drama. However that may be, in *Per Amica* he develops the theory that the poet in the act of creation is not seeking his self, but a mask which is his anti-self, the antithesis of all that he is in life.[1]

The tentative suggestions in this passage need implementation; they do not give a satisfactory answer to the problem which Professor Hough is presumably dismissing when he says 'However that may be' – the problem of how and when Yeats's ideas on the Mask began to exist. The theory advanced that, as many of Yeats's ideas seemed to come to him initially as verbal suggestions, the origin of this idea can be sought in an earlier poem, is misleading, because it gets us away from answering the problem with all the resources at our command. Yeats was such an introspective and self-centred poet, writing out of his moods and emotions as well as his intellect, that we cannot afford to neglect the biographical element in examining his ideas. To obtain this biographical element requires a close study of the poet's personal papers.

Inevitably, when seeking the first occurrence of this theory of the mask in Yeats's writings the researcher is brought face to face with the Donne-like quality of Yeats's mind, his frequent repetition of ideas and images at varying intervals of time, sometimes in slightly altered guise, a restless circling, or a swinging to and fro in antithetical movement.

[1] Graham Hough, 'A Study of Yeats' (conclusion), *The Cambridge Journal*, Mar 1949.

Indeed Yeats once said to his wife that he had spent the whole of his life saying the same thing in different ways.[2] His theory of the Mask is based upon antithesis in character, upon the differences between a natural and a chosen personality, upon contrariety. Joseph Hone suggested[3] that many instances in the early poems where shadows are described are a contributory part of the beginning of the theory. There is, however, a more direct very early statement of the idea in 'Quatrains and Aphorisms', included in *The Wanderings of Oisin and Other Poems* (1889):

> The child who chases lizards in the grass,
> The sage who deep in central nature delves,
> The preacher watching for the ill hour to pass –
> All these are souls who fly from their dread selves.

These lines do not differ essentially from the ideas of the *Per Amica* period.[4] Then, too, there is another early poem 'Fergus and the Druid', included in *The Countess Kathleen and Various Legends and Lyrics* (1892), in which Fergus gives up his kingdom and wants to learn the druid's dreaming wisdom.[5] This poem's theme is repeated later in the *Per Amica* period in 'The Saint and the Hunchback'[6] though with a slight twist. The later poem is more subtle, it opposes to the saint a figure who is balked of worldly achievement but can indicate it sufficiently to act as a foil for the saint, who, in Professor Hough's words, 'assumes his masks for ever, and puts away the world and reduces his life to a round of customary duties'. Apart from the more vigorous writing in the later poem and the images in it from *A Vision*, its saint closely resembles the earlier druid:

> Look on my thin grey hair and hollow cheeks
> And on these hands that may not lift the sword,
> This body trembling like a wind-blown reed.
> No woman's loved me, no man sought my help.[7]

---

[2] Cf. G. D. P. Allt, 'Yeats and the Revision of his Early Verse', *Hermathena*, Nov 1944.

[3] Joseph Hone, *W. B. Yeats 1865–1939* (1942) p. 114.

[4] Cf. Peter Ure, 'The Integrity of Yeats', *The Cambridge Journal*, Nov 1949, p. 85.

[5] WBY, *Collected Poems* (1950), p. 36.

[6] Ibid., p. 189. For yet another example of Yeats's repetition of imagery and ideas, this poem should be compared to stanza vi of 'Among School Children', op. cit., p. 242, where the 'taws' are taken over. In the manuscript version of the later poem 'Caesar Augustus' appeared, but may have been banished because he had been used in the early poem. Cf. the present writer's article, 'Yeats and his Methods of Writing Verse', *The Nineteenth Century and After*, Mar 1946, for the manuscript version in question.

[7] WBY, Collected Poems, p. 56.

How did the idea of the mask arise in Yeats's mind? It is clear that he met the idea of contrarieties in Blake, and dealt with their occurrence in his notes to the three-volume edition of Blake which Edwin Ellis and he produced in 1893. Blake's ideas were neatly summarised by Denis Saurat in his book *Blake and Modern Thought*:

> Without contraries there is no progression. Attraction and Repulsion, Reason and Energy, Love and Hate, are necessary to Human existence. From these contraries spring what the religious call Good and Evil. Good is the passive that obeys Reason. Evil is the active springing from Energy. Good is heaven. Evil is hell.[8]

Yeats fully agreed with this summing-up of Blake's thought, for he pencilled opposite this passage in his copy of *Blake and Modern Thought* the comment: 'I think there was no such thought known in England in Blake's day. It is fundamental in Blake.' This careful qualification, that Blake was the first in England to have these thoughts, suggests that Yeats was also acquainted with the idea in an earlier non-English source. Jacob Boehme seems very likely; Yeats had studied his work with some care. To Boehme, as to Blake, the idea of contrariety was fascinating, and he considered it of the first importance.[9] But the likelihood of these two authors acting as intellectual sources is not enough to answer 'how' Yeats's theories came about, though it does help to put the date back to the 1890s as another period when Yeats, if not then consciously occupied with the theory himself, would have been meeting it in these two authors.[10] But this brings us directly to the biographical approach.

In the first place, an element of observation is present. Joseph Hone demonstrated that the idea of self and anti-self, of contrary types of character, was germinating in Yeats's mind before the turn of the century; he drew on a letter from the poet to Mrs Shakespear, in which Yeats suggested that a character in one of her novels should be an actively athletic but passively artistic young man, and went on to stress the contradiction between Morris's table manners and the tact of the characters in his romances. Yeats used his observation of Morris again as an example of his ideas in *Per Amica Silentia Lunae*, and the collection there of other similar contradictory characters shows clearly that observed behaviour had its part in the formulation of Yeats's theory: a

---

[8] Denis Saurat, *Blake and Modern Thought* (1929) p. 19.
[9] Cf. H. L. Martensen, *Jacob Boehme* (1885) p. 77.
[10] Cf. WBY, *Autobiographies* (1955) p. 188, where he writes that his mind had begun to drift towards the idea of the mask during the 1887–91 period.

friend, who judged her friends harshly, writing indulgent comedies; an
actress, in private life 'like the captain of some buccaneer ship holding
his crews to good behaviour at the mouth of a blunderbuss', on the
stage the epitome of women who arouse pity; Synge, when ill, writing
of romantic daredevils; Landor, writing in calm nobility, raging in
savage passion; Keats making imaginary delights to compensate his
lack of luxury; all these instances of contraries excited Yeats.[11] Most of
all, however, he was influenced by Wilde, who told him that 'nothing
in life interests me but the mask'.[12] In Wilde he had an example of
poise that he envied, a blend of scholar and man of the world, a man
who had come from Dublin to London, and had become famous, who
made Yeats conscious of his own youthful sheepishness.[13]

Observation of others, however, is only a part of the idea, and a
small one, compared to Yeats's own experience, his personal feelings,
his needs. His development of the theory seems fundamentally bound
up with his deep interest in his own personality. This interest, and its
connection with the mask, can be seen most clearly in his 1909–12
diary.[14] Part of this has been published as *Estrangement: Being Some
Fifty Thoughts from a Diary kept by William Butler Yeats in the Year
Nineteen Hundred and Nine*, a Cuala Press edition of 1926,[15] and one of
the published sections reveals that Yeats, even at the age of forty-four,
was both shy and yet highly desirous of appearing to be in complete
command of himself:

> But when one shrinks from all business with a stranger and is unnatural with
> all who are not intimate friends, because one underrates or overrates unknown
> people, one cannot venture forth. The artist grows more and more distinct,
> more and more a being in his own right as it were, but more and more loses
> grasp of the always more complete world. Some day setting out to find know-
> ledge, like some pilgrim to the Holy Land he will become the most romantic
> of characters. He will play with masks.[16]

The unpublished sections of the diary show Yeats in a state of anxiety

[11] WBY, *Essays*, pp. 487 ff.   [12] WBY, *Autobiographies*, p. 205.
[13] WBY, unpublished material.
[14] Both R. Ellmann, *Yeats: the Man and the Masks* (1948; rev. edn 1961) chs. 6–9, and
the present writer, *Yeats: Man and Poet* (1949; rev. edn 1962) chs 3, 5–8, have suggested
the importance of *John Sherman* (1891) and of the later Michael Robartes and Owen
Aherne, who represent in more complex fashion Yeats's self-dramatisation, Robartes the
mystical element, Aherne the formal.
[15] Republished in a large edition by Macmillan in 1936. This contains an essay, 'The
Death of Synge', previously published by the Cuala Press in 1928 as *The Death of Synge
and Other Passages From An Old Diary*; this is also taken from the diary of the period
1909–12.   [16] WBY, *Estrangement*, p. 11.

caused by the conflicting claims which his roles as poet and as man of action were making upon him. After 1902 he had taken on the organisation of the Irish theatrical movement, and his output of verse fell as a result of his venturing into a much fuller life, one directed by more practical aims than before. The poem 'All Things can tempt Me from this Craft of Verse' reflect some of this inner struggle. Yeats had ceased to live a life dominated by poetic aims, and he was worried:

> Am I perhaps going against Nature in my constant attempt to fill my life with work? Is my mind as rich as in idle days? Is not perhaps the poet's labour a mere reflection? If he seeks purity – the ridding of his life of all but poetry – will not inspiration come? Can one reach God by toil? He gives himself to the pure in heart. He asks nothing but attention.[17]

In a later entry the masks are becoming important:

> I have been looking at some Venetian costumes of the sixteenth century as pictured in the mask. All fantastic bodily form hidden or disguised. . . . Life had become so leisured and courtly, that men and women dressed with no thought of bodily activity. They no longer toiled much. One feels that if they still fought and hunted their imagination was not with these things. Does not the same thing happen to our passions when we grow contemplative and so liberate them from use. They also become fantastic and create the strange life of poets and artists.[18]

Another entry shows how intensely the contradictions in his own character affected Yeats:

> I see always this one thing, that in practical life . . . the Mask is more than the face. I believe that I am speaking with more self-condemnation than self-defence when I say it. There are moments of life when one must say 'Such and such an act proves such and such a man to be a cad or a fool' and not 'such and such a man has shown himself by this or that good action to be neither cad nor fool so why did he do this?' Then one must say 'such and such a person could never have done such and such a thing' even though one's imagination suggests an endless array of circumstances in which anyone might be moved to do anything. Thus one must continually feel and believe what one's reason denies. I am so unfortunate that I can only conceive of this as a kind of play acting. I feel no emotion enough to act upon it, but faint lyrical emotion, which only affects life indirectly. Then there is the difference that words are with me a means of investigation rather than a means of action. O masters of life give me confidence in something even if it be my own reason. I can never believe in anything else now for I have accused the impulses of too many sins. I know that reason is almost a blaspheming thing, a claim to infinity of being, while we are limited social creatures, truly artificial. Twenty, no, a hundred times, if I had acted upon impulse and against reason, I should have gone from

[17] WBY, diary entry, 22 Sept 1919. [18] WBY, diary entry, 27 Oct 1909.

my world. The passionate man must believe he obeys his reason. Reason is the stopping of the pendulum, a kind of death. Life is a perpetual injustice.[19]

Two more quotations reveal more of Yeats's inner doubtings and how he was unable to rationalise any experience directly. The concluding note of the first passage is still emotionally subjective and dissatisfied:

To-night as I sat in idleness, my eyes too tired to read or write, I saw plainly how I could not only change the constitution of the United Arts Club so as to make the club more vigorous but . . . I was triumphant. I saw before me victory over those who least understand the manhood of mere art. Then I remembered that the renunciation of the artist is of those things which in others are virtue, and I did not go to find the man I would have had to persuade. Why have I these faculties which I cannot use? I know I have them and I know they are the chief temptation of life. It is easy to give up the thought of wealth and domestic life even, but it is hard to give up those generalizations through which the will flings itself upon the world, those gleams of future victory, that come to one as though one cried aloud, all that makes one, for a moment, of the race of the eagles. Did the first of us all hate the kindness that kept him from the oblivion of activity?[20]

Later, however, he came to a provisional conclusion, a temporary crystallisation of his views on the use of the Mask:

I think all happiness depends on having the energy to assume the mask of some other self; that all joyous or creative life is a rebirth as something not oneself – something created in a moment and perpetually renewed; in playing a game like that of a child where one loses the infinite pain of self-realisation, a grotesque or solemn painted face put on that one may haste from the terrors of judgment. An imaginative saturnalia that one may forget reality.[21] Perhaps all the sense and the energies of the world are but the world's flight from the infinite blending beam.[22]

The poem from The Player Queen, to which Professor Hough refers as a possible verbal source for the ideas on the Mask, is written down in the Diary immediately after two passages where Yeats – in a letter to one of his friends (Robert Gregory) which was never sent (explaining

[19] WBY, diary entry, Aug 1910.
[20] WBY, diary entry marked section 71.
[21] This thought can be found in 'The Grey Rock'. Collected Poems, p. 115, where, as J. Bronowski has pointed out, in The Poet's Defence (1939) p. 233, Yeats avoids an end by escaping to his imaginative saturnalia:
> And she with Goban's wine adrip
> No more remembering what had been
> Stared at the gods with laughing lip.
[22] WBY, diary entry marked section 104.

his attitude to a crisis which had arisen over an apparent insult given to his friend's mother by Gosse) – wrote:

I have understood that I am trying to put myself right with myself even more than with you. I want you to understand that once one makes a thing subject to reason, as distinguished from impulse, one plays with it, even if it is a very serious thing. I am more ashamed because of the things I have played with in life than of any other thing. All my moral endeavour for years has been an attempt to recreate practical interest in myself. I can only conceive of it as a kind of acting.

After a week he applied this particular analysis to general life, while denouncing generalisation at the same time:

Why do I write all this? I suppose that I may learn at last to keep to my own in every situation in life. To discover and create in myself as I grow old that thing which is to life what syle is to letters – moral radiance, a personal quality of universal meaning in action and in thought. I can see now how I lost myself. 'I must have been trying to recreate in myself the passion' I wrote. Yes, but for me they must flow from reason itself. My talent would fade if I trafficked in general standards and yet Punchinello is ancient. They dug up a statue of him among the ruins of Rome. Is not all life the struggle of experience, naked, unarmed, timid, but immortal, against generalized thought, only the personal history in this is the reverse of the world's history. We see all arts and societies passing from experience to generalization whereas the young begin with generalization and end with experience, and that is to say not what we call the 'results' which are generalizations but with its presence its energy. All good art is experience, all popular art generalization.

Other questions remain. Why should Yeats's introspective interest in his personality have led him to the Mask? Or, why was he interested in the idea of contraries? Or, why should we find him developing the theory during the second decade of this century? From his youth onwards Yeats was both sensitive and proud. He had the necessary histrionic ability to make use of his indecisive, often timid nature. For instance, his Irish sense of pride at being different from and indeed feeling superior to his English schoolfellows at the Godolphin School in Hammersmith was countered by his sense of physical inferiority. He attempted to overcome this defect by acquiring an excess of unusual vigour, a natural defence for a delicate child to adopt. He took care not to appear out of breath after running. Having fallen off a diving-board by mistake, he thence dived from greater heights than his fellows and used to make himself swim under water, pretending not to be out of breath when he emerged. His great triumph was the winning of a cup for running, for this was a demonstration that he could do the things the others valued. All these activities arose from his attempts to mould himself differently, to reverse his natural bent. And yet, paradoxically, he thought while at the school that he would become a famous man but in a way which would be different from the commonplace ambitions of the other boys; he felt he must dedicate himself to an end worthy of an artist's son. John Butler Yeats had probably contributed to this division within his son, telling him when he was a child in Sligo that he must try to do well all the things the Pollexfens – his mother's people – respected, thus indicating the need to counterbalance the dreaming intellectual strain of the Yeats line with some of the activity of the Pollexfens.[23]

As Yeats grew older he developed his capacity to play a part. He found Hamlet 'an image of heroic self-possession for the poses of childhood and youth to copy, a combatant of the battle within myself'; he even adopted, when at the School of Art in Dublin, an artificial stride in memory of Hamlet. At about this time, when the Yeats family was living at Howth, he had begun to imagine himself as a Manfred, an Alastor, or an Athanase; and he acted the parts in his own poems aloud to himself. When he met Maud Gonne in 1889 and fell in love with her there was need of another role. She was obviously one of his Shelleyan heroines, but was he a suitable hero, shy and poor as he was? He saw a copy of *Tristan of Lyonesse* upon her table, and when she told him she wanted a play to act in Dublin, he told her he wished to become an Irish Victor Hugo, and offered to write *The Countess Kathleen* for her. He had read some bad verse-translations of Hugo when at school but, writing long afterwards in his unpublished autobiography, he wondered whether he had been wholly sincere in telling her he wished to emulate Victor Hugo; but he had seen the book on her table along with *Les Contemplations*: 'besides, it was natural to commend myself by a very public talent, for her beauty as I saw it in those days seemed incompatible with private intimate life.'[24] Elsewhere he wrote: '. . . I was sedentary and thoughtful; but Maud Gonne was not sedentary.' At their first meeting he had told her of his hopes for a new and great Irish literature founded on the old legends. At the time he was collecting material in the British Museum for his *Fairy and Folk Tales of the Irish Peasantry*, and for his *Representative Irish Tales*, and his mind had by then begun, he tells us in *Autobiographies*,[25] to drift towards the idea of the Mask, which convinced him that every passionate man 'is, as it

[23] See 'John Butler Yeats', below, p. 121.   [24] WBY, unpublished material.
[25] WBY, *Autobiography*, p. 188.

were, linked with another age, historical or imaginary, where alone he finds images that rouse his enemy'. But his love for Maud became intertwined in his hopes for Ireland; was she not the living embodiment of beauty and did she not represent the person of Ireland, all the young grace and old wisdom of Cathleen ni Houlihan? She turned his attention from dreaming of a heroic age to the everyday realities, some of them, it must be admitted, fantastic enough, of revolutionary politics. Such was his love for her that he suppressed dislike of some aspects of her personality in order to worship the ideal qualities his imagination saw in her, to gaze upon her from behind the mask the great love poets, Dante and Petrarch, had worn before him.[26] His love was not returned by Maud, though she valued his friendship, and he strove all the more to please and serve her, the poetic, thoughtful side of him, however, often despising the man of action who had begun to emerge in the shy youth:

> All the while I worked with this idea of founding societies that became quickly or slowly everything that I despised, one part of me looking on mischievous and mocking, and the other part spoke words which were more and more unreal as the attitude of mind became more and more strained and difficult.[27]

Yeats grew disillusioned in love and politics about the turn of the century:

> In our age it is impossible to create as I had dreamed, an heroic and passionate conception of life, worthy of the study of men elsewhere and in other lands, and to make this conception the especial dream of the Irish people.[28]

The masks were thrown aside, and in his diary the mask of love was turned inside out after he had received the news of Maud Gonne's marriage to John MacBride:

> My dear is angry, that of late
> I cry all base blood down,
> As if she had not taught me hate
> By kisses to a clown.[29]

His adoration of Maud, only apparently uncritical for many years, had lasted so long because he had compelled it to take the shape of a mask: much later he was to call his relationship to her of 1897

> a miserable love affair that had but for one brief interruption absorbed my thought for years past, and would for years yet. My devotion might as well

---

[26] Cf. WBY, *Dramatis Personae* (Dublin, 1935; London, 1936) p. 49: 'I thought one woman whether wife, mistress or incitement to platonic love, enough for a lifetime.'
[27] WBY, *Essays and Introductions* (1961) p. 249.   [28] WBY, diary entry, Mar 1909.
[29] WBY, unpublished poem included in the 1909–12 diary.

have been offered to an image in a milliner's window, or to a statue in a museum, but romantic devotion had reached its extreme development.[30]

But even after her marriage in 1903 he continued to see love as the province of the mask:

> It seems to me that true love is a discipline, and it needs so much wisdom that the love of Solomon and Sheba must have lasted for all the silences of the scriptures. Each derives the secret self of the other, and, refusing to believe in the more daily self, creates a mirror where the lover or the beloved sees an image to copy in daily life; for love also creates the mask.[31]

The reason for Yeats's interest in the mask after he had apparently left romantic ideals of life behind was that he had vacillated to another extreme in his desire for a practical life. Up to the end of the nineteenth century his life had in many ways been very unreal, and in facing a fuller life he needed to acquire a new manner. He knew that the early devotion had been more literary than literal:

> That had she done so who can say
> What would have shaken from the sieve?
> I might have thrown poor words away
> And been content to live.[32]

For the new business of living, where all things could tempt him from his craft of verse, he had a double-edged gift of extreme sensitivity:

> I cry continually against my life. I have sleepless nights, thinking of the time that I must take from poetry – last night I could not sleep – and yet, perhaps, I must do all these things that I may set myself into a life of action and express not the traditional poet but that forgotten thing the normal active man.[33]

His concern with his manner is almost adolescent and reveals much inner uncertainty, as well as an ability to remodel himself as a human being, a degree of plasticity which is so unusual and extraordinary – what other poet has cried out in old age 'Myself must I remake',[34] and carried out the change of style so effectively? His interest in the Irish theatre doubtless acted as a stimulus in his forties:

> There is a relation between discipline and the theatrical sense. If we cannot imagine ourselves as different from what we are and assume that second self, we cannot impose a discipline upon ourselves, though we may accept one from others. Active virtue as distinguished from the passive acceptance of a current code is therefore theatrical, consciously dramatic, the wearing of a mask.[35]

The need was deeply felt; he lacked control over himself, as an entry

30 WBY, *Dramatis Personae*, p. 18.
31 WBY, *Estrangement*. See also *Autobiographies*, p. 464.
32 WBY, *Collected Poems*, p. 101.   33 WBY, *Estrangement*, p. 109.
34 WBY, 'An Acre of Grass', *Collected Poems*, p. 347.   35 WBY, *Estrangement*, p. 87.

in his diary, probably written after his visit to Paris in 1908, indicates:

> The other day in Paris I found that for days I lost all social presence of mind through the very ordinary folly of a very ordinary person. I heard in every word she spoke ancient enemies of vanity and sentimentality and became rude and accordingly miserable. This is my worst fault rooted in ♂♄☽). I must watch myself carefully recording errors that I may become interested in their cure perhaps I ought [to] seek out people I dislike till I have conquered this petulant combativeness. It is always inexcusable to lose self-possession. It always comes from impatience from a kind of spiritual fright of someone who is here and now more powerful even if only from stupidity. I am never angry with those in my power. I fear strangers and I fear the representatives of the collective opinion and so rage stupidly and rudely exaggerating what I feel and think.

In the following January he was at a meeting of the Arts Club and managed to restrain himself enough not to use arguments to answer something that was said, afterwards commenting in his diary:

> Logic is a machine, one can leave it to itself; unhelped it will force those present to exhaust the subject, the fool is as likely as the sage to speak the appropriate answer to any statement, and if the answer is forgotten somebody will go home miserable. You throw your money on the table and you receive so much change. Style, personality, deliberately adopted and therefore a mask is the only escape from the hot-faced bargainers and the money changers.[36]

A mask could therefore be employed as a protection against irritation, as well as against logic, for logic employed against Yeats must usually have caused him irritation. Another entry in the diary is frank:

> I had to subdue a kind of Jacobin rage. I escaped from it all as a writer through my sense of style. Is not our art made out of the struggle in one's soul. Is not beauty a victory over one's self.

Gradually the idea was worked out:

> I began in, I think, 1907, a verse tragedy, but at that time the thought I have set forth in Per Amica Silentia Lunae was coming into my head, and I found examples of it everywhere. I wasted the best working months of several years in an attempt to write a poetical play where every character became an example

---

[36] His father disliked logic too, but he knew how to play on his son's dislike of it. See John Butler Yeats, Letters, p. 168, where he writes: 'I have no doubt you will do nothing illogical, but it is better to be illogical than INHUMAN. To be sure a Frenchman will never be illogical. It is their pride in business and in everything; and it is a poor kind of pride and belongs to a people who aim at instructing the world and succeed in being rhetorical and eloquent and always charmingly lucid – yet they might do better – if their poetry was greater——The Frenchman is most charming when he is thinking about others, and so he works and lives and writes in the bondage of logic. Victor Hugo gloried in the servitude – and was splendidly ostentatious about it, it delighted his countrymen, and amazed other people, its naïveté was astonishing – the naïveté of logic not the naïveté of the feelings.'

of the finding or not finding of what I have called the Antithetical Self; and because passion and not thought makes tragedy, what I made had neither simplicity nor life. I knew precisely what was wrong and yet could neither escape from thought nor give up my play. At last it came into my head all of a sudden that I could get rid of the play if I turned it into a farce; and never did I do anything so easily, for I think that I wrote the present play in about a month.[37]

It appeared in various forms in *Per Amica Silentia Lunae*, the poems, and *A Vision*. Yeats had needed experience of the reverse of the masks before he could understand their function in his life and dogmatise about them accordingly. If in the later poetry they do not appear quite so often they are none the less theatrically effective. In 'Meeting' there is probably a memory of the contrary passions which underlay that early devotion, cause in its day of so much beautiful love poetry:

> Hidden by old age awhile
> In masker's cloak and hood
> Each hating what the other loved,
> Face to face we stood.[38]

The simplicity of these lines returns us once more, as so often in Yeats, to Blake, and reminds us of how eagerly Yeats read and enjoyed the contrariety of Blake's poetry.[39] And Yeats himself still fought the struggle, as Professor Hough has said, to the end of his days, but with moments, of course, when he had lived so long behind a particular mask that it had worn away and the features beneath it still bore its shape. The masks gave him the necessary cover he required for his changes; and he insisted that 'there is always a living face behind the mask'. He saw in very active natures a desire to pose, or if the pose had become a second self 'a preoccupation with the effect they are producing'. Therein lay the danger of the mask.

[37] WBY, *Plays in Prose and Verse* (1922) p. 429.

[38] WBY, *Collected Poems*, p. 314. In the Introduction to *Wheels and Butterflies* (1934) he wrote: 'Young, we discover an opposite through our love; old, we discover our love through some opposite neither hate nor despair can destroy, because it is another self, a self that we have fled in vain.' Text from *Explorations* (1962) p. 378.

[39] See his *Letters*, p. 758, where he describes in a letter to Olivia Shakespear of 2 Mar [1929] a dream (which became the poem 'Crazy Jane Grown Old looks at the Dancers', *Collected Poems*, p. 295) and adds, 'I suppose it was Blake's old thought "sexual love is spiritual hate".' Again, in *On the Boiler* (1939) p. 22, he comments that Heraclitus was in the right:

'Opposites are everywhere face to face, dying each other's life, living each other's death. When a man loves a girl it should be because her face and character offer what he lacks, the more profound his nature the more should he realise his lack and the greater be the difference. It is as though he wanted to take his own death into his arms and beget a stronger life upon that death.'

Yeats, Public Man

W H E N Yeats wrote of his twenties as 'crammed with toil' he was referring to more than stitching and unstitching of lines, more than reading Gaelic legends or occult philosophy. For in his twenties he was struggling against shyness, battling for self-possession, and driven by a desire to be able to play with hostile minds as Hamlet played. In his late teens he had joined a club founded by Charles Oldham and had begun to practise oratory at its meetings, reliving them afterwards, going over and over his own words and getting the wrong ones right. Then he joined a Young Ireland Society presided over by John O'Leary and made more speeches there. What he learned of public speaking in these two societies in Dublin was reinforced in London by Madame Blavatsky's advice when, after his stumbling attempt at a speech in the Theosophical Society, she made him throw away his notes and 'say his say'.

During his membership of the Young Ireland Society he formed an idea of bringing Protestant and Catholic elements in Ireland together in a national literature. This literature was to make Ireland beautiful in the memory and yet be freed from provincialism by rigorous criticism. This aim went further than his father's Home Rule beliefs and was influenced by John O'Leary; it was part of his developing independence.

Public men are made, not born: when a born poet decides to become a public man his struggle has a peculiar intensity about it, for he must manage two personalities, at times divergent in their aims and interests. And this pull between public, political life and private, literary life is part of the conflict that raged incessantly within Yeats throughout his life. A late poem puts it strongly:

> How can I, that girl standing there,
> My attention fix
> On Roman or on Russian
> Or on Spanish politics?
> Yet here's a travelled man that knows
> What he talks about,

And there's a politician
That has read and thought,
And maybe what they say is true
Of war and war's alarms,
But O that I were young again
And held her in my arms![1]

Love, literature and politics were all part of Yeats's being. He had an immense capacity to love and serve; his creation of a literary movement arose out of his desire to show his love of Ireland by serving her publicly: but there was also a parallel, personal reason for this patriotic work. As a boy and in his teens he had dreamed of one great love, a Shelleyan heroine, whose wild beauty he would sing with all the tragic hopelessness of a Pre-Raphaelite knight: all would be for her approval, all in her service. At the age of twenty-three he met Maud Gonne and, as he wrote in a diary, the trouble of his life began. She was beautiful, she was wealthy, and she was a revolutionary nationalist. He fell in love with her and at once sharply experienced the tension caused by the conflicting claims of a private literary life and a public, political one. Her beauty seemed to him incompatible with private, intimate life. She was a public figure; she enjoyed publicity and he felt he must commend himself to her by a public talent, by showing her that he also could serve Ireland publicly. He began to translate his aims for a literary renaissance into action; he wrote *The Countess Kathleen* for Maud Gonne and in the lull that followed Parnell's death in 1891 he formed an Irish literary society in London, and followed this up by establishing the National Literary Society in Dublin. His career as a public man had begun. His attitude to it was similar to his search for some certainty about the supernatural, for it was touched with an innate scepticism.[2] Yet this action, created out of crusading conversational committees, was not sufficiently dynamic for Maud Gonne's taste. Though she helped to form branches of the National Literary Society in country towns, her interests were primarily political. She liked more obvious action than the literary movement seemed to offer; she liked visible results; she involved herself in the cause of evicted tenants, and then in the work of the Irish Republican Brotherhood and the '98 Association, with both of which Yeats became associated.

---

[1] WBY, 'Politics', *Collected Poems*, p. 392.
[2] A passage in 'Poetry and Tradition', *Essays and Introductions*, p. 249, quoted above, p. 11, describes how the societies he founded became everything he despised, and how part of him looked on, mischievous and mocking, while the other part spoke words which became more and more unreal, as his attitude of mind became more strained and difficult.

Yeats was extending his dreams. He had taught himself to speak in public, his first effective performance taking place at the Thesophical Society after he accepted Madame Blavatsky's advice and spoke without his notes.[3] Though public speaking was an ordeal at first he became more proficient and after his apprenticeship in the Contemporary Club and the Young Ireland Society in Dublin, and at gatherings in William Morris's house, he was ready for public life. He thought that a man 'must know to speak in Ireland just as in old times he had to carry a sword'. As President of the '98 Association he attempted to heal the split between Parnellites and anti-Parnellites. He accompanied Maud Gonne on her speech-making tours; her beauty and passionate oratory swayed crowds; and he was fascinated, yet deeply disturbed, by the spectacle. He found these months, he said later, the worst in his life. Public speaking did not come easily: he rehearsed his speeches and went over them again and again afterwards to improve them. In private conversation he could easily lose his temper, but in the various committees of nationalist and literary societies where 'the technical forms' give him time to deliberate he was very effective indeed.

During the nineties Yeats was withdrawing from Dublin Unionist society, against which he had, as he wrote in his unpublished autobiography, 'a blind anger'. This meant excluding himself from the houses where his family was welcome, and, instead, acting the role of nationalist with vigour, even rolling up red carpets laid to welcome vice-royalty to Dublin. His shyness and timidity lessened; but his sensitivity increased. The violence that developed among the rioting Dublin crowds during Queen Victoria's Jubilee brought home to him the ultimate responsibility of his own role: he writes of this in *Autobiographies*,[4] describing how Maud Gonne and he had come from the City Hall to the National Club in Rutland Square and found a great crowd in the street which surrounded them and followed them. Then the crowd began to stone the windows of houses decorated in honour of Queen Victoria's Jubilee. When Yeats tried to restore order he found he had lost his voice 'through much speaking at the Convention'. He records how he could only whisper and gesticulate, and thus freed from responsibility shared the emotion of the crowd, seeing Maud Gonne's exultation as she walked 'with her laughing head thrown back'.[5]

[3] See *Lady Gregory's Journals*, ed. Lennox Robinson (1946) p. 263.
[4] WBY, 'The Stirring of the Bones', *Autobiographies*, pp. 367-8.
[5] See p. 86 for a full quotation of the passage.

Responsibility thrust itself upon him in the meetings of the I.R.B.
also when he and Maud Gonne argued long – and successfully – against
the murder of a man called O'Donnell. They subsequently left this
organisation and Maud Gonne joined Arthur Griffith's Sinn Féin movement, her nationalist fervour unquenched. Yeats, however, still hoped
to win her from politics, to the quietude of a life among artists and
writers who reverenced beauty. He realised that 'the political movement she was associated with, finding it hard to build up any fine lasting
thing, became content to attack little persons and little things'.[6] But he
was still searching for self-possession, still torn between his public and
his personal aims. His surrender, as he later put it, to the artist's chief
temptation, 'creation without toil', led him to one final gesture as
devoted nationalist and devoted lover. He wrote *Cathleen ni Houlihan*
for Maud Gonne, and she played the title role in it in the National
Dramatic Society's production of 1902. This was explosive material
which stirred its audience deeply: in later life Yeats wondered

> Did that play of mine
> Send out certain men the English shot?[7]

Stephen Gwynn, writing years afterwards of the first production of
this play, said that he had never seen an audience so moved, and that
he had asked himself whether such plays should be produced unless one
was prepared for people to go out to shoot and be shot.

This play was a final gesture because Maud Gonne married John
MacBride in 1903, and Yeats's part of *cavalier serviente* was suddenly
ended. While Yeats was to write some magnificent poetry about her in
this period of disillusionment he was also to learn how to express strong
hate rather than devoted love, turning to a satiric portrayal of the people
for whom both he and Maud Gonne had been working. Already dis-
concerted by learning what mob violence meant – for Maud Gonne
would have taught 'to ignorant men most violent ways' – and by re-
garding the nationalist politicians he had met as ineffective, he was to
become increasingly bitter as he discovered that his positive aim, to 'be
counted one with Davis, Mangan, Ferguson', was not likely to be
understood or appreciated by the philistines whose power was as strong
as that of the nationalist politicians was weak.

His early poetry had moved through several phases, from echoes of
Shelley to local legends, through the wider symbolism of *The Wander-*

[6] WBY, 'Poetry and Tradition', *Essays and Introductions*, p. 249.
[7] WBY, 'The Man and the Echo', *Collected Poems*, p. 393.

ings of Oisin to the twilight romance of Innisfree and Faeryland, and thence to Irish legends seen through the techniques of European symbolism. It was often sad, melancholic, weak, impersonal love poetry; it bore no relationship to current events. It was abstracted from life; it languished in vague misty affirmation of ideal beauty and an ideal Ireland. It showed no signs of Yeats's actual political activities in the real Ireland. His political activity, however, was followed by an increasing interest in playwriting and through his work for the establishment of an Irish drama and an Irish theatre he was forced to realise that the public disliked the great art which he was striving to bring into being.

In his middle period Yeats emerged from the twilight of aestheticism into a cold dawn of sardonic directness as he began to allow public themes their place in this new poetry, stripped of decoration, through which he now pursued equally naked truth. His experience of political life aided his work for the theatre, for he and Lady Gregory had to push the presentation of plays which were true to their creators' visions of truth rather than to popular prejudice. And his poetry became polemical in two controversies in which he despised and rejected the new Irish middle classes and the mob.

The first controversy arose when some of the audience demonstrated against Synge's *The Playboy of the Western World* in 1907. Yeats fought the *Playboy*'s case against a hostile audience at a public meeting. He had had this kind of trouble earlier in his own career when *The Countess Kathleen* had been attacked, because in it the heroine sold her soul to save her starving people, but this occasion seemed an attack on all his plans for moulding a new cultural outlook in Ireland; he began to think that his 'blind bitter land' was so twisted by political hatreds that it could appreciate neither literature nor art. Synge was a Homeric figure (whom he had, in a sense, created) and so any attack on Synge was an attack upon genius which must be opposed. The play was performed and Yeats faced the mob with dignity and courage. But the cost was great; the row compelled him to face the difference between what he had hoped it would be to write for his own race and the reality of writing and working for it, which he described savagely in 'The Fisherman':

> The living men that I hate,
> The dead man that I loved,
> The craven man in his seat,
> The insolent unreproved,
> And no knave brought to book

> Who has won a drunken cheer,
> The witty man and his joke
> Aimed at the commonest ear,
> The clever man who cries
> The catch-cries of the clown,
> The beating down of the wise
> And great Art beaten down.[8]

The controversy over Sir Hugh Lane's pictures followed. Lane had offered these pictures to Dublin on condition they were suitably housed – he favoured Lutyens's plans for a gallery over the Liffey – but this idea did not gain popular support, and to Yeats it seemed another occasion when he must fight for the rightful position of genius and art in the community. The language of his poetry was rapidly altering from a 'poetic' vocabulary to one which used the accents of ordinary speech. He had abandoned ideal beauty removed from the ugly realities of life; he now imbued his new scornful, undecorated poems with savage political rhetoric:

> You gave, but will not give again
> Until enough of Paudeen's pence
> By Biddy's halfpennies have lain
> To be 'some sort of evidence',
> Before you'll put your guineas down,
> That things it were a pride to give
> Are what the blind and ignorantt own
> Imagines best to make it thrive.
> What cared Duke Ercole, that bid
> His mummers to the market-place,
> What th' onion-sellers thought or did
> So that his Plautus set the pace
> For the Italian comedies?
> And Guidobaldo, when he made
> That grammar school of courtesies
> Where wit and beauty learned their trade
> Upon Urbino's windy hill,
> Had sent no runners to and fro
> That he might learn the shepherds' will.[9]

He was weighing the whole romantic glory of the past against his experiences in committee rooms, processions and public meetings, in riots in streets and theatre. Parnell was dead and so was O'Leary; against them the present seemed a poor thing. Glory had departed,

[8] WBY, *Collected Poems*, p. 166.
[9] WBY, 'To a wealthy man who promised a second subscription to the Dublin Municipal Gallery if it were proved the People wanted Pictures', *Collected Poems*, p. 119.

romantic Ireland was dead and gone, and now in a poem addressed to Parnell's ghost he records how Parnell's enemy, 'an old foul mouth' (William Martin Murphy, the proprietor of the two Dublin newspapers which opposed the Lane project), had 'set the pack'[10] on Lane,

> a man
> of your own passionate kind who had brought
> In his full hands what, had they only known
> Had given their children's children loftier thought
> Sweeter emotion working in their veins
> Like gentle blood.[11]

Lane had had insult heaped on him for his pains, and Yeats had rallied to his defence. He appreciated Lane's generosity of spirit and largeness of view. They fitted into the theories he was beginning to formulate, based on his dreaming of 'the noble and the beggarman'. Summers spent since 1897 in the ordered routine of life at Coole Park, Lady Gregory's house in Galway, a visit with her and her son to the glories of Renaissance Italy in 1907 as well as his reading in Castiglione, Spenser and Sidney, had provided him with rich images of aristocratic life; and he returned to his earlier interest in peasant lore and speech while he accompanied Lady Gregory on her expeditions to collect folklore. He began to think that Ireland needed 'the ablest minds' in a national legislature, that an independent Ireland would remedy defects of national character, for he regarded the life of Ireland, in 1913, as 'under the image of a stagnant stream'.[12] But into this dreaming, after his spirited defence of Synge, the classless artist, and Lane, the aristocratic patron, came once again the jarring note of Dublin's mockery. This time his own heritage was the target, for George Moore wrote an article in *The English Review* which commented with lively malice on Yeats's ancestry and a speech he had made in Dublin after a lecture tour in America:

> He began to thunder like Ben Tillett himself against the middle classes, and all because the middle classes did not dip their hands into their pockets and give Lane the money he craved for his contribution . . . and we asked ourselves why Willie Yeats should feel himself called upon to denounce the class to which he himself belonged essentially: one side excellent mercantile millers and ship-owners, and on the other side a portrait painter of rare talent. . . .[13]

---

[10] A phrase derived from Eckermann's Conversations with Goethe, 7 Apr 1829, describing Irish jealousy, and the Irish as 'like a pack of hounds, always dragging down some noble stag'.　　　　[11] WBY, 'To a Shade', *Collected Poems*, p. 123.

[12] Speech of January 1913 explaining why he was an Irish nationalist, quoted by Michael Yeats, 'Yeats: The Public Man', *Southern Review*, v, N.S., 3 (July 1969) p. 878.

[13] Cf. George Moore, *Vale* (1947 ed.) pp. 113–15.

Yeats was deeply offended; Moore had mixed up two of his speeches and misunderstood them. To be misunderstood, to have his motives maligned, to have his antecedents attacked was but part of the purgation of public life. He had yet more to experience: the realisation that he had himself misjudged others. This came with the 1916 Rebellion, which took him by surprise. He recorded this in a poem which has been called a palinode, 'Easter 1916':

> I have met them at close of day
> Coming with vivid faces
> From counter or desk among grey
> Eighteenth-century houses.
> I have passed with a nod of the head
> Or polite meaningless words,
> Or have lingered awhile and said
> Polite meaningless words,
> And thought before I had done
> Of a mocking tale or a gibe
> To please a companion
> Around the fire at the club,
> Being certain that they and I
> But lived where motley is worn:
> All changed, changed utterly:
> A terrible beauty is born.[14]

At the time, he wrote to Lady Gregory, it seemed that all the work of years had been overturned, all the freeing of Irish literature and criticism from politics.

Yeats had then, by 1917, experienced two extremes of public life: a youthful creative period when he dreamed that his literary movement would remodel a new Ireland freed from the bitterness of politics; that his cultural drive would remodel an ideal, idiosyncratic state on heroic models deriving from earlier Gaelic literature. This he later described as a period filled by creation without toil. There followed a middle-aged period of toil when creation seemed unwelcomed by the public he had hoped to change; it was one of disillusionment, deepening as he fought for others' work. The ideal Ireland he had celebrated in the delicate beautiful poetry of his youth was no longer a druid land, but had become a blind bitter land in the astringency of his middle age. As the literary movement gained strength and reputation so the forces of philistinism created greater obstacles. He had hauled others up the craggy heights of patriotic fervour when *Cathleen ni Houlihan* was per-

[14] WBY, *Collected Poems*, p. 202.

formed; when Synge and Lane seemed likely to be thrown down where
Parnell's memory lay, he himself descended the declivities, in order to
assert the rightful place of his friends upon the peaks of public life. And
then Moore's malicious mockery about his own personal position had
followed. Thus, by the time of his marriage, in 1917 when he was
fifty-two, he had experienced the heights and depths of public life, just
as his poetry had swung from a romantic extreme to a realistic. And
then, almost miraculously, came the sudden great flowering, for now
Yeats began the new, exciting poetry, founded, in part, upon the ideas
he included in his book *A Vision* with its vistas of history, its views of
man and of the supernatural, and in part upon the reflections he based
upon the experiences of his own life. His poetry could now include
beauty *and* realism, and magically he fused these extremes into emotive
rhetoric. He could use both self and soul in one poem and compel them
into a unity, of the whole man, of the poetic personality.

Yeats's later poetry reflected a continuous achievement based upon
the positive and complex nature of his last twenty years. In the early
1920s he had at last put down his roots into his Anglo-Irish heritage;
his Norman tower in Galway was a visible symbol of this. He had a
daughter and a son and so the Yeats line would continue. The Abbey
Theatre was an essential part of Dublin's life; the award of the Nobel
Prize recognised the achievement of the poet whose inspiration Dubliners had thought finished when he had published his *Collected Works*
in 1908; and the erstwhile idealistic revolutionary turned disillusioned
scoffer, now became a Senator in the new Irish Free State. The Senators,
himself included, seemed to him like coral insects with some design in
their heads of the ultimate island. His attitudes of mind were complex.
While he had sympathised with the allied cause in the First World War
he kept himself aloof from it. He had been deeply moved by the
tragedy of the 1916 Rising, and in 1921 he spoke with eloquent moving
force in the Oxford Union condemning the conduct of British forces in
Ireland. When the treaty between England and Ireland was agreed he
supported it, and attempted to mediate between pro- and anti-treaty
forces in Ireland once the civil war broke out. In the Senate he generally
supported the government policy of the time. His own contribution
to the deliberations of the Senate rested upon a complex foundation of
the aesthetic ideas he had formed before the end of the nineteenth
century and tested out in the twentieth; a foundation of adventurous
reading, lively originality and sceptical common sense. His knowledge
of 'theatre business, management of men' stood him in good stead,

and his management of the Abbey had taught him to cover his shyness with a mask,[15] in order to keep to his own in every situation in life 'to discover and create in myself as I grow old that thing which is to life what style is to letters – moral radiance, a personal quality of universal meaning in action and thought'.

This moral radiance drove him later into the plain speech he discovered and enjoyed in the Anglo-Irish tradition, in Swift and Berkeley, in Goldsmith and Burke. He was rediscovering this literary inheritance in the twenties and some of his controversial speeches in the Senate stem from a desire to express minority views as he conceived them. He had before him

> an ideal expression in which all that I have, clay and spirits, assists; it is as though I most approximate towards that expression when I carry with me the greatest amount of hereditary thought and feeling, even national and family hatred and pride.[16]

Out of this feeling came the controversial speeches: in the Abbey Theatre defending Sean O'Casey's play *The Plough and the Stars*, for he thought O'Casey was receiving a repetition of the treatment given to Synge: in the Senate on divorce and censorship, for he thought the Protestant minority's freedom threatened by Roman Catholic doctrine. Above all, he wanted his public life to be sincere. He knew the political risks of the speeches, that they might undo the effect of his patient committee work. Some remarks he made about Synge in 1908 could well be applied to his own senatorship:

> When a country produces a man of genius he never is what it wants or believes it wants; he is always unlike the idea of itself. In the eighteenth century Scotland believed itself very religious, moral and gloomy, and its national poet Burns came not to speak of these things but to speak of lust and drink and drunken gaiety. Ireland, since the Young Irelanders, has given itself up to apologetics. Every impression of life or impulse of imagination has been examined to see if it helped or hurt the glory of Ireland or the political claim of Ireland. A sincere impression of life became at last impossible, all was apologetics. There was no longer an impartial imagination, delighting in whatever is naturally exciting. Synge was the rushing up of the buried fire, an explosion of all that had been denied or refused, a furious impartiality, an indifferent turbulent sorrow. His work, like that of Burns, was to say all the people did not want to have said. He was able to do this because Nature had made him incapable of a political idea.[17]

---

15 'When one shrinks from all business with a stranger and is unnatural with all who are intimate friends, because one underrates or overrates unknown people one cannot venture forth.'   16 WBY, *Explorations* (1962) p. 293.
17 WBY, 'The Death of Synge', *Autobiographies*, p. 520.

Yeats himself was far from being incapable of a political thought; but now he did not want to play the part of popular politician. In 1928 he decided not to stand again for the Senate; his health and the new pressures of political parties were factors in this decision. He wanted to develop the role of art in society; his aims were, ultimately, educational. His early hopeful desire had been to create 'some new *Prometheus Un-bound*; Patrick or Columcille, Oisin or Finn, in Prometheus' stead; and, instead of Caucasus, Cro-Patrick or Ben Bulben'. He realised that he had written a bad poem on the occasion of Parnell's death entitled 'Mourn and then onward' and he excluded it from collections of his poems. He had wanted to fill the vacuum caused by Parnell's death, but he wanted to get away from the endemic Irish frustration of political squabblings. At all times he was primarily a poet, and even in his period of disillusionment, when his ideals were apparently being rejected, he saw the need for an intellectual movement: 'the Irish people till they are better educated must dream impermanent dreams'. His concern was to help his countrymen to dream them, and so we find this man, original, creative, imaginative, and strong, was almost inevitably involved, like Milton and Marvell before him, in public, political life. He was listened to with respect when he applied his shaping skill to such subjects as the Irish Manuscripts, Literary Copyright, the Lane pictures, the National Museum, the National Gallery and Art School, and a proposed 'Federation of the Arts' in Ireland.[18] The report of the Commission on Coinage of which he was Chairman is a model of lucidity and freshness, and is Yeats's most notable contribution to the proceedings of the Senate, for, though he would himself have preferred the designs of another artist, he presented his Commission's findings and its selection of Percy Metcalf's designs brilliantly, and so because of his work and the Commission's Ireland possesses a superbly designed coinage.

Yeats founded the Irish Academy of Letters in order to strengthen the position of Irish authors within the new state. (He had been sharply reminded of the need yet again when he had had to defend O'Casey's play *The Plough and the Stars*.) He believed that the permanent dreams of a country are rooted in its literature, and that an enthusiasm for literature should therefore be fostered in children. He became increasingly interested in education; he toured schools; he made advanced

[18] See W. B. Stanford, 'Yeats in the Irish Senate' (a review of *The Senate Speeches of W. B. Yeats*, ed. Donald R. Pearce (1960), *A Review of English Literature*, IV (3 July 1963) p. 77.

and constructive speeches on the need for improved buildings and for a curriculum which would seem 'one lesson and not a mass of unrelated topics'. His friend Joseph O'Neill, the Secretary of the Department of Education, provided him with information; he met

> teacher after teacher who has said to me that young people are anarchic and violent and that we have to show them what the state is and what they owe to it. All over the world during the Great War, the young people became anarchic and violent and in Ireland it is worse than everywhere for we have in a sense been at war for generations and of late that war has taken the form of burning and destruction under the eyes of the children. They respect nothing, one teacher said to me, I cannot take them through Stephen's Green because they would pull up the plants. Go anywhere in Ireland and you will hear the same complaint. The children everyone will tell you are intelligent and friendly, yet have so little sense of their duty to community and neighbour that if they meet an empty house in a lonely place they will smash all the windows . . . the proper remedy is the teaching of religion.[19]

Yeats's speeches in the Senate make fascinating reading; they reveal his intensely practical (and occasionally unpractised) attitude to public affairs,[20] his sharp insistence upon minority viewpoints and his occasional flashes of realistic and sardonic wit. 'Public speech' was a phrase applied to his poetry by Archibald MacLeish and it gave Yeats great pleasure. The authority which underpinned his great poetry of the twenties and thirties was parly due to the confidence that 'getting it all in order' in A Vision had given him (his horror at the 1914–18 holocaust continued in his concern for Europe where 'the cruelty of Governments' grew greater in the thirties, where 'the ceremony of innocence' was doomed and the ruin of civilisation seemed to ap-

[19] From a typescript draft. This appears, in a more polished form, as 'The Child and the State', a speech made to the Irish Literary Society on 30 Nov 1925, the text of which is included in The Senate Speeches of W. B. Yeats, ed. Donald R. Pearce (1960) p. 172.
[20] For example, see his penetrating comments in On the Boiler (1940) p. 12:
'When I was first a member of the Irish Senate I discovered to my surprise that one learned in three months more about every Senator's character and capacity than could have been learned from years of ordinary life . . . the thirty men nominated by President Cosgrave were plainly the most able and the most educated. I attached myself to a small group led by an old friend of my father's, Andrew Jameson, for I knew that he would leave me free to speak my mind. The few able men among the elected Senators had been nominated for election by ministers. As the nominated element began to die out – almost all were old men – the Senate declined in ability and prestige. In its early days some old banker or lawyer would dominate the House, leaning upon the back of the chair in front, speaking with undisturbed self-possession as at some table in a board room. My imagination sets up against him some typical elected man, emotional as a youthful chimpanzee, hot and vague, always disturbed, always hating something or other.'

proach); partly to the international recognition of his achievement
(typified by the Nobel Prize); but not least to his senatorial experience,
which gave him clear proof that his early idealism about the intellectual
and artistic regeneration of Ireland, tempered as it was by the experience of middle age, had not been in vain. He drew upon the eighteenth-
century Anglo-Irish writers and statesmen for inspiration, and,
paradoxically, could unite their convervatism with his early revolutionary nationalism. He could apply the wisdom he had gained, and, as his
muse grew younger, could apply irony, could write the great haunting
meditative poems of his maturity in which he accepts life affirmatively,
private and public life fused together now. 'Among School Children'
demonstrates the nature of this achievement: it moves from youth,
from the wonder of the children to the public man and his private
passionate recollection of the past, from his cold thought on the pre-
dicament of individual man to both the abstract and the real preoccupation of women, and then from the decrepitude of age to a great
exultant, inclusive cry at the ironic complexiites of human life:

> I walk through the long schoolroom questioning;
> A kind old nun in a white hood replies;
> The children learn to cipher and to sing,
> To study reading-books and histories,
> To cut and sew, be neat in everything
> In the best modern way – the children's eyes
> In momentary wonder stare upon
> A sixty-year-old public man.
>
> I dream of a Ledaean body, bent
> Above a sinking fire, a tale that she
> Told of a harsh reproof, or trivial event
> That changed some childish day to tragedy –
> Told, and it seemed that our two natures blent
> Into a sphere from youthful sympathy,
> Or else, to alter Plato's parable,
> Into the yolk and white of the one shell.
>
> And thinking of that fit of grief or rage
> I look upon one child or t'other there
> And wonder if she stood so at that age –
> For even daughters of the swan can share
> Something of every paddler's heritage –
> And had that colour upon cheek or hair,
> And thereupon my heart is driven wild:
> She stands before me as a living child.

Her present image floats into the mind –
Did Quattrocento finger fashion it
Hollow of cheek as though it drank the wind
And took a mess of shadows for its meat?
And I though never of Ledaean kind
Had pretty plumage once – enough of that,
Better to smile on all that smile, and show
There is a comfortable kind of old scarecrow.

What youthful mother, a shape upon her lap
Honey of generation had betrayed,
And that must sleep, shriek, struggle to escape
As recollection or the drug decide,
Would think her son, did she but see that shape
With sixty or more winters on its head,
A compensation for the pang of his birth,
Or the uncertainty of his setting forth?

Plato thought nature but a spume that plays
Upon a ghostly paradigm of things;
Solider Aristotle played the taws
Upon the bottom of a king of kings;
World-famous golden-thighed Pythagoras
Fingered upon a fiddle-stick or strings
What a star sang and careless Muses heard;
Old clothes upon old sticks to scare a bird.

Both nuns and mothers worship images,
But those the candles light are not as those
That animate a mother's reveries,
But keep a marble or a bronze repose.
And yet they too break hearts – O Presences
That passion, piety or affection knows,
And that all heavenly glory symbolise –
O self-born mockers of man's enterprise;

Labour is blossoming or dancing where
The body is not bruised to pleasure soul,
Nor beauty born out of its own despair,
Nor blear-eyed wisdom out of midnight oil.
O chestnut-tree, great-rooted blossomer,
Are you the leaf, the blossom or the bole?
O body swayed to music, O brightening glance,
How can we know the dancer from the dance?[21]

---

[21] WBY, 'Among School Children', *Collected Poems*, p. 242.

Poet's Tower

MR FALCONER, the exquisite and sensitive, if passive, hero of *Gryll Grange* was so haunted by the daydream Milton sketched in *Il Penseroso*, of living remote in 'some high lonely tower', that he purchased a tower and, until he met Miss Gryll, lived in it a life of quiet studious ease. There was another inspiration besides that of Milton; he also wished to imitate a recluse, whom he called Lord Noirmont, who lived on the top of a tower, attended by a daughter or niece, until the latter departed to get married. Mr Falconer told Dr Opimian that he thought

> This was associated with some affliction that was cured, or some mystery that was solved, and that the hermit returned into the everyday world. I do not know when I read it, but I have always liked the idea of living like Lord Noirmont, when I shall have become a sufficiently disappointed man.

Peacock does not give the source of Mr Falconer's Lord Noirmont, but he may have owed the idea to Shelley, a great creator of towers and solitary inhabitants. Mr Falconer may, in fact, be a Peacockian parody of the melancholy Prince Athanase, brought into a firmly nineteenth-century epicurean setting, well nourished by madeira before pronouncing that

> We are all born to disappointment. It is as well to be prospective. Our happiness is not in what is, but in what is to be. We may be disappointed in our everyday realities and if not, we may make an ideality of the unattainable, and quarrel with Nature for giving what she has not to give.

But whether or not Peacock took his ideas from Milton and Shelley there is no doubt of Yeats having done so. Not only did he brood upon their imagery, but he gave it an unique reality. In 1917 he bought a Norman castle at Ballylee, County Galway, and subsequently used the castle as a summer residence until 1929. The purchase of the castle, its renovation and its symbolic value in the later poems of its owner are the fitting outcome of his early interest in towers as poetical symbols and his long-felt delight in this particular old tower and its legendary neighbourhood.

As a youth Yeats was greatly influenced by the poetry of Shelley: he had begun 'to write poetry in imitation of Shelley and Edmund Spenser, play after play'. The effect of these poets upon his early style is marked; he described *The Wanderings of Oisin* in retrospect as full of the Italian colour of Shelley. More than mere style was influenced, however, for he began to imagine himself as a Shelleyan character. A passage in *Autobiographies* records this phase:

> I had many idols, and as I climbed along the narrow ledge I was now Man-fred on his glacier, and now Prince Athanase with his solitary lamp, but I soon chose Alastor for my chief of men, and longed to share his melancholy, and may be at last to disappear from everybody's sight as he disappeared drifting in a boat along some slow moving river between great trees.[1]

The solitary nature of these characters first excited Yeats's imagination. After his adolescent preoccupation with loneliness had waned he found that Shelley's characters united with their lonely lives a love of intel-lectual beauty; he was also to find that a similar search for wisdom underlay and inspired his own work. Two of Shelley's symbolic char-acters especially interested him. He wrote in later years that his mind

> gave itself to gregarious Shelley's dream of a young man, his hair blanched with sorrow, studying philosophy in some high lonely tower, or his old man, master of all human knowledge, hidden from sight in some shell strewn cavern on the Mediterranean shore.[2]

These dwellers in tower and cavern are both solitary; the first is a seeker after wisdom's power, the second has attained it. We can dis-regard the cavern-dweller, for he does not appear in Yeats's poetry until 'The Gyres', a late poem which probably reflects a mood when Yeats thought he had, like Shelley's old man, become preternaturally wise. The significance of the tower is indicated by Yeats in an essay on Shelley's poetry:

> As Shelley sailed along those great rivers and saw or imagined the cave that associated itself with rivers in his mind, he saw half-ruined towers upon the hilltops, and once at any rate a tower is used to symbolise a meaning that is the contrary to the meaning symbolised by caves. Cythna's lover is brought through the cave where there is a polluted fountain, to a high tower, for being man's far-seeing mind when the world has cast him out he must to 'the towers of thought's crowned powers'; nor is it possible for Shelley to have forgotten this first imprisonment when he made men imprison Lionel in a tower for a like offence; and beaause I know how hard it is to forget a symbolical meaning, once one has found it, I believe Shelley had more than a romantic scene in his mind when he made Prince Athanase follow his mysterious studies in a lighted

---

[1] *Autobiographies*, p. 64.   [2] Ibid., p. 171.

tower above the sea, and when he made the old hermit watch over Laon in his sickness in a half-ruined tower, wherein the sea, here doubtless as to Cythna's 'the one mind' threw 'spangled sands' and 'rarest seashells'. The tower, important in Maeterlinck, as in Shelley, is, like the sea, and rivers, and caves with fountains, a very ancient symbol, and could perhaps, as years went by, have grown more important in his poetry. The contrast between it and the cave in *Laon and Cythna* suggests a contrast between the mind looking outward on men and things and the mind looking inward on itself, which may or may not have been in Shelley's mind, but certainly helps, with one knows not how many dim meanings, to give the poem mystery and shadow. It is only by ancient symbols, by symbols that have numberless meanings beside the one or two the writer lays an emphasis upon, or the half score he knows of, that any subjective art can escape from the barrenness and shallowness of a too conscious arrangement, into the abundance and depth of nature. The poet of essence and pure ideas must seek in the half-lights that glimmer from symbol to symbol as if to the ends of the earth, all that the epic and dramatic poet finds of mystery and shadow in the accidental circumstances of life.[3]

When Yeats wrote of Prince Athanase studying philosophy in his tower:

> . . . a youth who, as with toil and travel,
> Had grown quite grey before his time,
> Nor what religion fables of the grave
> Feared he, Philosophy's accepted guest

he did not mention the famous passage in *Il Penseroso*, quoted by Mr Falconer to Dr Opimian, but he later drew attention to it. The Miltonic lines

> Or let my Lamp, at midnight hour,
> Be seen in some high lonely Tower,
> Where I may oft outwatch the *Bear*,
> With thrice great *Hermes*, or unspheare
> The spirit of Plato, to unfold
> What worlds, or what vast regions hold
> The immortal mind that hath forsook
> Her mansion in this fleshly nook . . .

may well have been a source for Shelley's imagery in *Prince Athanase*. In the copy of Shelley's works presented to Yeats by Katharine Tynan in 1888, page 510 was turned down opposite this passage of *Prince Athanase*:

> His soul had wedded wisdom, and her dower
> Is love and justice: clothed in which she sate
> Apart from men, as in a lonely tower,
> Pitying the tumult of their dark estate.

---

[3] WBY, 'Ideas of Good and Evil', *Essays and Introductions*, pp. 86–7.

CA B 2

Apart from the fact that Milton and Shelley each end a line with the words 'lonely tower' there are other similarities in their poems. Milton's 'lamp at midnight hour' which is 'seen in some high lonely tower' is echoed by Shelley's

> The Balearic fisher, driven from shore,
> Hanging upon the peaked wave afar,
> Then saw their lamp from Laian's turret gleam,
> Piercing the stormy darkness, like a star. . . .

A reference to the Bear in *Il Penseroso* is matched by Shelley's line

> Bright Arcturus through yon pines is glowing

and Milton's praise of 'the spirit of Plato' is reflected by the old man who comforts Athanase:

> Then Plato's words of light in thee and me
> Lingered like moonlight in the moonless east
> Fore we had just then read – thy memory
> Is faithful now – the story of the feast;
> And Agathon and Diotima seemed
> From death and dark forgetfulness released.

Yeats was probably hinting at this similarity when he described himself as having

> . . . found, after the manner of his kind,
> Mere images; chosen this place to live in
> Because, it may be, of the candle-light
> From the far tower where Milton's Platonist
> Sat late, or Shelley's visionary prince:
> The lonely light that Samuel Palmer engraved,
> An image of mysterious wisdom won by toil.[4]

The last two lines of this passage refer to an illustration by Palmer in *The Shorter Poems of John Milton*:[5] this is entitled 'The Lonely Tower' and the following description accompanies the quotation of four lines from *Il Penseroso*:

> Here poetic loneliness has been attempted; not the loneliness of a desert, but a secluded spot in a genial pastoral country, enriched also by antique relics such as the so-called druidic stones upon the distant hill. The constellation of the 'Bear' may help to explain that the building is the tower of *Il Penseroso*. Two shepherds watching their flocks speak together of the mysterious light above them.

---

4 WBY, 'The Phases of the Moon', *Collected Poems*, p. 184.
5 Seeley & Co., London, 1889.

Yet another source for towers as symbols of a search for wisdom is
Villiers de l'Isle-Adam's *Axël*, of which Yeats wrote in his edition to
the Jarrold edition of 1925:

> Now that I have read it again in Mr. Finberg's translation and recalled that
> first impression [he had read *Axel* in French before he went to Paris in 1894] I
> can see how those symbols dominated my thought. . . . Is it only because I
> opened the book for the first time when I had vivid senses of youth that I must
> see that tower room always and hear always that thunder?

It is obvious that this tower in *Axël* is akin to Shelley's symbol in
Prince Athanase, for Axël, Count of Auersperg,

> deprives himself of all the joys of his age! And spends the best years of his life
> sitting up there in the tower, night and night, studying by lamplight, poring
> over ancient manuscripts with the doctor.

To sum up the effect of these literary sources upon Yeats would be
an easier matter if we were dealing with their effect upon his adolescence
and youth alone: but the problem is to allot them their due importance
in the tower poetry, almost all of which he wrote after his acquisition
of the tower at Ballylee in 1917. We could realise clearly what the possession of a tower would have meant to the young Yeats, who associated towers with those Shelleyan characters who were such a formative
influence upon his early development: towers were almost a *sine qua
non* for Shelley's romantic atmosphere, and the possession of one would
have meant the realisation of many of Yeats's own youthful dreams of
being a solitary hero. The secondary meaning of Shelley's tower symbolism, however, must have grown in importance for Yeats as his
years of study accumulated. What he called 'making his soul' would
have included and laid stress upon the importance of intellect which
Shelley associated with the inhabitants of his towers. As both these
symbolic meanings, of romantic loneliness and the search for wisdom,
appear in the tower poetry of Yeats we can see that elements, at least,
of early memories and desires underlay his purchase of a tower in later
life.

There were other reasons which led Yeats to his acquisition of a
tower, and these also colour the tower poetry. In an essay which first
appeared in *The Dome* of October 1899 and later in *The Celtic Twilight*
(1902) he described the neighbourhood of the tower, his early visits [6]

[6] He first visited Coole Park in 1896, on his tour of the west of Ireland with his friend
Arthur Symons.

there in search of folklore, and the semi-literary associations which
endeared the place to him:

> I have lately been to a little group of houses, not many enough to be called a
> village, in the barony of Kiltartan in County Galway, whose name, Ballylee,
> is known throughout all the west of Ireland. There is the old square castle,
> Ballylee, inhabited by a farmer and his wife, and a cottage where their daughter
> and their son-in-law live, and a little mill with an old miller, and old ash-trees
> throwing green shadows upon a little river and great stepping stones.[7]

Later in the essay he writes that he will

> be back there again before it is autumn, because Mary Hynes, a beautiful
> woman whose name is still a wonder by turf fires, died there sixty years ago;
> for our feet would linger where beauty has lived its life of sorrow to make us
> understand that it is not of the world.

Raftery, the famous Irish poet,[8] made a song in Irish about Mary
Hynes which Yeats quoted in a version translated by a friend (probably
Lady Gregory[9] rather than Douglas Hyde) from the singing of an old
woman who lived in Ballylee and remembered Raftery and Mary
Hynes.[10] In 1926 Yeats returned to the theme of Mary Hynes in *The
Tower*, describing the images and memories which surrounded his
dwelling:

> Some few remembered still when I was young
> A peasant girl commended by a song,
> Who'd lived somewhere upon that rocky place,
> And praised the colour of her face,
> And had the greater joy in praising her,
> Remembering that, if walked she there,
> Farmers jostled at the fair
> So great a glory did the song confer.

Mary Hynes's beauty led to the death of John Madden, one of her
drunken admirers, by drowning in the great bog of Cloone. The old
woman had other violent anecdotes. And at Peterswell, near by, there
occurred in 1778 the grisly clipping of a farmer's ears by a servant of
Mrs French. Yeats got this story from the lively *Recollections* of her
grandson, Sir Jonah Barrington.

[7] See WBY, 'Dust hath closed Helen's Eye', *Mythologies* (1959) pp. 22 ff.
[8] Anthony Raftery (1784–1835), a blind Gaelic poet. See also Yeats's reference to him
in *Autobiographies* (1956) pp. 561 ff.
[9] See her article 'Raftery, the Poet of the Poor', *Tuam Herald*, 28 Oct 1899, and her
Poets and Dreamers (Dublin, 1903). Mary Hynes died in the 1840s. See Douglas Hyde's
account of her, *Songs Ascribed to Raftery* (Dublin, 1903) pp. 327–9. She, like Maud Gonne
in Yeats's poetry, was compared to Helen of Troy.
[10] WBY, *Mythologies*, pp. 24–5, and *Autobiographies*, pp. 561–2.

Another important reason underlying Yeats's purchase of the tower of Ballylee was its proximity to Coole, Lady Gregory's residence. He visited her at Coole Park almost every summer from 1897 onwards. He stressed the proximity of the tower to Coole in a poem entitled 'Coole Park and Ballylee, 1931':

> Under my window-ledge the waters race,
> Otters below and moor-hens on the top,
> Run for a mile undimmed in Heaven's face
> Then darkening through 'dark' Raftery's 'cellar' drop,
> Run underground, rise in a rocky place
> In Coole demesne, and there to finish up
> Spread to a lake and drop into a hole.
> What's water but the generated soul?

Some time before Yeats's marriage, which took place in October 1917, Robert Gregory, Lady Gregory's son, had urged him to buy the castle,[11] and when the Congested Districts Board was splitting up some of the Gregory Estate into smaller holdings Yeats entered into negotiations for the purchase of Ballylee. He first mentioned it in a letter he wrote to his friend Mrs Shakespear on 8 November 1916, alluding to it as 'my castle', delighting in the fact that there was a sound cottage at its foot so he might be there even before the castle was roofed, and adding: 'If I get it I shall plant fruit trees as soon as possible – apple trees for the sake of the blossoms and because it will make me popular with the little boys who will eat my apples in the early mornings.'[12] In a memo dated 19 February 1917 H. R. Vereker, the Board's Chief Land Inspector, reported to Sir Henry Doran as follows:

> I was at Ballylee on the 14th instant. This is the most perfectly preserved old castle I have ever seen, not a stone in the outer walls being displaced. It stands on the edge of a river of some considerable size, and is approached by a very substantial bridge twenty feet wide. Inside the castle, the floors of the rooms are, of course, gone, and only a small proportion of the slated roof remains. Its value as a residence is sentimental and therefore problematical, as in my opinion it would take between £300 and £400 to make it habitable. The tenant of the holding on which the castle stands had his house built against one side of it, and has used the tower portion as a stable. . . . A bye road, which serves two large villages approaches the river on the opposite side of the castle. When the river is low it is shallow enough to go across, and the arrangement of flags laid on dry stone piers enables foot passengers to cross.

The report went on to object to the proposed sale of the castle to Yeats, because the Board would have to build a new bridge at the site

---

11 He had spoken to John Quinn in 1904 of his dream of one day buying the tower.

12 *Letters*, ed. Allan Wade (1954) p. 615.

of the ford to improve the bye road, and this would cost them £150 – whereas they were selling the castle to Yeats for £80 and its bridge could be converted to public use quite cheaply. Sir Henry Doran concluded a letter to Bailey Bailey, dated 23 February 1917, in these words:

> If Mr. Yeats agreed to have an open roadway through the castle yard from the existing bridge above referred to, the Board might agree to take less than £80.

It was probably after a little haggling that the Board eventually wrote to Yeats to say that although legal transfer could not yet be completed he could take possession of his new property in April 1917; the price he was to pay was £35. On 12 May 1917 he wrote to his father to say that he had come to Coole Park

> to take over my Tower, Ballylee Castle. I shall make it habitable at no great expense and store there so many of my possessions that I shall be able to have less rooms in London. [In May 1916 he had written to John Quinn, announcing that he had taken over the floor below his rooms in 18 Woburn Building and so had practically all the house. In this letter he talked of returning to Dublin. See *Letters*, p. 614.] The Castle will be an economy, counting the capital I spend so much a year, and it is certainly a beautiful place. There are trout in the river under the window. Jack [his brother, the artist Jack Butler Years] can come there when he wants Connaught people to paint.[13]

For his outlay Yeats obtained

> An ancient bridge, and a more ancient tower,
> A Farmhouse that is shattered by its wall,
> An acre of stony ground,
> Where the symbolic rose can break in flower,
> Old ragged elms, old thorns innumerable,
> The sound of the rain or sound
> Of every wind that blows.[14]

The castle was originally built by the de Burgo family, probably in the fourteenth century; in 1585 it belonged to an Edmond McUlick de Burgo (or Burke) who died in it in 1597.[15] The prolific de Burgo family had owned much land in the western part of Ireland, but their power and wealth vanished in the eighteenth century. The tower had come into the possession of the Earl of Clanrickarde in 1617 and in 1783 the property was part of the Gregory Estate. In 1837 Patrick

[13] *Letters*, p. 624. See also J. B. Yeats, *Letters to his son W. B. Yeats and Others, 1869–1922*, ed. J. Hone (1944) p. 238.
[14] WBY, 'Meditations in Time of Civil War, II', *Collected Poems*, p. 226.
[15] See Mary Hanley, *Thoor Ballylee, Home of William Butler Yeats* (1965) p. 2. She cites *The Compossicion Booke of Connought*, transcribed A. Martin Freeman (Dublin, 1936), for this information.

Carrick (or Carrig) was the tenant. He was probably the 'ancient bankrupt master' of the house to whom Yeats alludes in 'The Tower'.[16] In
1861 the tower was offered to Patrick Spellman by his uncle James
Carrick, who owned Kilcornan Castle.[17] This Spellman 'had his house
against one side' of the tower, and an excited letter from Yeats to
Mrs Shakespear of 15 May 1917 describes how he had been at Coole
Park, looking after the castle chiefly, and deciding to leave the restora-
tion of the tower until after the repairing of the cottages beside it:

> The architect has been down and I know what I am going to do. The little
> cottage is to be repaired and extended so as to put in a quite comfortable and
> modern part – kitchen, bathroom, sitting room, three bedrooms. I am then to
> go on to the castle at my leisure. The cottage on the island will be arranged so
> as to give me privacy shutting me off from the road thus. [*Here follows a rough
> plan.*] The cottage will make a kind of cloister and will be thatched.
>
> [*Here follows a rough sketch, marked* 'very bad drawing'.]
>
> This will give me a little garden shut in by these and by the river. The
> cottage will cost I believe £200. The old outhouses to supply the stonework.
> My idea is to keep the contrast between the mediaeval castle and the peasant's
> cottage. As I shall have the necessities in the cottage I can devote the castle to a
> couple of great rooms and for very little money.
>
> I shall never be in good health but in the country. I have been better since
> I came here than I have been for months. I have never been here in spring
> before. The woods full of crabtrees in flower and here and there double cherries
> in flower. The fruit trees in the garden too a mass of flowers.[18]

The next month he wrote again to his father that he was going to
give lectures in Paris and perhaps Milan to 'earn enough to roof the
castle'.[19] In July he wrote to Mrs Shakespear about starting the builders
on the castle. In August he wrote several letters from France to Lady
Gregory asking her to get Thomas Rafferty ('Raftery' in the *Letters* –
he was the local builder) to begin work under the directions of William
A. Scott (Professor of Architecture in the National University of Ireland from 1911). The builder's estimate was as he expected, and in
September another letter asked Lady Gregory if Rafferty was at work.

After his marriage Yeats decided that he and his wife would live at
Ballylee for part of each year. Mrs Yeats took over the correspondence
with Rafferty; the cottages which adjoined the square bulk of the castle
were repaired and had room for kitchen, bathroom, sitting-room, and

16 *Collected Poems*, p. 221. See also Donald T. Torchiana, *W. B. Yeats and Georgian
Ireland* (1966) p. 301.
17 Letter from Gerard K. Brady *to Irish Times*.
18 *Letters*, pp. 625–6.   19 *Letters*, p. 627.

bedrooms. Yeats's eagerness to live in the tower increased. He wrote to
Lady Gregory (who had offered to lend them Ballinamantane House,
near Gort):

> We shall be with you at Easter as you are so kind [as] still to wish it. Raftery
> gets on slowly but fairly steadily with his work at Ballylee, and has just written
> that the rats are eating the thatch. Scott has asked for dimensions of fireplaces
> so evidently will send designs and the Castle has been cleaned out. It looks as
> if this Spring may see the roof on but I don't want my wife to spend more
> money till she has seen the place. We have heard of a shop in Dublin that could
> hire us furniture for Ballinamantane should we go there. . . . Ballinamantane is
> our main thought but we are very vague and know nothing yet of the expense
> of hiring furniture.[20]

They went to Coole Park in May, occupied Ballinamantane House
in June 1918, and Mrs Yeats had a man digging in front of the cottage
to plant flowers 'as we expect to be there in a month'.[21] They enjoyed
trout and salmon caught in Ballylee river, and the excitement of getting
into the castle mounted. Yeats wrote to John Quinn on 22 July:

> My dear Quinn, This heading is written in hope, that is to say, I hope it will
> be true a day or two after this letter reaches you, at the latest. We are sur-
> rounded with plans. This morning designs arrived from the drunken man of
> genius, Scott, for two beds. The war is improving the work for, being unable
> to import anything, we have bought the whole contents of an old mill – great
> beams and three-inch planks, and old paving stones; and the local carpenter
> and mason and blacksmith are at work for us. On a great stone beside the front
> door will be inscribed these lines:

> > I, the poet, William Yeats,
> > With common sedge and broken slates
> > And smithy work from the Gort forge,
> > Restored this tower for my wife George;
> > And on my heirs I lay a curse
> > If they should alter for the worse,
> > From fashion or an empty mind,
> > What Raftery built and Scott designed.[22]

> Raftery is the love builder . . .
>
> I am making a setting for my old age, a place to influence lawless youth,
> with its severity and antiquity.

The opening of 'In Memory of Major Robert Gregory' was written in
this hope of the work being completed:

> Now that we're almost settled in our house.

[20] *Letters*, p. 647.   [21] *Letters*, p. 650.
[22] This is an early form of 'To be carved on a Stone at Ballylee', *Collected Poems*, p. 214.

A letter to Clement Shorter of September conveys some of the impatience:

> We are hoping every day to get into our castle where we are, or it is, constantly looking after carpenters and the like. We shall live on the road like a country man, our white walled cottage with its border of flowers like any country cottage and then the gaunt castle.[23]

And a poem written in 1918, 'A Prayer on going into my House', reveals the poet's delight in his new home:

> God grant a blessing on this tower and cottage
> And on my heirs, if all remain unspoiled,
> No table or chair or stool not simple enough
> For shepherd lads in Galilee; and grant
> That I myself for portions of the year
> May handle nothing and set eyes on nothing
> But what the great and passionage have used
> Throughout so many varying centuries.[24]

The tables, chairs and two large beds were made from local elm wood by local craftsmen. Some of the furniture still remains within the tower; it was constructed *in situ* and could not be moved down the winding stair.

In the summer of 1919 the family was installed in Ballylee. Anne Butler Yeats had been born on 26 February and Yeats, offered two years in a Japanese University, found the additions to his life of wife, child – and tower – elements to weigh against 'a spirited old age'. But would he ever come back? He wrote to John Quinn on 1 July 1919:

> And would I mind if Sinn Fein took possession of my old tower here to store arms in, or the young scholars from the school broke all the new windows? I think my chief difficulty in accepting will be my tower, which needs another year's work under our own eyes before it is a fitting monument and symbol, and my garden, which will need several years if it is to be green and shady during my lifetime. Ballylee is a good house for a child to grow up in – a place full of history and romance, with plenty to do every day.[25]

A letter which Yeats wrote to his father on 16 July 1919 gives an idyllic picture of Ballylee:

> Anne and George [Mrs Yeats] were there too, George sewing and Anne lying in her seventeenth century cradle. I am writing this in the great ground floor of the castle – the pleasantest room I have yet seen, a great wide window opening over the river and a round arched door leading to the thatched hall.

---

[23] *Letters*, p. 652.   [24] *Collected Poems*, p. 183.   [25] *Letters*, pp. 658–9.

[*Drawing.*] A very bad drawing but I am put out by having the object in front of me, 'nature puts me out'. There is a stone floor and a stone-roofed entrance-hall with the door to winding stair to left, and then a larger thatched hall, beyond which is a cottage and kitchen. In the thatched hall imagine a great copper hanging lantern (which is, however, not there yet but will be, I hope, next year). I am writing at a great trestle table which George keeps covered with wild flowers.[26]

Gradually the tower itself was made habitable. Yeats wrote to John Quinn on 5 June 1922

Our bedroom is upstairs in the Castle and is a delight to us, and the third floor which is to be my study is almost ready. Our dining room on the ground floor was finished three years ago. This is the first year in which we have been able to sleep in the Castle itself. We have added an extra cottage, which is ultimately to be a garage, though not for anything nobler than a Ford and not even that till next year at the earliest. This country is still so disturbed that even Ford cars don't stay with their owners. None of these improvements has cost much. The stone for the cottage was dug out of our garden and the slates were bought two years ago for the Castle, which has to be concreted over instead, for our builder declares that no slate would withstand the storms.[27] I went on my last American tour for Ballylee and that money is not all gone yet.[28]

It is a great pleasure to live in a place where George makes at every moment a fourteenth century picture. And out of doors, with the hawthorn all in blossom all along the river banks, everything is so beautiful that to go else-where is to leave beauty behind.[29]

A letter to Mrs Shakespear, written two days later, told her

The castle which we call *Thoor* (Tower)[30] and escape from associations of modern gothic, is a joy to us both and the country all white with the may flower full of plenty. Stone stairs to my surprise are the most silent of all stairs and sitting as I am now upstairs in the Tower I have a sense of solitude and silence. As yet we have no stranger's room, mainly because there is so little labour to be had. It will be the room above this, a beautiful room high in the tower. It is ready but for futniture and a door.[31]

He wrote that letter and another to Sir Herbert Grierson on the same

[26] Quoted by J. Hone, *W. B. Yeats 1865–1939*, p. 319.
[27] An ornate design for a roof of sea-green slates had been prepared in Lutyens's office.
[28] Ezra Pound wrote flippantly to John Quinn on 24 March 1920 about this lecture tour: 'Besides he'll have made enough to buy a few shingles for his phallic symbol on the Bogs. Ballyphallus or whatever he calls it with the river on the first floor.' See B. L. Reid, *The Man from New York*, p. 419.
[29] *Letters*, pp. 682–3.
[30] He had written to Mrs Shakespear in the previous April: 'What do you think of our address – Thoor Ballylee? Thoor is Irish for tower and it will keep people from suspecting us of modern Gothic and a deer park. I think the harsh sound of "Thoor" amends the softness of the rest.' *Letters*, p. 680.   [31] *Letters*, p. 686.

day from the first-floor bedroom of the tower which was also 'for the most part' his study. Here there was

an open fire of turf, and a great elm-wood bed made with great skill by a neighbouring carpenter, but designed by that late drunken genius Scott; and over my head is a wooden ceiling made according to his design. Some day it will be painted in brilliant colours.[32]

The spring and summer of 1922 were spent quietly at Ballylee, the family often all day in the garden 'George gardening – I writing and Michael[33] under a tree asleep'.[34] It was, however, not a quiet summer for Ireland. The period of the Black and Tans was over; the Treaty had been signed; but Yeats's letters from the tower reflected his increasing distress at the situation. All their locks had been broken before they arrived in April and some windows but these had been repaired, and nothing was missing but a garden syringe. There had been 'troubles' of various kinds in the area; then there followed the civil war in the summer 'and for weeks we had neither railways, newspapers nor posts'. In 'Meditations in Time of Civil War' the contrast between the quiet of the tower and the turbulent world outside was emphasised. The railway bridges were blown up, the roads blocked:

> We are closed in, and the key is turned
> On our uncertainty; somewhere
> A man is killed, or a house burned,
> Yet no clear fact to be discerned:
> Come build in the empty house of the stare.

> A barricade of stone or of wood;
> Some fourteen days of civil war;
> Last night they trundled down the road
> That dead young soldier in his blood:
> Come build in the empty house of the stare.[35]

Results of the violence were, indeed, in evidence:

One never knew what was happening on the other side of the hill or of the line of trees. Ford cars passed the house from time to time with coffins standing upon and between the seats and sometimes at night we heard an explosion, and one day saw the smoke made by the burning of a great neighbouring house. Men must have lived so through many tumultuous centuries.[36]

---

[32] *Letters*, p. 687.
[33] The poet's son, Michael Butler Yeats, born 22 Aug 1921.
[34] See *Letters*, p. 688.
[35] WBY, 'Meditations in Time of Civil War, VI', *Collected Poems*, p. 230.
[36] WBY, *The Bounty of Sweden* (Dublin, 1925) p. 50.

His contemplative life was weighed against the purposeful activity of a soldier's: his predecessor in the tower, the man-at-arms who gathered a score of horse and spent his days in this tumultuous place occurred as contrast to himself, and yet he found for himself in the tower 'befitting emblems of adversity'. He felt himself aged in comparison to the youthful Free State soldiers and their Republican enemies:

> An affable Irregular,
> A heavily-built Falstaffian man,
> Comes cracking jokes of civil war
> As though to die by gunshot were
> The finest play under the sun.
>
> A brown Lieutenant and his men,
> Half dressed in national uniform,
> Stand at my door, and I complain
> Of the foul weather, hail and rain,
> A pear-tree broken by the storm.[37]

He envied their youth, their insouciance; and turned back to the tower. The 'Meditations' revolve around it: it will act as a monument to him and his descendants; the stares (a west of Ireland name for starlings) nest in a hole over his bedroom window and become a symbol; from its top he surveys the countryside

> . . . and on the stair
> Wonder how many times I could have proved my worth
> In something that all others understand or share;[38]

The Republicans blew up the bridge, and thus dammed the river:[39] the water rose two feet in the kitchen the day the Yeats family left for Dublin at the end of the summer in 1922. (One of the reasons that the tower was only usable in the summer was a liability to winter flooding of the ground-floor level.) The tower had to be roofed, for the stone floors served but imperfectly in this capacity. A concrete top was built and Yeats could climb here and could see 'at no great distance a green field where stood once the thatched cottage of a famous country beauty

---

[37] WBY, 'The Road at My Door', *Collected Poems*, p. 229.
[38] WBY, 'Meditations in Time of Civil War, VII', *Collected Poems*, p. 232.
[39] Cf. his note in that volume (p. 534): 'Before they were finished the Republicans blew up our "ancient bridge" one midnight. They forbade us to leave the house, but were otherwise polite, even saying at last "Good-night, thank you," as though we had given them the bridge.'

[Mary Hynes], the mistress of a small local landed proprietor'.[40] He could also

> . . . pace upon the battlements and stare
> On the foundations of a house, or where
> Tree, like a sooty finger, starts from the earth;
> And send imagination forth
> Under the day's declining beam, and call
> Images and memories
> From ruin or from ancient trees. . . .[41]

In 1927, perhaps remembering the story of Swift and the tree half-dead at the top[42] Yeats thought of the waste room at the top of the tower where butterflies came in through the loop-hole and died against the window-panes:

> Upon the dusty, glittering windows cling,
> And seem to cling upon the moonlit skies,
> Tortoiseshell butterflies, peacock butterflies,
> A couple of night-moths are on the wing.
> Is every modern nation like the tower,
> Half dead at the top? No matter what I said,
> For wisdom is the property of the dead,
> A something incompatible with life; and power,
> Like everything that has the stain of blood,
> A property of the living; but no stain
> Can come upon the visage of the moon
> When it has looked in glory from a cloud.[43]

In January 1924, after the *annus mirabilis* of joining the Senate, the award of the Nobel Prize, and finishing *A Vision* and the new uniform edition of his work for Macmillan, Yeats and his wife were not in a mood to spend much on it.[44] Now the whole symbolism of the tower was complete. Yeats continued to enjoy it, as many phrases in letters indicate. In May 1926 he was writing poetry 'as I always do here'.[45] He liked the absence of events 'for nothing happens in this blessed place, but a stray beggar or a heron';[46] he felt he owed health to the tower.[47] In the summer of 1927 he recorded its 'perfect tranquility – no children, no telephone, no callers. No companion but a large white dog which

---

[40] WBY, *Autobiographies* (1956) p. 561.
[41] WBY, 'The Tower, II', *Collected Poems*, p. 219.
[42] WBY, 'Blood and the Moon, IV', *Collected Poems*, p. 269.
[43] See also a later poem 'Three Songs to the Same Tune, III', *Collected Poems*, p. 323:
> When nations are empty up there at the top
> When order has weakened or faction is strong
[44] *Letters*, p. 703.   [45] *Letters*, p. 714.   [46] *Letters*, p. 715.   [47] *Letters*, p. 716.

has a face like the Prince Consort, or a mid-Victorian statue – "capable of error but not of sin"'.[48] In this tranquillity he was writing the intense poems of *A Woman Young and Old*. The poem entitled 'The Tower' was published in 1927 in *October Blast*, a Cuala Press limited edition, and in 1928 by Macmillan in *The Tower*. Yeats continued to write new 'tower' poems in 1927 – including 'The Woman Young and Old', 'Blood and the Moon' and 'Sword and Tower' (later 'A Dialogue of Self and Soul') – which appeared in *The Winding Stair* (1929), published by the Fountain Press, New York, in October 1929, and later in *The Winding Stair* (1933).

In the winter of 1927–8 Yeats was planning the summer visit to Ballylee as one thing certain,[49] but from the distance of Switzerland the walk between Ballylee and Coole seemed likely to become overlong for him as his health deteriorated.[50] In February 1928 he wrote to T. Sturge Moore that he might see but little of the tower henceforth.[51] Its dampness and the absence of various comforts and amenities at Ballylee meant that 1929 was the last summer that the tower was occupied.

The symbolism of the tower poems was probably based upon a deliberate aim. In *The Cutting of an Agate* Yeats had written

> In European poetry I remember Shelley's continually repeated fountain and cave, his broad stream and solitary star.[52]

And Yeats continually repeats his own symbols (with a lack of inessential detail): the bridge, the river, the water-hens, the trees, the wind, the cottages, the tower, the stone chambers, the winding stair, the light, the battlement, the tower's top. The cover design for *The Tower* by T. Sturge Moore had 'a fine picture of Ballylee'[53] to add to these verbal images. Yeats sent the artist a bundle of photographs, asking him for an imaginative impression of the impressive building; the tower was not to be too unlike the real object. 'Do what you want with cloud and bird, day and night, but leave the great walls as they are', he wrote,[54] and later found when he got the first sketch for the cover that Sturge Moore 'had completed the Tower symbolism by surrounding it with water'.

[48] *Letters*, p. 725.   [49] *Letters*, p. 737.   [50] *Letters*, p. 739.
[51] WBY and T. Sturge Moore, *Correspondence* (1953) p. 123.
[52] WBY, 'Certain Noble Plays of Japan', *Essays and Introductions*, p. 235. Cf. also his reference to Shelley's recurring images of towers and rivers etc in 'Discoveries', *Essays and Introductions*, p. 294.   [53] *Letters*, p. 738.
[54] See WBY and T. Sturge Moore, *Correspondence*, pp. 109, 114 and 123.

The tower poetry is personal, the region peopled with the unusual, vivid characters who impressed themselves upon or originated in Yeats's imagination: Mary Hynes, Mrs French, Hanrahan, older inhabitants of the tower, contemporary soldiers and irregulars: all of them linked with the earlier poets' images, and the great eighteenth-century Anglo-Irish writers, Swift, Goldsmith, Berkeley and Burke. When young Yeats had thought it the duty of an Irish poet to describe some particular place in Ireland – as Allingham had Ballyshannon – and he had asserted his own lineage, poetic and social, in selecting the tower.

Its proximity to Coole where Lady Gregory seemed to have created an Irish Urbino was important to Yeats, who valued the public service and the private leisure of a cultivated aristocracy (as well as enjoying – perhaps even envying – the physical bravery sometimes displayed by its wilder members). Beyond the social and literary associations lay historical ones, of those generations of violence culminating in the Irish Civil War; but the tower remained as an image of wisdom. From it the poet could contemplate ruin and decay as well as the lively life of the birds, animals and fish along the banks of the river that vanished into the limestone, and that of the bees which might remind men that there had been more than enough hatred in the little room of the island. The bitterness of the tower poems later surprised Yeats. But this was part of his achievement, of his becoming his own subject. He had found cause for bitterness in his earlier experience of the bitterness of Irish life. He had early hoped to unite pagan and Christian elements in Irish tradition; then he developed the Gaelic legends as material for poetry while gaining from his experience of the tradition of English verse: his experience of nationalist politics, his creation of the Irish literary movement and the Abbey Theatre, his fusion of the Gaelic and the Anglo-Irish finally brought him back into an admiration of the eighteenth-century Anglo-Irish tradition – of intellectual freedom, of disregard for the mob:

> I declare this tower is my symbol; I declare
> This winding, gyring, spiring treadmill of a stair is my ancestral stair;
> That Goldsmith and the Dean, Berkeley and Burke have travelled there.[55]

After Yeats's death his gloomy picture of a possible decay could be remembered:

> . . . this laborious stair and this stark tower
> Become a roofless ruin that the owl

---

[55] WBY, 'Blood and the Moon', *Collected Poems*, p. 268.

> May build in the cracked masonry and cry
> Her desolation to the desolate sky.[56]

The inscription 'To be carved on a stone at Thoor Ballylee' was more explicit:

> I, the poet William Yeats,
> With old mill boards and sea-green slates,
> And smithy work from the Gort forge,
> Restored this tower for my wife George;
> And may these characters remain
> When all is ruin once again.[57]

The cottages fell in, Mrs Yeats's garden disappeared, much of the furniture was removed, and for many years the jackdaws chattered and screamed around the loop-holes, accentuating by their activity the loneliness of the gaunt building, its strength accentuated by the decaying cottages.[58]

Then, in 1963, Mrs Yeats placed the property in trust, and the Irish Tourist Board, *Bord Failte*, restored the buildings and opened the tower to the public in 1965. The Board and the Kiltartan Society, founded by Mrs Mary Hanley in 1961, co-operated in the renovation, based on Professor Scott's original drawings. Some of the original furniture was discovered, some was replaced by new pieces made by a local craftsman, and both the interior walls and the thatched roofs are now as they were in the 1920s. Padraic Colum opened the tower in June 1965, the centenary month and year of Yeats's birth. It was worth remembering that the poet once wrote to his friend Sturge Moore that he liked to think of the building

> As a permanent symbol of my work plainly visible to the passer-by. As you know, all my art theories depend on just this – rooting of mythology in the earth.[59]

[56] WBY, 'My Descendants', *Collected Poems*, p. 229.
[57] WBY, *Collected Poems*, p. 214. The stone was not set up in Yeats's lifetime: it was erected by the Board of the Abbey Theatre in 1948.
[58] For further information see Mary Hanley, *Thoor Ballylee* (Dublin, 1965).
[59] WBY and T. Sturge Moore, *Correspondence*, p. 114.

Yeats, critic

The true ambition is to make criticism as international, and literature as National, as possible.[1]

YEATS wrote criticism more or less continuously throughout his life. He read very widely. Not only did he assimilate what he read but he had a flair for finding in the works of others what he wanted for his own poetic purposes, and in his reading he sought confirmation for his own ideas and beliefs.[2] He talked freely of his discoveries, using them to bolster his own theories and convictions; and he also wrote freely about them, using prose as a means of exploring and explaining his thoughts. He was primarily interested in the emotions and impulses that create literature.

His early critical work is obviously part of this explorative process. In his family the exploration and explanation of ideas was often a lively business, carried on by arguments which were very energetically pursued. On one occasion, for instance, he differed from his father, the artist John Butler Yeats, on the subject of Ruskin's *Unto This Last* and was ejected from the room by his father so violently that he broke the glass of a picture with the back of his head. On another occasion his father wanted to fight him, but Yeats said he couldn't fight his own father. 'I don't see why you shouldn't', replied the artist, whose several views on the nature of Irish family life were obviously based on his own experience, both as a young man and as a father. The bright Irish boy, he wrote in an essay, experienced so much frank conversation at home that

> His intellect is in constant exercise. He is full of intellectual curiosity, so much conversation keeping it alive. . . .
> He is at once sceptical and credulous but, provided his opinions are expressed gaily and frankly, no one minds. With us intellect takes the place which in the English home is occupied by the business faculty.[3]

In his teens Yeats grew up under the influence of his father's lively,

[1] WBY, Letter to the Editor, *United Ireland*, 10 Nov [1894], in *Letters*, ed. Allan Wade, p. 239.
[2] A point made by Alexander Zwerdling, *Yeats and the Heroic Ideal* (1966) p. 77.
[3] John Butler Yeats, *Essays Irish and American* (1918) p. 30.

questioning mind. J. B. Yeats admired Shakespeare and Scott, Balzac
and the Pre-Raphaelites: but he had little time for the orthodoxies:

> Wordsworth, notwithstanding his genius, is to my mind a dull dog and his
> intensities and enthusiasms have something forced and factitious in them. . . ,
> Shelley again has always seemed a little crazy, a little of a fanatic . . . Byron, –
> talent rather than genius. . . . Browning was the non-conformist conscience
> trying to make itself vocal and musical – all *his* humanity gone away into some
> such channels; he thought poorly of human nature. . . . The stripling Keats,
> had he not died of consumption, would have died spiritually in the intellectual
> penury of the time; and as to Tennyson and his musical inanities – whom do
> they grip?[4]

When his son was set a school essay on the theme 'Men may rise
on the stepping-stones of their dead selves to higher things' the artist
was indignant, and suggested that Shakespeare's lines 'To thine own
self be true, and it must follow, as the night the day, thou canst not
then be false to any man' would make a better subject. He would attack
the concept of duty savagely; his iconoclasm must have been stimulat-
ing and exciting. It was not, however, the product of a destructive mind,
for John Butler Yeats appreciated writers who were humane; he was
convinced that poets would find their salvation in writing for the
public theatre. Though Yeats later came to believe that a lot of what his
father had said to him in his teens was right, he regretted that he had
not been taken away from school and taught Latin and Greek: this
would have made him 'a properly educated man' who would not have
had 'to look in useless longing at books that have been, through the
poor mechanism of translation, the builders of my soul nor to face
authority with the timidity born of excuse and evasion'.

John Butler Yeats disliked over-much trust in the intellect; he held
that all valuable education 'was but a stirring up of the emotions'. He
was himself a rationalist, much swayed by reading John Stuart Mill as a
young man: his son, however, moved away from his influence as he
developed his own interest in psychical research and mystical philosophy, and began to form his own political ideas. The father had killed
the son's capacity for belief but not his capacity to search at once wish-
fully and sceptically for it; and where the father was a Home Ruler,
the son became a nationalist. He later described himself as a particular
kind of Irish nationalist, of the school of John O'Leary. O'Leary (1830–

---

[4] Cf. a similar expression of dislike of Wordsworth, and comment on Shelley and
Browning in a letter to WBY of 5 Mar 1910, included in *J. B. Yeats: Letters to his son
W. B. Yeats and Others*, ed. J. Hone (1944) p. 124.

1907)[5] had been sentenced to twenty years' penal servitude in 1865: he was released under amnesty in 1871 and lived in Belgium and later in Paris. When his sentence expired in 1885, he returned to Dublin where he became President of the Young Ireland Society. He was an idealist who exercised much influence over Yeats, and introduced him to a new literary and social world unlike that of his father and his father's friends. In Dublin these had included Edward Dowden, the first Professor of English Literature at Trinity College, Dublin, the biographer of Shelley and the author of a study of Shakespeare. He was an interesting critic, who did not, however, rate Irish literature highly – though he encouraged W. B.'s early writing, which first appeared in the *Dublin University Review* in 1885. In England John Butler Yeats was a member of a Pre-Raphaelite group, and his son described him as 'living in a free world accustomed to the gay exaggeration of the talk of equals, of men who talk and write to discover truth, and not for popular instruction'. When the family lived at Bedford Park in North London they met York Powell, Professor of History at Oxford, who spent his week-ends in his house in this new suburb. Powell was kind to the young poet, but neither the early encouragement of Dowden nor the subsequent aid of Powell was as important to him as his friendship with O'Leary. The literary, social, and political milieu into which the old Fenian brought the young poet was very different from the Protestant establishment to which his father belonged by birth and education.

Through O'Leary Yeats discovered the work of patriotic Irish writers, and he began to learn something of Irish Catholic life through his friendship with Katharine Tynan, who introduced him to other living Irish writers. O'Leary lent him small sums of money and Irish books, and suggested others he should read. In particular he drew Yeats's attention to the Gaelic legends as they existed in useful but little-known pioneering but pedestrian translations. Thus in addition to reading the poems of Thomas Davis, Jeremiah Joseph Callanan and James Clarence Mangan, Yeats read the translations of Gaelic legend by David Comyn, Nicholas O'Kearney, John O'Daly, Eugene O'Curry and Brian O'Looney. Sir Samuel Ferguson's adaptations and Standish O'Grady's histories and prose epics (and later his novels) had more effect on his imagination than any of the others.

Through Katharine Tynan Yeats met Father Matthew Russell, who

5 See Desmond Ryan, *The Fenian Chief: A Biography of James Stephens* (1967) p. 361' for a brief biography of John O'Leary.

edited *The Irish Monthly*, and his work began to be published in this journal and in another, *The Irish Fireside*, from 1886 onwards. John O'Leary recommended him to John Boyle O'Reilly (1844-98), who, like O'Leary, had been arrested in 1865. He was sentenced to death, his sentence was commuted to twenty years' penal servitude, and, after three attempts to escape from prison, he was transported to Western Australia in 1868. In 1869 he escaped to the United States and became Editor of the *Boston Pilot* in 1876. This paper paid well for Yeats's articles, published under the heading 'The Celt in London', and, together with *The Providence Sunday Journal*, gave him an entry into an American readership, as well as a means of exploring his ideas through journalism. By 1889 he had also appeared in *The Gael, United Ireland, The Leisure Hour* and *East and West*, and W. E. Henley published his work in the *Scots Observer*.

His early prose records his adventuring into new literary areas. His first article, which appeared in *The Irish Fireside* in October 1886, was on 'The Poetry of Sir Samuel Ferguson', a bold move towards the revelation of his own aims, for in it he stated his aim of bringing Catholic and Protestant together in a new literary movement, an aim he later glossed in his *Autobiographies*:

> I had noticed that Irish Catholics among whom had been born so many political martyrs had not the good taste, the household courtesy and decency of the Protestant Ireland I had known, yet Protestant Ireland seemed to think of nothing but getting on in the world. I thought we might bring the halves together if we had a national literature that made Ireland beautiful in the memory, and yet had been freed from provincialism by an exacting criticism, a European pose.[6]

In Sir Samuel Ferguson's poems he found 'barbarous truth'; the older poet, who had died in 1886, had gone back to the Irish cycle of legends; he had restored the old Gaelic heroes to Ireland. Another article with the same title which appeared in the *Dublin University Review*, in November 1886, formulated some of Yeats's own ideas on the future of Irish literature. Ferguson had lacked the support of good critics, indeed Professor Dowden had failed to pay due attention to Irish writing. This was the first of Yeats's attacks on his father's friend (there may have been some element of sour grapes in Yeats's attacks on the dons of Trinity College[7]) and it was based on the idea that the

[6] WBY, *Autobiographies*, pp. 101-2.
[7] When he left the High School, Dublin, his ability to pass the easy Entrance examination was doubtful, and the money for fees difficult to find. See J. Hone, *W. B. Yeats 1865-1939*, p. 41, and A. Norman Jeffares, *W. B. Yeats: Man and Poet*, pp. 23-4.

most cultivated of Irish readers were only anxious to be academic:

and to be servile to English notions. If Sir Samuel Ferguson had written of
Arthur and of Guinevere, they would have received him gladly; that he chose
rather to tell of Congal and of desolate and queenly Deirdre, we give him full-
hearted thanks; he has restored to our hills and rivers their epic interest.[8] The
nation has found in Davis a battle call, as in Mangan the cry of despair; but he
only, the one Homeric poet of our time, could give us immortal companions
still wet with the dew of their primal world.

He added a typical young man's attack on the Establishment:

I do not appeal to the professional classes, who, in Ireland, at least, appear at no
time to have thought of the affairs of their country till they first feared for their
emoluments – nor do I appeal to the shoddy society of 'West Britonism' – but
to those young men clustered here and there throughout our land, whom the
emotion of patriotism has lifted into that world of selfless passion in which
heroic deeds are possible and heroic poetry credible.

Yeats realised the power of the Gaelic legends and stressed the Celtic,
heroic, and bardic qualities of Ferguson's poetry. Ferguson seemed to
him to view nature through a clear glass. He also found immediate
encouragement in the work of William Allingham, the poet of Ballyshannon, about whom he wrote in *The Providence Sunday Journal* on
2 September 1888, and in whom he recognised 'the entire emotion for
the place one grew up in'[9] which he had himself felt as a child in Sligo:

To remember how it was the centre of your world, how the mountains and the
rivers and the roads became a portion of your life for ever; to have loved with
a sense of possession even the roadside bushes where the roadside cottage hung
their clothes to dry. That sense of possession was the very centre of the matter.
Elsewhere you are only a passer-by, for everything is owned by so many that
it is owned by no one. Down there as you hummed over Allingham's *Fairies*
and looked up at the mountain where they lived it seemed to you that a portion of your life was the subject.[10]

Allingham, however, did not sufficiently sympathise with Ireland's
nationalism to gain Yeats's full approval.

His lifelong theme was already firmly established, that there is no
great literature without nationality, no great nationality without literature.[11] In pursuit of this idea he attacked George Savage-Armstrong, a
Cork poet and dramatist, in *United Ireland* on 23 July 1892, and in *The
Bookman* in September 1892, largely because he was a 'West-Briton'

8 See an essay 'Ireland and the Arts', *Essays and Introductions*, p. 206. This first appeared
in the *United Irishman*, 31 Aug 1904.   9 *Autobiographies*, p. 471.
10 WBY, *Letters to the New Island* (1934) p. 165.   11 Ibid., p. 104.

and because his poetry was largely 'noetry' – he found nothing but
'noetry' in seven out of this professor's nine volumes – and 'noetry'
mingled heavily with poetry in the remaining two volumes, though
Yeats thought Savage-Armstrong effective when he wrote of Wicklow.
This attack continued the strain of his article 'Dublin Scholasticism and
Trinity College' in *United Ireland*, 30 July 1892, in which Yeats
savagely remarked: 'As Dublin Castle with the help of the police keeps
Ireland for England, so Trinity College with the help of the school-
masters keeps the mind of Ireland for scholasticism with its accompanying weight of mediocrity.'

He continued to read more deeply in this Gaelic literature he was
discovering through the work of the translators and adaptors, and involved himself continuously in the process of working out a relationship between his literary and nationalistic aims. The Gaelic legends
came as means of escaping from the material of English Victorian
poets, from the Arthuriad of Tennyson, from the classicism of Arnold,
and from the medievalism of the Pre-Raphaelites. And it also offered
an escape from the present. In his pursuit of an Irish mythology he was
drawn into writing about many Irish authors. In the ten years from
1886, for instance, he dealt with Sir Samuel Ferguson, R. D. Joyce,
James Clarence Mangan, William Allingham, John Todhunter, William
Carleton, the Banim brothers, Jeremiah Curtin, Lady Wilde, Douglas
Hyde, Rose Kavanagh, Ellen O'Leary, Oscar Wilde, Standish O'Grady,
William Larminie, AE (George Russell), Thomas Davis and 'John
Eglinton' (W. K. Magee).

His enthusiasm led him to collect material from written and oral
sources for his *Irish Fairy and Folk Tales* (1888). He also edited *Stories
from Carleton* (1889) and *Representative Irish Tales* (1891), and he com-
piled *A book of Irish Verse* (1895).

His reviews and articles could be classified as literary journalism, his
editing described as hackwok, but for the fact that Yeats took all this
work very seriously indeed. It is true that he wrote to Robert Bridges
to remark modestly that his review of Bridges's *Return of Ulysses* was
'journalism like all my criticism so far, and done more quickly than I
would like'. But his reviewing and writing, his editing and anthologis-
ing had more to it than merely giving something of himself, giving his
criticism, as he explained in the same letter to Bridges 'to the devil
that one may live'.[12] He was deeply and seriously concerned as a
nationalist with the state of Irish culture and was prepared to work

[12] WBY, *Letters*, Sunday [June 1897[p. 286.

hard to reform it. His prose provided the propaganda necessary for the task; it was no light or easy struggle on which he had entered; and he knew it.

The 'Young Ireland' movement had produced political rhetoric rather than poetry, but to dethrone this patriotic literature in Ireland without appearing to be unpatriotic was extremely difficult. Sir Charles Gavan Duffy returned from Australia and took over Yeats's ideas for a New Irish Library, putting into it books which Yeats thought would kill the series. When he reviewed[13] three of the dull volumes in this Library Yeats used the occasion to stress his belief in the need for two kinds of literature, one which would appeal to the Irish countryfolk, the other to an educated, sophisticated Irish audience.[14] He also poured scorn on the 'jigging doggerel' which passed for Irish patriotic poetry and pointed out that neither 'the wholly uneducated peasant of the mountains' nor 'the wholly educated professional man of the cities' would have anything to do with this outmoded political didacticism. He attacked 'the half-educated country clerk or farmer's son' (who were later to become the philistine Irish middle class which he regarded with despair at the time of the Synge and Lane controversies while his dreams turned on the extremes of 'noble and beggarman'[15]), realising that his own doctrines were oversophisticated for political platforms.

Yeats's own writings were intended to make his readers aware that Ireland possessed very different traditions, totally different outlooks, from those of England. These were not necessarily attitudes he shared. At his English school he had not sympathised with his schoolfellows' patriotic thoughts about 'Cressy and Agincourt', but he had not, on the other hand, the Irish Catholic's memories of Limerick and the Yellow Ford to set against them, while he was to reject the conformism of Unionism, the Anti-Nationalist bias of his own ancestry. And so as a schoolboy he had fallen back on thoughts of mountain and lake in Sligo, of his grandfather there and of his 'grandfather's steamers plying between Liverpool and Sligo'. In his prose as well as in his verse he

---

[13] WBY, 'Some Irish National Books', *The Bookman*, Aug 1894.
[14] When he edited *A Book of Irish Verse* (1895) he remarked in his Introduction that it was 'not at all for Irish peasants'.
[15] See a lively passage in 'Poetry and Tradition', *Essays and Introductions*, p. 257: 'Three types of men have made all beautiful things, Aristocracies have made beautiful manners, because their place in the world puts them above the fear of life, and the countrymen have made beautiful stories and beliefs, because they have nothing to lose and so do not fear, and the artists have made all the rest, because Providence has filled them with recklessness.' The essay is dated 1907. See also ibid., p. 516.

regarded what he was trying to create as going back beyond more
recent Irish writing of the eighteenth and nineteenth centuries (at this
time he was, in general, excluding the eighteenth-century Anglo-Irish
writers from an Irish canon, though, amusingly enough, Dowden was
shortly to argue for them[16]) to the heroic Gaelic past and uniting with
this his own special interests – especially in folklore and the supernatural – while insisting upon more rigorous standards of writing and
criticism. He was, of course, in danger of falling between two stools,
of boring his new friends in the Rhymers' Club in London with too
much Celtic material,[17] and of irritating his Irish audience by criticising
accepted figures like Thomas Davis.[18] A condescending, apparently
over-confident tone pervaded some of his early prose – probably the
result of his secret unsureness, his longing to have been better educated.
While he could advise Miss Elizabeth White, an Irish writer, to
capitalise on Irish material[19] there was a defensiveness about his attitude
to his own writings:

> Nor may I less be counted one with Davis, Mangan, Ferguson.[20]

He wrote these lines[21] when his poetry was becoming more cryptic in
meaning, and he continued, appealing implicitly to the educated
sophisticated Irish reader:

> Because to him also ponders well
> My rhymes more than their rhyming tell . . .

His experience in England was that writers believed in poetry as an
end in itself while in Ireland, along with 'the robustness and rough
energy', which was so much in contrast with English writing, which
seemed the product of an age 'getting old and feeble', there went the
most utter indifference to art, the most dire carelessness, the most
dreadful intermixture of the commonplace.[22]

[16] Yeats's own views in his 1930 diary were concise; he thought 'that the thought of
Swift, enlarged and enriched by Burke, saddled and bitted reality, and that materialism
was hamstrung by Berkeley and ancient wisdom brought back; that modern Europe has
known no men more powerful' (text from *Explorations*, p. 297).

[17] See WBY, 'Hopes and Fears for Irish Literature', *United Ireland*, 15 Oct 1892.

[18] See his letter to the Editor of the Dublin *Daily Express*, 7 Feb 1895, which shows
how he was attacked in Ireland, for substituting 'the pursuit of high art for the old easy-
going days when every patriotic writer was as good as his neighbour'.

[19] WBY, letter of 30 Jan [1889], *Letters*, p. 103.

[20] WBY, 'To Ireland in the Coming Times', *Collected Poems*, p. 57.

[21] They were originally entitled 'An Apologia to Ireland . . .', in *The Countess Kathleen
and Various Legends and Lyrics* (1892).

[22] See his 'Hopes and Fears for Irish Literature', *United Ireland*, 15 Oct 1892, in which
he differentiates between cultivated people in the two islands.

The next development in his prose ran parallel to the path taken by his verse, though it did not become so complex for some time. His reviewing continued as direct propaganda for the Irish literary movement. He stressed the merits of those writers, and especially his friends, who were bringing into being what he considered good Irish literature. As early as 1887 he had praised Katharine Tynan's[23] work; by 1890 he was lamenting Ireland's lack of critical writing;[24] and in the same year he was emphasising the melancholy of Irish legends and peasant minds,[25] entitling his review 'Tales from the Twilight'. The Irish literary movement was often summed up as the 'Celtic twilight' movement, a description deriving from *The Celtic Twilight*, Yeats's collection of poems and prose pieces which appeared in 1893. Some of this prose included material which joined together his interests in folklore and the supernatural: for instance, 'Village Ghosts',[26] Drumcliff and Rosses',[27] 'The Three O'Byrnes and the Evil Faeries'[28] and a review of Douglas Hyde's *Beside the Fire: a collection of Irish Gaelic Folk Tales*.[29] The poems developed the twilight mood, of dim far-off things.

The Celtic Twilight consolidated the success of *The Wandering of Oisin* (1889) and *The Countess Kathleen and Various Legends and Lyrics* (1892), and led forward to the achievement of *Poems* (1895). By the middle nineties, however, Yeats was moving into a new sophistication. Reviewing for the *Scots Observer* and even more for *The Bookman* had established him firmly in London's literary life and had given him a most useful non-Irish platform for his views on what Irish literature should be.

The advantage of appearing in *The Bookman* can be seen if the unhappy controversy between Yeats and Dowden (which can be followed in the Dublin *Daily Express*[30]) is compared with the four excellent articles Yeats wrote on 'Irish National Literature' between July and October in *The Bookman*. In these four articles, in which he had sufficient space and time for reflection, Yeats was at his best, praising the merits of those writers whom he admired, and having an opportunity to develop his views on the old and the new literatures of Ireland

[23] Review of her *Shamrocks* in *The Irish Fireside*, 9 July 1887.
[24] In a review of Sophie Bryant's *Celtic Ireland*, in the *Scots Observer*, 4 Jan 1890.
[25] In review of Lady Wilde's *Ancient Cures, Charms and Usages of Ireland* in the *Scots Observer*, 1 Mar 1890.
[26] Originally appeared in the *Scots Observer*, 11 May 1889.
[27] Originally appeared in the *Scots Observer*, 5 Oct 1889.
[28] Originally appeared in 'Irish Faeries', *The Leisure Hour*, Oct 1890.
[29] Originally appeared in *The National Observer*, 28 Feb 1891.
[30] See issues of 26 Jan, 7 Feb, 27 Feb and 8 Mar 1895.

CA C

at some length. This was a more positive way for him to express his anger at Dowden and Unionist Ireland in general.[31] They had, he wrote in his unpublished autobiography:

> opposed to our movement their mere weight and indifference, and had written and spoken as if the finest literature of Ireland – certain old ballads in English, the Gaelic heroic tales, the new literature of A.E., Johnson, Standish O'Grady, of myself, was itself provincial and barbarous.

In the first of his four articles Yeats defined his idea of the scope of Irish writing: it consisted of work written 'under Irish influence and of Irish subjects'. This gave him a free hand to dismiss from consideration such writers as Swift, Berkeley and Burke, whom, ironically enough, he was later – when he had actually read them in middle age – to take up with enthusiasm, seeing the eighteenth century as the one period of Irish history without confusion. He found the absence of tradition in Irish writing harmful: English-speaking Ireland was a new country, he thought, and the Irish writers who had been effective in the nineteenth century had used English techniques. His dethroning of past Irish literary gods was effective. Thomas Moore 'quenched an admirable Celtic lyricism in an artificial glitter learned from the eighteenth century' (in Yeats's old age he dismissed him more harshly in *On the Boiler* as that 'cringing Firbolg Tom Moore'); Thomas Davis borrowed the 'strange help' of Macaulay, Scott and Lockhart; and John Mitchel, whose magnificent *Jail Journal* he praised discerningly, none the less used a thunder that was half-Carlyle's. These men were not priests of the 'Immortal Moods' but they were the kind of writer Yeats had had in mind when he wrote in *United Ireland* on 23 December 1893:

> I did not say the man of letters should keep out of politics but I remember the examples of Hugo, and Milton, and Dante, but only that he should, no matter how strong be his political instincts, endeavour to become a master of his craft, and be ever careful to keep rhetoric, or the tendency to think of his audience rather than of the Perfect and the True, out of his writing.

He detected his own kind of writing in the poems of Callanan, who possessed 'the cold vehemence, the arid definiteness, the tumultuous movement, the immeasurable dreaming of the Gaelic literature', while

---

[31] In a review of Lady Ferguson's *Sir Samuel Ferguson in the Ireland of his Day*, in *The Bookman*, May 1896, he returned to the attack, suggesting that the hardness and heaviness in Ferguson's rhythm and language came from the 'dead world' around him of 'dignitaries, professional condemners of the multitude, and archbishops and bishops, deans and archdeacons, professors and members of learned societies, Lord Chancellors and leaders of the Bar . . .'.

in those of Aubrey de Vere the 'Immortal Moods' found 'the one perfect ritual fashioned for their honour by Irish hands'. Mangan's half-
dozen lyrics of 'indescribable, vehement beauty' provided passion of a
European romantic nature, while Sir Samuel Ferguson, despite lapses
into verse that could be monotonous and clumsy, possessed a 'massy
strength or tranquil beauty'. In Carleton there was to be found the
peasant Chaucer of a new tradition.

In the prose writers, however, there was not enough imaginative
artistry to satisfy Yeats. Indeed Standish O'Grady was 'the only Irish
historian' who was 'anything of an artist'. He received generous praise
for his *History of Ireland: Heroic Period* (1878), which had 'done more
than anything else to create that preoccupation with Irish folklore and
legend and epic which is called the Irish literary movement'.

Here Yeats was, perforce, being manifestly unfair to himself. He
had reached a capacity for more balanced judgement of others, however, for while he could see O'Grady's faults – 'Despite his breathless
generalisations,' he wrote, 'his slipshod style, his ungovernable likings
and dislikings' – he insisted on his merits as 'the first man who has tried
to write the true history of Ireland'.

Yeats was labouring under the difficulties often experienced today by
those who write about the emergent literatures of Africa, as he attempted to write a truer history of contemporary Irish writing than
either extreme Irish nationalists or Unionists could achieve. In his
second article,[32] on the prose authors, Miss Emily Lawless was described as a twofold slanderer of Irish and English national character
because she followed stereotypes; Miss Jane Barlow was the creator of
peasants who were 'passive, melancholy and gentle' whereas, Yeats
wryly pointed out, they are 'often as not grim as their limestone, or
fiery as a shaken torch'. Such touches of realism show Yeats's capacity
for common sense, though those who followed his own prescriptions
for Irish literature were more gently treated, Nora Hopper, for instance,
being praised for a book that had 'the beauty of dim twilight'. A balance
was sought in his account of Douglas Hyde, who at his worst was
'shapeless enough', at his best 'an admirable artist'. There is a single
sharp discerning sentence to indicate the merits of the Somerville and
Ross novel of Irish middle-class life, *The Real Charlotte*.

Among the poets, in his third article,[33] Yeats seemed more at ease,
and here he returned to his idiosyncratic ideas of literary history, that
Ireland was in a ballad or epic stage where England was in the decadent

[32] *The Bookman*, Aug 1895.   [33] *The Bookman*, Sept 1895.

period of a lyric stage of literature. In pronouncing that Art is a revelation not a criticism, he was reinforced by his own escape from Arnold-
ian ideas, from the flux of contemporary Victorian life, back into a
Gaelic past. 'The Irish Celt', he declared, 'has an unexhausted and in-
exhaustible mythology to give him symbols and personages, and his
nature has been profoundly emotional from the beginning.' Thus,
Douglas Hyde's *Love Songs from Connacht* have in them the search for
something beyond expression and AE had 'a perfect understanding
that the business of poetry is not to enforce an opinion or expound an
action but to bring us into communication with the moods and passions
which are the creative powers behind the universe'. The previous year
he had reviewed AE's *Homeward Songs by the Way*[34] and though he was
severe with the faults he found in plenty in this volume – 'certain
rhymes are repeated too often, the longer lines stumble now and again,
and here and there a stanza is needlessly obscure' – he was able to
praise AE because of his mystic qualities. This was 'the most haunting
book' he had seen 'these many days'. Such praise, because discriminating, was indeed effective.

In his fourth article on Irish literature, Yeats drew up a list of the
best Irish books; he was able to point out that in a literature which was
not only new, but without recognised criticism any list was a good
deed in a disordered world. In effect he was saying that there were now
enough Irish writers before the public for the literature to be taken
seriously. He included his own anthology *A Book of Irish Verse* (1895)
on the grounds that an anthology was necessary, and that he disliked
those already in existence. The last of the four articles has a polemic air
about it: it returns to the attack on Dowden, but there is also a touch
of weariness about it, as though the battle had been fought too long.

Yeats longed to escape from criticism: he felt it took undue time
from his poetry. He had made his distinctions in various reviews
between poetry and prose, between poet and critic. His passionate
interest in style, especially in symbolism, was continuously developing.
He was influenced by Oscar Wilde and Walter Pater as his prose
became more mannered – though he later regarded Wilde as over-
artificial,[35] and he had learned much about the French symbolists from

[34] *The Bookman*, Aug 1894.
[35] In a review, 'Oscar Wilde's Last Book', *United Ireland*, 26 Sept 1891, he described
him as partially 'Irish of the Irish', seeing in his life and works 'an extravagant Celtic
crusade against Anglo-Saxon stupidity. "I labour under a perpetual fear of not being
misunderstood", he wrote. . . .' Pater's idea of culture seemed to him, by 1909, to be only
able to create feminine souls' (*Estrangement*, text from *Autobiographies*, p. 477).

Arthur Symons, with whom he shared a flat in the Temple in 1896.
This was the year when he hoped to achieve his escape from journalism
by attempting to write stories and novels. (The stories of *The Secret
Rose* (1897) ensued, but the novel was never finished.) He had been
enormously influenced by the English poets he had met at the Rhymers'
Club; their example reinforced his belief that all Irish people needed to
respect craftsmanship more – Davis, Mangan, Carleton were examples
of Irish writers who had not achieved their proper success. Craftsmanship had to be sought in England.[36] He himself had rejected the lure of
regular employment there earlier in his career – to his father's relief.
But he envied the assurance and scholarship of Dowden, or Wilde, or
Lionel Johnson (whose stately style he regarded as better than Hardy's),
and he set himself to shaping his own form of dignity and courtliness.
This was not easy particularly when he had to write for a living, and
one which paid him little. In order to survive and to preserve his
literary ideals he had to call into existence his own form of what he
called in 1930 'the Anglo-Irish solitude'.[37] As early as 1892 he had
faced the problem:

> he who would write a memorable song must be ready to give often days to a
> few lines, and be ready, perhaps, to pay for it afterwards with certain other
> days of dire exhaustion and depression, and, if he would be remembered when
> he is in his grave, he must give to his art the devotion the Crusaders of old gave
> to their cause and be content to be alone among men, apart alike from their
> joys and sorrows, having for companions the multitude of his dreams and for
> reward the kingdom of his pride.[38]

He sought to purge from his work what he saw as impurities
(curiosities about politics, science, history, religion) in the writings of
Swinburne, Browning and Tennyson. He wanted to create once more
'the pure art'. The paradox was that as he sought this, his own interest
in occultism, magic, psychical research, astrology and the Hermetic
tradition deepened. And so his prose became richer in texture, more
elaborate and allusive. Here is an example of it:

> Painting, music, science, politics, and even religion, because they have felt a
> growing belief that we know nothing but the fading and flowering of the
> world, have changed in numberless elaborate ways. Man has wooed and won
> the world, and has fallen weary, and not, I think, for a time, but with a weari-
> ness that will not end until the last autumn, when the stars shall be blown away

---

36 WBY, letter to Olivia Shakespear, 12 Apr 1895, *Letters*, ed. Allan Wade, p. 257.
37 WBY, *Explorations*, p. 325.
38 WBY, 'Hopes and Fears for Irish Literature', *United Ireland*, 15 Oct 1892. This is the
doctrine stated again in 'Adam's Curse', *Collected Poems*, p. 88: 'A line will take us hours
maybe . . .'.

like withered leaves. He grew weary when he said, 'These things that I touch and see and hear are alone real', for he saw them without illusion at last, and found them but air and dust and moisture. And now he must be philosophical above everything, even about the arts, for he can only return the way he came, and so escape from weariness, by philosophy. The arts are, I believe, about to take upon their shoulders the burdens that have fallen from the shoulders of priests, and to lead us back upon our journey by filling our thoughts with the essences of things, and not with things. We are about to substitute once more the distillation of alchemy for the analyses of chemistry and for some other sciences; and certain of us are looking everywhere for the perfect alembic that no silver or golden drop may escape. Mr. Symons has written lately on Mallarmé's method, and has quoted him as saying that we should 'abolish the pretension, aesthetically an error, despite its dominion over almost all the masterpieces, to enclose within the subtle paper other than – for example – the horror of the forest or the silent thunder in the leaves, not the intense dense wood of the trees', and as desiring to substitute for 'the old lyric afflatus or the enthusiastic personal direction of the phrase' words 'that take light from mutual reflection, like an actual trail of fire over precious stones', and 'to make an entire word hitherto unknown to the language' 'out of many vocables'. Mr. Symons understands these and other sentences to mean that poetry will henceforth be a poetry of essences, separated one from another in little and intense poems. I think there will be much poetry of this kind, because of an ever more arduous search for an almost disembodied ecstasy, but I think we will not cease to write long poems, but rather that we will write them more and more as our new belief makes the world plastic under our hands again. I think that we will learn again how to describe at great length an old man wandering among enchanted islands, his return home at last, his slow-gathering vengeance, a flitting shape of a goddess, and a flight of arrows, and yet to make all of these so different things 'take light from mutual reflection, like an actual trail of fire over precious stones', and become 'an entire word', the signature or symbol of a mood of the divine imagination as imponderable as 'the horror of the forest or the silent thunder in the leaves'.[39]

The reasons for the allusiveness exemplified in this passage are themselves complex. As Yeats had wanted his verse to be beautiful, to occupy itself with essences and with moods, to be a thing of beauty, free of the immediate and the realistic, he kept many of his political and occult interests out of his verse for some time, and so, in the same way, he kept his prose allusive. Up to a point, at this period of his life, he *wanted* to be obscure. And in part he wanted obscurity as a cloak. The 'excuse and evasion' which timidity had led him to adopt in the face of authority meant that he was unsure of himself, unready to assert his views. Instead, he tended to use rhetorical questions.

[39] WBY, 'The Autumn of the Body', *Ideas of Good and Evil* (1903). This first appeared under the title 'The Autumn of the Flesh' in the Dublin *Daily Express*, 3 Dec 1898, and was reprinted in *Literary Ideals in Ireland* (1899).

While his own prose became more elaborate, so in his comments on his reading the names of more obscure writers were increasingly mentioned, and their names began to appear almost as decorative elements in his style. Often, however, they were invoked to lend their authority to statements themselves shadowy, which were imbued with Pre-Raphaelite melancholia and were generalisations upon the theme of art and the artist, for Yeats did not make large distinctions between art and literature.

In *Literary Ideals in Ireland* (1899) he wrote of the renewal of belief the 'great movement of our time' which would liberate the arts from their age, and leave them free to lose themselves in beauty, the accumulated beauty of the age. Men would reject the idea that poetry was a criticism of life: they would regard painting, poetry and music as 'the only means of conversing with eternity left to man on earth' (p. 37).

His concept of literature was, in part, emotional. The best poetry contained images of a better world than this: the poets were not to be involved in the actual world which was full of weeping. But this concept could not be maintained after the turn of the century, even though the writers who had originally affected Yeats's critical views continued to influence his thought. Shelley's affirmations, Blake's revelations, even Hallam's advocacy of unpopular art[40] underlay much of his thinking about literature: his prose of the 1890s reflects the background to his own development as a poet, his continuous linking of art and literature.

His critical articles in the nineties include comment upon the performance of Villiers de l'Isle-Adam's symbolist drama *Axël*, which he saw in Paris in 1894, on the symbolist paintings of Althea Gyles (a young artist with whom he had formed a friendship in London), on symbolism in poetry, on the philosophy of Shelley's poetry, and on Blake's symbolic art.

His reviews of work on Blake reveal him acting the part of outraged scholar and defender of the text. When reviewing Laurence Housman's *Selections from the Writings of William Blake* in *The Bookman*, August 1893, he attacked Housman for using doctored texts and omitting material, and for the matter of his Introduction. An editor had a perfect

---

[40] Yeats's review of *The Poems of Arthur Henry Hallam* in *The Speaker*, 22 July 1893, is a clear statement of the dangers of popular art; Yeats thought Hallam 'philosophical'; he saw in his writings an early statement of the principles of the aesthetic movement – beauty being 'the beginning and end of all things in art'. See also the essay 'Art and Ideas', dated 1913, in *Essays and Introductions*, p. 349.

right, he wrote, to think the Prophetic Books nonsense even before
he read them, but let him keep from editing Blake; and again if he
has to edit Blake, let him keep from all comment on the prophetic.
This fury was not manifested in his later review of Richard Garnett's
William Blake, in *The Bookman*, April 1896. Yeats's views on Swedenborg and Boehme emerge again as in the earlier review, there is a
mild thwacking for repetition of old errors and some acid comment on
Garnett's apparent use of Rossetti's edition, and finally a qualified re-
commendation – the book would help all who could learn a little of
one of the most creative minds of modern days: its futilities were
wholly, its errors almost wholly in the parts where it touched mysticism. As a result of his own work Yeats had a proprietorial attitude to
Blake, his master, as he proudly called him.

An essay on Magic (1901) began to reveal how his own early fascination with the supernatural, with the fairies and ghosts of Irish tradition,
had become more sophisticated, more involved (because of the conflict
between his desire to believe in something and his innate scepticism),
and perhaps all the more committed to exploring the undercurrents of
European and Eastern traditions in mysticism and in occultism. His
experience of Theosophy, of Rosicrucianism, of magical societies, of
spiritualist groups, of cabbalistic ideas, of astrology, underlay his prose
writing every bit as much as it informed his poetry.

There was yet another change in his prose style after the turn of the
century. His essay on Magic is direct and forthright:

> I believe in the practice and philosophy of what we have agreed to call magic,
> in what I must call the evocation of spirits, though I do not know what they
> are, in the power of creating magical illusions, in the visions of truth in the
> depths of the mind when the eyes are closed; and I believe in three doctrines,
> which have, as I think, been handed down from early times, and been the
> foundations of nearly all magical practices. These doctrines are:
> (1) That the borders of our mind are ever shifting, and that many minds can
> flow into one another, as it were, and create or reveal a single mind, a single
> energy.
> (2) That the borders of our memories are as shifting, and that our memories
> are a part of one great memory, the memory of Nature herself.
> (3) That this great mind and great memory can be evoked by symbols.
> I often think I would put this belief in magic from me if I could, for I have
> come to see or to imagine, in men and women, in houses, in handicrafts, in
> nearly all sights and sounds, a certain evil, a certain ugliness, that comes from
> the slow perishing through the centuries of a quality of mind that made this
> belief and its evidences common over the world.[41]

---

41 WBY, 'Ideas of Good and Evil', *Essays and Introductions*, p. 28.

He wrote an excellent essay on Spenser as an Introduction to a selection he made of his poetry; he wrote another on Stratford-upon-Avon where his praise of Shakespeare is discriminating and imaginative. These essays are much more forthright than those written out of his earlier, fashionable *fin-de-siècle* melancholia and despair.

A letter to John Quinn gives Yeats's own views of what was happening to him and his art:

> Whatever I do from this art will, I think, be more creative. I will express myself, so far as I express myself in criticism at all, by that sort of thought that leads straight to action, straight to some sort of craft. I have always felt that the soul has two movements primarily: one to transcend forms, and the other to create forms. Nietzsche to whom you have been the first to introduce me, calls these the Dionysiac and the Apollonic, respectively. I think I have to some extent got weary of that wild god Dionysus and am hoping that the Far-Darter will come in his place.[42]

By 1904 he wrote to AE of the exaggeration of sentiment and sentimental beauty in his own lyric verse and in his play *The Land of Heart's Desire* (1894); he had been fighting the prevailing decadence for years but there was a region of shadows 'full of fleshly waters and vapours which kill the spirit and the will, ecstasy and joy equally';[43] and he now dreaded this region, adding in his PS.: 'Let us have no emotions, however abstract, in which there is not an athletic joy.' In 'Discoveries' of 1906 he was writing that 'we should ascend out of common interests, the thoughts of the newspapers, of the market-place, of men of science, but only as far as we can carry the normal, passionate, reasoning self'.

When his work to create a national theatre for Ireland forced him – perhaps less unwillingly than he would have admitted – back into the role of propagandist and teacher once more Yeats became more direct and lively. He had his old problems: the conversion of an Irish audience from political preoccupations into a consideration of the role of a national literature, or rather, the creation of a new audience which could sympathise with his special aims in the theatre. He had to be understood. But he had also to fight on another front: against the existing concepts of the commercial theatre. Shaw, too, fought these but his answer did not appeal to Yeats. Any movement towards realism seemed to him to mean a decline in dramatic energy, and the theatre managers were to blame in this increase in what he called 'externalism'

---

[42] Letter to John Quinn, 15 May 1903, in *Letters*, p. 402.
[43] Letter published in *Dublin Magazine*, July 1939.

or visual realism. He insisted upon the importance of the words, the speech rather than the settings, the costumes or the acting.[44] The actor with his words would make the scene significant; what was needed was an art of the theatre rather than a technology. He, like Lady Gregory and Synge, worked his own way from short one-act prose plays, as a discipline. He began to see into the major dramatists' techniques. *King Lear*, for instance, was less the history of one man and his sorrows than the history of a whole evil time, and the subplot was the main plot working itself out in ordinary people thus calling up 'the image of multitude'.[45] The new dramatist had to be freed from convention, as the new Irish writers had earlier to be freed from political rhetoric. But middle-class morality – Puritanism and shopkeeping timidity as he saw it – linked to the disappearance of an oral tradition had ended English drama's possibilities: it could not become impassioned without making somebody gushing and sentimental.[46] Ireland, on the other hand, was at a stage of history where imagination needed dramatic expression.[47]

Yeats had learned much from his prose writing in the eighties and early nineties. But the limpidity of that period was replaced by another kind of simplicity: he wrote out of a more mature, complex attitude to art. The virtue of his new writing on drama was that it conveyed not only, despite Yeats's disclaimers, the theatre manager's awareness of an audience to be captured, held and educated, but the poet's self-communing about the nature of poetic drama.[48] In part his new habits of composition helped: he had taken to dictating, probably as a result of his bad sight. For instance, he dictated 6000 words of the 1904 *Samhain* to Lady Gregory. He read over what he had dictated – in this case to John Quinn, who recorded that Yeats 'after dictation writes out entire thing which is the work of many days in his own hand for the purpose of getting the sound – every sentence of his first tried as a specimen sentence and for its sound'.[49]

---

[44] See 'The Theatre', in *Essays and Introductions*, p. 169, for his views of what was wrong with the theatre and what could be achieved. The essay is dated May 1899.

[45] WBY, *Essays and Introductions*, p. 215.

[46] Ibid., p. 274.

[47] *Explorations*, p. 74.

[48] See, for instance, his remarks in *Explorations*, p. 199: 'If I had written to convince others I would have asked myself not "Is that exactly what I think and feel?" but "How would that strike so-and-so? How will they think and feel when they have read it?" And all would be oratorical and insincere.' He often wrote with himself as critical audience.

[49] B. L. Reid, *The Man from New York: John Quinn and his Friends* (New York, 1968) p. 30.

He continually formulated his ideas of what a theatre ought to be, what popular art ought to be:

> What attracts me to drama is that it is, in the most obvious way, what all the arts are upon a last analysis. A farce and a tragedy are alike in this, that they are a moment of intense life. An action is taken out of all other actions; it is reduced to its simplest form, or at any rate to as simple a form as it can be brought to without our losing the sense of its place in the world. The characters that are involved in it are freed from everything that is not a part of that action; and whether it is, as in the less important kinds of drama, a mere bodily activity, a hairbreadth escape or the like, or as it is in the more important kinds, an activity of the souls of the characters, it is an energy, an eddy of life purified from everything but itself. The dramatist must picture life in action, with an unpreoccupied mind, as the musician pictures it in sound and the sculptor in form.[50]

An essay such as 'First Principles' from which the preceding passage has been quoted stands the test of time very well indeed. It reveals the largeness of Yeats's concepts of a national literature. He continues to explain his attitude and his own aims for Ireland:

> A writer is not less National because he shows the influence of other countries and of the great writers of the world. No nation, since the beginning of history, has ever drawn all its life out of itself. Even the Well of English Undefiled, the the Father of English Poetry himself, borrowed his metres, and much of his way of looking at the world, from French writers, and it is possible that the influence of Italy was more powerful among the Elizabethan poets than any literary influence out of England herself. Many years ago, when I was contending with Sir Charles Gavan Duffy over what seemed to me a too narrow definition of Irish interests, Professor York Powell either said or wrote to me that the creative power of England was always at its greatest when her receptive power was greatest. If Ireland is about to produce a literature that is important to her, it must be the result of the influences that flow in upon the mind of an educated Irishman today, and, in a greater degree, of what came into the world with himself. Gaelic can hardly fail to do a portion of the work, but one cannot say whether it may not be some French or German writer who will do most to make him an articulate man. If he really achieve the miracle, if he really make all that he has seen and felt and known a portion of his own intense nature, if he puts it all into the fire of his energy, he need not fear being a stranger among his own people in the end. There never have been men more unlike an Englishman's idea of himself than Keats and Shelley, while Campbell, whose emotion came out of a shallow well, was very like that idea. We call certain minds creative because they are among the moulders of their nation and are not made upon its mould, and they resemble one another in this only – they have never been foreknown or fulfilled an expectation.[51]

---

50 WBY, 'The Irish Dramatic Movement', *Explorations*, pp. 153–4. The essay 'First Principles' is from *Samhain: 1904*.
51 WBY, 'The Irish Dramatic Movement', *Explorations*, pp. 157–9.

Many of the essays published in *Samhain*, *Beltaine* and *The Arrow*, occasional publications put out by the Abbey Theatre, achieve a high critical standard, and there are many of Yeats's critical comments on the drama elsewhere, the retrospective pieces such as 'A People's Theatre' (1919) and 'The Irish Dramatic Movement', a survey delivered in a lecture to the Royal Academy of Sweden (1923) which convey the richness and originality of his thinking.[52]

The attempt to bring a theatre based on folklore and poetic drama to Dublin failed because the modern world with its 'town mind' intruded, and so the Dublin playgoers preferred plays about their own trades, professions and classes.[53] And Yeats, having unselfishly worked for the theatre which did not go his way, began to think on other lines, inspired by Japanese drama, with its allusive art, with its myth and symbolism. His Introduction to *Certain Noble Plays of Japan*[54] gives some of his ideas about what he now wanted to create, an 'unpopular theatre and an audience like a secret society',[55] of about fifty people admitted 'by favour' to some great dining-room or drawing-room. But the nature of *The Plays for Dancers* precluded his writing much propaganda criticism about them. There was no need to seek a large audience.

Realism, he remarked in this essay, is created for the common people; whereas with the help of the Noh plays, in Fenollosa's translation finished by Ezra Pound, he had invented an aristocratic form of drama, a true theatre of beauty.

What appealed to him in the *Noh* drama was the absence of the 'clear and logical constructions' which came from France and had every aspect of high literature except the emotion of multitude.[56] His criticism often demands, like his poetry, a familiarity on the part of the reader: his deliberate attempt to keep his thoughts casual led to what were often an isolated series of insights, phrases sometimes gnomic or over-abstract (despite his hatred of abstraction), over-generalised for quick reception at the hands of those trained in academic orthodoxy.

Thus his vocabulary was his own. His use of 'reverie', for instance, indicated a positive force rather than a negative capability.[57] His skilful

---

[52] In a letter to A. H. Bullen of 16 Mar 1913, *Letters*, p. 578, he wrote that a proposed volume of his dramatic criticism would be 'the only serious criticism of the new craft of the theatre'.

[53] WBY, *Explorations*, p. 253.   [54] *Essays and Introductions*, pp. 221 ff.

[55] *Explorations*, p. 254.   [56] *Essays and Introductions*, p. 215.

[57] See his essay on 'The Tragic Theatre', *Essays and Introductions*, p. 245, and also his essay 'Art and Ideas', *Essays and Introductions*, p. 355.

delineation of personalities to illustrate his points, his occasional obscurity, his desire to retain a priest-like sense of mystery and power through his service of literature, and his insistence upon the emotions often make him difficult to assimilate, especially for readers brought up upon new criticism or twentieth-century academicism. Indeed he can at times seem naïve, over-decorative in a nineteenth-century way. Yet the impulse behind his prose technique was the same as that which made his verse seem spontaneous, striking speech. He wanted to appear to talk in his prose without caring whether one idea followed another. Yet the paradox was also there since he was using criticism deliberately, to conserve his nervous vitality,[58] just as pose and gesture were part of the measures he used to keep his mind under control.

Yeats's constant deliberations on problems of personality, on the relationship of the artist with society, and, ultimately, on man in time, were recorded in his diaries – and portions of his 1909 diary were subsequently published in 1929 under the title *Estrangement* (parts had appeared in *The Manchester Playgoer* in 1911). These are raw material for poems and essays, and both poems and essays of this period are closely related. For instance, the complex essays in *Per Amica Silentia Lunae* (1918) are complementary to the difficult poems 'Ego Dominus Tuus' and 'The Phases of the Moon', included in *The Wild Swans at Coole* (1917). 'A People's Theatre', too, often discusses these poems, attributing them to 'a certain friend of mine':

> The two great energies of the world that in Shakespeare's day penetrated each other have fallen apart as speech and music fall apart at the Renaissance, and that has brought each to greater freedom, and we have to prepare a stage for the whole wealth of modern lyricism, for an art that is close to pure music, for those energies that would free the arts from imitation, that would ally acting to decoration and to the dance. We are not yet conscious, for as yet we have no philosophy, while the opposite energy is conscious. All visible history, the discoveries of science, the discussions of politics, are with it; but as I read the world, the sudden changes, or rather the sudden revelations of future changes, are not from visible history but from its anti-self. Blake says somewhere in a 'Prophetic Book' that things must complete themselves before they pass away, and every new logical development of the objective energy intensified in an exact correspondence a counter-energy, or rather adds to an always deepening unanalysable longing. That counter-longing, having no visible past, can only become a conscious energy suddenly, in those moments of revelation which are as a flash of lightning. Are we approaching a supreme moment of self-consciousness, the two halves of the soul separate and face to face? A certain friend of mine has written upon this subject a couple of intricate poems called

---

[58] See *Autobiographies*, p. 318.

The Phases of the Moon and *The Double Vision* respectively, which are my con-
tinual study, and I must refer the reader to these poems for the necessary
mathematical calculations. Were it not for that other gyre turning inward in
exact measure with the outward whirl of its fellow, we would fall in a generation or so under some tyranny that would cease at last to be a tyranny, so
perfect our acquiescence.

> Constrained, arraigned, baffled, bent and unbent
> By those wire-jointed jaws and limbs of wood,
> Themselves obedient,
> Knowing not evil and good;
>
> Obedient to some hidden magical breath.
> They do not even feel, so abstract are they,
> So dead beyond our death,
> Triumph that we obey.[59]

Similarly, many of Yeats's poems written after his marriage in 1917
are related to *A Vision* (1926), the prose work in which he wrestled
with his ideas on man and history.[60] *A Vision* itself, of course, contains
criticism. Yeats exercised his critical powers constantly; he had his
favourite authors (one of his pleasantest pieces of appreciation is 'The
Happiest of the Poets', an essay on William Morris of 1902). He had
his favourite quotations (one of the most effective is from Nashe, 'Dust
hath closed Helen's eye' – which he also used as the title of an essay of
1902 on the poetic associations of Ballylee Castle, the subject of his
'Tower' poetry of the 1920s and early 1930s); and he had the spur of
dislike of others' ideas. In discussing Hamlet at the graveside he felt he
was in the presence of a soul lingering on the storm-beaten threshold
of sanctity: 'Has not that threshold always been terrible, even crime-
haunted?' And thinking of Shakespeare he rejected the professorial view
yet again: 'Surely Shakespeare, in those last seeming idle years, was no
quiet country gentleman, enjoying, as men like Dowden think, the
temporal reward of an unvalued toil'.[61]

His criticism runs through very many of his letters: early letters to
Katharine Tynan; letters to his father up to 1922, the year that lively,
exciting, civilised man – 'all interested in the future' – died in New
York in his eighty-third year; letters to his friends, especially to Olivia
Shakespear, to whom he felt he could say anything; to Lady Gregory;

---

[59] WBY, 'The Irish Dramatic Movement', *Explorations*, pp. 258–9.
[60] He wrote of it to Mrs Shakespear in Feb 1931 (*Letters*, p. 781) that even his simplest
poems would be the better for it, that he had 'constructed a myth, but then one can
believe in a myth – one only assents to philosophy'.
[61] *Autobiographies*, p. 522.

and, in his old age, to Dorothy Wellesley. Here is a passage from a
letter to Olivia Shakespear:

> . . . Of course Lawrence is an emphasis directed against modern abstraction. I
> find the whole book interesting and not merely the sexual parts. They are
> something that he sets up as against the abstraction of an age that he thinks
> dead from the waist downward. Of course happiness is not where he seems to
> place it. We are happy when for everything inside us there is an equivalent
> something outside us. I think it was Goethe said this. One should add the con-
> verse. It is terrible to desire and not possess, and terrible to possess and not
> desire. Because of this we long for an age which has the unity which Plato
> somewhere defined as sorrowing and rejoicing over the same things. How else
> escape the Bank Holiday crowd?
>   I have bought a suit of rough blue serge.
>
> Yours,
>
> W. B. YEATS.
>
> Read *Twenty Years a-Growing* or some of it. I once told you that you would
> be happy if you had twelve children and lived on limpets. There are limpets
> on the Great Blasket.[62]

His criticism runs, too, through the Introductions to his plays – those
to *The Words upon the Window-pane* and *Fighting the Waves* are particularly rewarding, for they show us very clearly indeed the results of
Yeats's deepening thought in the 1920s and 1930s. He was still suspicious of science:

> Science has driven out the legends, stories, superstitions that protected the
> immature and the ignorant with symbol, and now that the flower has crossed
> our rooms, science must take their place and demonstrate as philosophy has in
> all ages, that States are justified, not by multiplying or, as it would seem, com-
> forting those that are inherently miserable, but because sustained by those for
> whom the hour seems 'awful', and by those born out of themselves, the best
> born of the best.
>
> Since my twentieth year these thoughts have been in my mind, and now
> that I am old I sing them to the Garrets and the Cellars:
>
> > Move upon Newton's town,
> > The town of Hobbes and of Locke,
> > Pine, spruce, come down
> > Cliff, ravine, rock:
> > What can disturb the corn?
> > What makes its shudder and bend?
> > The rose brings her thorn,
> > The Absolute walks behind.
>
> Yet it may be that our science, our modern philosophy, keep a subconscious
> knowledge that their raft, roped together at the end of the seventeenth century,

---

[62] WBY, *Letters*, ed. Allan Wade, pp. 810–11.

must, if they so much as glance at that slow-moving flower, part and abandon
us to the storm, or it may be, as Professor Richet suggests at the end of his
long survey of psychical research from the first experiments of Sir William
Crookes to the present moment, that all it can do is, after a steady scrutiny, to
prove the poverty of the human intellect, that we are lost amid alien intellects,
near but incomprehensible, more incomprehensible than the most distant stars.
We may, whether it scrutinise or not, lacking its convenient happy explana-
tions, plunge as Rome did in the fourth century according to some philosopher
of that day into 'a fabulous, formless darkness'.

> Should H. G. Wells afflict you,
> Put whitewash in a pail;
> Paint: 'Science – opium of the suburbs'
> On some waste wall.[63]

In addition to philosophy and history Yeats had been reading Anglo-
Irish authors, partially, no doubt, because he saw himself as an inheritor
of the Anglo-Irish tradition and as its upholder in the Irish Senate,
partially because he found in the Anglo-Irish writers the kind of clarity
and directness of speech he sought in his own work, the 'public speech'
of Archibald MacLeish's phrase that he liked so much. He had not read
deeply in the eighteenth-century Anglo-Irish writers before, and he
found much to praise in them; much of his own thought was affected
by them; and they gave a sanction for the forthrightness of his later
prose, just as the nineteenth-century Irish writers had earlier reinforced
his instinctive delight in folklore, legends and local poetry. Yeats's
ability to absorb what he read and synthesise it informed his comments
on Berkeley (in an essay of 1937), and his references to Burke, while
Swift, of course, was always round the corner, particularly in *The
Words upon the Window-pane*. Yeats's earlier introductions to Synge's
work in 1907 had prepared him for this kind of impassioned appraisal;
he made the writers on whom he wrote part of his own great pageant
of literature and life. There was, in particular, the heroic gesture, his
own concept: part and parcel of his romanticism was his attitude to
what he called creative joy: he found this in the supreme moments of
tragedy. This heroic gesture was captured in poems such as 'Lapis
Lazuli', and it was possessed by those he admired. In his essay on
'J. M. Synge and the Ireland of his Time', for instance, Yeats suggested that there is in creative joy

> an acceptance of what life brings, because we have understood the beauty of
> what it brings, or a hatred of death for what it takes away, which arouses
> within us, through some sympathy perhaps with all other men, an energy so

noble, so powerful, that we laugh aloud and mock, in the terror or the sweetness of our exultation, at death and oblivion.[64]

This concentration upon a heightened dramatic moment, an affirmation of life, allowed him to select and stress aspects of the lives and the work of authors he admired and in doing so he presented new aspects of their achievement. This he did also in his poetry: he condensed his comments and epitomised the writers in the brilliant phrases of 'Blood and the Moon' which, once read, continue to colour our views:

> I declare this tower is my symbol; I declare
> This winding, gyring, spiring treadmill of a stair is my ancestral stair;
> That Goldsmith and the Dean, Berkeley and Burke have travelled there.
>
> Swift beating on his breast in sibylline frenzy blind
> Because the heart in his blood-sodden breast had dragged him down into
>   mankind,
> Goldsmith deliberately sipping at the honey-pot of his mind,
>
> And haughtier-headed Burke that proved the State a tree,
> That this unconquerable labyrinth of the birds, century after century,
> Cast but dead leaves to mathematical equality;
>
> And God-appointed Berkeley that proved all things a dream,
> That this pragmatical, preposterous pig of a world, its farrow that so solid
>   seem,
> Must vanish on the instant if the mind but change its theme;
>
> *Saeva Indignatio* and the labourer's hire,
> The strength that gives our blood and state magnanimity of its own desire;
> Everything that is not God consumed with intellectual fire.[65]

His prose no less than his poetry explored the nature of moments of intense, heightened perception.[66] 'I know', he once wrote while discussing Standish O'Grady, 'of no other criticism than a candid impressionism.' Sometimes it is hard to judge whether prose or verse is the better vehicle for conveying his experience; here, for instance, he puts an idea in a poem; it is the fourth section of 'Vacillation', published in *The Winding Stair and Other Poems* (1933):

> My fiftieth year had come and gone,
> I sat, a solitary man,
> In a crowded London shop,
> An open book and empty cup
> On the marble table-top.

---

[64] *Essays and Introductions*, p. 322.   [65] *Collected Poems*, p. 268.
[66] Letter to the Editor, Dublin *Daily Express*, 8 Mar 1895.

> While on the shop and street I gazed
> My body of a sudden blazed;
> And twenty minutes more or less
> It seemed, so great my happiness,
> That I was blessèd and could bless.[67]

The prose version was included in his *Essays* (1924):

At certain moments, always unforeseen, I become happy, most commonly
when at hazard I have opened some book of verse. Sometimes it is my own
verse when, instead of discovering new technical flaws, I read with all the
excitement of the first writing. Perhaps I am sitting in some crowded restaurant, the open book beside me, or closed, my excitement having over-brimmed
the page. I look at the strangers near as if I had known them all my life, and it
seems strange that I cannot speak to them: everything fills me with affection,
I have no longer any fears or any needs; I do not even remember that this
happy mood must come to an end. It seems as if the vehicle had suddenly
grown pure and far extended and so luminous that the images from *Anima
Mundi*, embodied there and drunk with that sweetness, would, like a country
drunkard who has thrown a wisp into his own thatch, burn up time.[68]

Towards the end of his life Yeats wrote broadcasts and Introductions
in which he surveyed the work of his youthful friends, the poets of the
'Cheshire Cheese', whom he had earlier described brilliantly in *Autobiographies*; he also re-examined his own work. This criticism appeared
in both his prose and verse. He had written prophetically in *Anima
Hominis* in 1917 of what his old age might be:

A poet, when he is growing old, will ask himself if he cannot keep his mask
and his vision without new bitterness, new disappointment. Could he if he
would, knowing how frail his vigour from youth up, copy Landor who lived
loving and hating, ridiculous and unconquered, into extreme old age, all lost
but the favour of his Muses?

> The Mother of the Muses, we are taught,
> Is Memory; she has left me; they remain,
> And shake my shoulder, urging me to sing.

Surely, he may think, now that I have found vision and mask I need not
suffer any longer. He will buy perhaps some small old house, where, like
Ariosto, he can dig his garden, and think that in the return of birds and leaves,
or moon and sun, and in the evening flights of the rooks he may discover
rhythm and pattern like those in sleep and so never awake out of vision. Then
he will remember Wordsworth withering into eighty years, honoured and
empty-witted, and climb to some waste room and find, forgotten there by
youth, some bitter crust.[69]

[67] *Collected Poems*, p. 283.   [68] *Mythologies*, pp. 364–5.
[69] WBY, 'Per Amica Silentia Lunae', *Mythologies*, p. 342.

And in his last years he realised he had achieved this state, and described
it in 'An Acre of Grass':

> Picture and book remain,
> An acre of green grass
> For air and exercise,
> Now strength of body goes;
> Midnight, an old house
> Where nothing stirs but a mouse.
>
> My temptation is quiet.
> Here at life's end
> Neither loose imagination,
> Nor the mill of the mind
> Consuming its rag and bone,
> Can make the truth known.
>
> Grant me an old man's frenzy,
> Myself must I remake
> Till I am Timon and Lear
> Or that William Blake
> Who beat upon the wall
> Till Truth obeyed his call;
>
> A mind Michael Angelo knew
> That can pierce the clouds,
> Or inspired by frenzy
> Shake the dead in their shrouds;
> Forgotten else by mankind,
> An old man's eagle mind.[70]

These last years were the period of his Introduction to the *Oxford
Book of Modern Verse*, in which his prose, purged of rhetoric, poured
out his sweepingly assertive views of modern poetry. He regarded
his task, he wrote to Olivia Shakespear, as solving the problem of
'How far do I like the Ezra, Auden, Eliot school, and if I do not,
why not?' Then he saw the further problem, 'Why do the younger
generation like it so much?'[71] He could be discerning about work unlike his own. Take, for example, his brilliant comments on T. S. Eliot
with their movement into the parallels which graphic art afforded him
in his view of literature: he had always a passionately concentrated
visual sensibility:

Eliot has produced his great effect upon his generation because he has
described men and women that get out of bed into it from mere habit; in

describing this life that has lost heart his own art seems grey, cold, dry. He is an Alexander Pope, working without apparent imagination, producing his effects by a rejection of all rhythms and metaphors used by the more popular romantics rather than by the discovery of his own, this rejection giving his work an un-exaggerated plainness that has the effect of novelty. He has the rhythmical flatness of *The Essay on Man* – despite Miss Sitwell's advocacy I see Pope as Blake and Keats saw him – later, in *The Waste Land*, amid much that is moving in symbol and imagery there is much monotony of accent:

> When lovely woman stoops to folly and
> Paces about her room again, alone,
> She smooths her hair with automatic hand,
> And puts a record on the gramophone.

I was affected, as I am by these lines, when I saw for the first time a painting by Manet. I longed for the vivid colour and light of Rousseau and Courbet, I could not endure the grey middle-tint – and even today Manet gives me an incomplete pleasure; he had left the procession. Nor can I put the Eliot of these poems among those that descend from Shakespeare and the translators of the Bible. I think of him as satirist rather than poet. Once only does that early work speak in the great manner:

> The host with someone indistinct
> Converses at the door apart,
> The nightingales are singing near
> The Convent of the Sacred Heart,
>
> And sang within the bloody wood
> When Agamemnon cried aloud,
> And let their liquid siftings fall
> To stain the stiff dishonoured shroud.

Not until *The Hollow Men* and *Ash-Wednesday*, where he is helped by the short lines, and in the dramatic poems where his remarkable sense of actor, chanter, scene, sweeps him away, is there rhythmical animation. Two or three of my friends attribute the change to an emotional enrichment from religion, but his religion compared to that of John Gray, Francis Thompson, Lionel Johnson in *The Dark Angel*, lacks all strong emotion; a New England Protestant by descent, there is little self-surrender in his personal relation to God and the soul. *Murder in the Cathedral* is a powerful stage play because the actor, the monkish habit, certain repeated words, symbolise what we know, not what the author knows. Nowhere has the author explained how Becket and the King differ in aim; Becket's people have been robbed and persecuted in his absence; like the King he demands a strong government. Speaking through Becket's mouth Eliot confronts a world growing always more terrible with a religion like that of some great statesman, a pity not less poignant because it tempers the prayer book with the results of mathematical philosophy.[72]

---

[72] *The Oxford Book of Modern Verse 1892–1935*, ed. W. B. Yeats (1936) pp. xxi–xxiii.

Yeats was a man of extremes; his expression of them is dramatic, intense, imaginative. While, as L. A. G. Strong put it, he could reject 'whole masses of work' he had formed loyalties to certain kinds of literature, and, especially, to certain writers. Last of the romantics, he found his favourite poetry in the writings of his friends: he was Irish, he valued personality, the expression of individualism. Ireland still made this possible, he thought, because she still had a living folk tradition. And personality was all-important: it was the only bulwark against abstraction and specialisation, against the isolation of modern life. Personal utterance could be, he thought as a young man, and continued to think, 'as fine an escape from rhetoric and abstraction as drama itself'.[73]

His comments, in a radio talk on modern poetry,[74] are a good example of how his mind could range in its appreciation of a particular person's poetry, through addressing an audience, and finally bring to mind another poet's work and words. Yeats's praise of his friends in the Introduction to the *Oxford Book of Modern Verse* often seems odd to the modern critic. But he was a man who had grown up through nationalist struggles, and in a world of often sharpened enmities he knew the value of friendship.[75] In his poem on 'The Municipal Gallery Revisited' he stated his belief proudly to those who judge him:

> You that would judge me, do not judge alone
> This book or that, come to this hallowed place
> Where my friends' portraits hang and look thereon;
> Ireland's history in their lineaments trace;
> Think where man's glory most begins and ends,
> And saw my glory was I had such friends.[76]

In these lines the quality of his mind emerges in the directness of his speech, speech achieved through endless toiling for the right word in the right place. He drew attention to the work that underlay the apparent ease of style he so admired (and had himself achieved) in his radio talk of 1936: he appreciated hard work, and praised it constantly (as for instance in 'Adam's Curse'); it had, however, to give the effect of

---

[73] *Autobiographies*, p. 102. His praise of the poetry of W. J. Turner and Dorothy Wellesley in his Introduction to the *Oxford Book of Modern Verse* is based on his view of the history of intellectual movement – a movement from the mirror to the lamp. This is, as it were, a development of his earlier views of literary history in terms of ballad and lyric stages, etc.

[74] See *Essays and Introductions*, pp. 491–508.

[75] He had originally intended to call his essay on the Irish Dramatic Movement 'Friends and Enemies'; see *Letters*, p. 507.   [76] *Collected Poems*, p. 368.

casual conversation – to have both the naturalness of peasant speech, the elegance and epigrammatic quality of courtly poetry.[77] He valued the work of Gogarty, a minor poet and his friend, because it had these qualities and this passage about Gogarty also indicates Yeats's generosity of mind, his never-ceasing care for poetry:

> Some twelve years ago political enemies came to Senator Gogarty's house while they knew he would be in his bath and so unable to reach his revolver, made him dress, brought him to an empty house on the edge of the Liffey. They told him nothing, but he felt certain he was to be kept as hostage and shot after the inevitable execution of a certain man then in prison. Self-possessed and daring, he escaped, and while swimming the cold December river, vowed two swans to it if it would land him safely. I was present some weeks later when, in the presence of the Head of the State and other notables, the two swans were launched. That story shows the man – scholar, wit, poet, gay adventurer. In one poem, written years afterwards, the man who dedicated the swans dedicates the poems, and the mood has not changed:

> Tall unpopular men,
> Slim proud women who move
> As women walked in the islands when
> Temples were built to Love,
> I sing to you. With you
> Beauty at best can live,
> Beauty that dwells with the rare and few,
> Cold and imperative.
> He who had Caesar's ear
> Sang to the lonely and strong.
> Virgil made an austere
> Venus Muse of his song.

Here is another poem characteristic of those poems which have restored the emotion of heroism to lyric poetry:

> Our friends go with us as we go
>   Down the long path where Beauty wends,
> Where all we love forgathers, so
>   Why should we fear to join our friends?

[77] A letter to his father of 5 Mar 1912 (*Letters*, p. 568), about how he was writing an introduction to Lady Gregory's book of Fairy Belief, shows his concern to preserve this quality along with sincerity: 'I think I have made the first philosophic generalization that has been made from the facts of spiritism and the facts of folklore in combination. I have got nearly all the thought down now on paper, but I shall have to spend a long time making it vivid to the senses and making it emotionally sincere. It is always such a long research getting down to one's exact impression, one's exact ignorance and knowledge. I remember your writing to me, that all good art is good just in so far as it is intimate. It always seems to me that that intimacy comes only from personal sincerity. If you write on a subject it is usual to assume that you know all the facts that are known and have all the necessary faculties to interpret them. Yet this assumption is never really true.'

> Who would survive them to outlast
> His children; to outwear his fame –
> Left when the Triumph has gone past –
> To win from Age, not Time, a name?
>
> Then do not shudder at the knife
> That Death's indifferent hand drives home,
> But with the Strivers leave the Strife,
> Nor, after Caesar, skulk in Rome.

When I have read you a poem I have tried to read it rhythmically; I may be a bad reader; or read badly because I am out of sorts, or self-conscious; but there is no other method. A poem is an elaboration of the rhythms of common speech and their association with profound feeling. To read a poem like prose, that hearers unaccustomed to poetry may find it easy to understand, is to turn it into bad florid prose. If anybody reads or recites poetry as if it were prose from some public platform, I ask you, speaking for poets, living, dead, or unborn, to protest in whatever way occurs to your perhaps youthful minds; if they recite or read by wireless, I ask you to express your indignation by letter. William Morris, coming out of a hall where somebody had read or recited his *Sigurd the Volsung*, said: 'It cost me a lot of damned hard work to get that thing into verse.'[78]

---

[78] WBY, 'Modern Poetry', *Essays and Introductions*, pp. 507–8.

Women in Yeats's Poetry

'WOMEN', Yeats wrote in an unpublished account of his early twenties in London, 'filled me with curiosity, and my mind seemed never to escape from the disturbances of my senses.'[1] He had many women friends on whom he used to call to discuss ideas he could not bring to a man without meeting some competing thought, but apart from these intimate intellectual exchanges he was timid and abashed.[2] Yet that curiosity and that disturbance of his senses lasted throughout his life, and much of his finest poetry is concerned with matters of love, with the heart-mysteries of his own life.

His dreams alternated between adventurous love and arduous intellectual austerity. In his teens, he was a romantic, his head full of the mysterious women of Rossetti; he saw the hesitating faces painted by Burne-Jones as always awaiting some Alastor at the end of a long journey. Himself he imagined in many roles, as a kind of Hamlet, for instance, but more significantly as an Alastor: lonely and melancholic and given to dreaming. When he thought of women, they were modelled on those of his favourite poets. They loved in brief tragedy, or else, like the girl in *The Revolt of Islam*, they accompanied their lovers through all manner of wild places, lawless women without homes and without children.

From Shelley and the Romantic poets came an idea of perfect love. 'Perhaps', Yeats wrote, 'I should never marry in Church but I would love one woman all my life.'[3] This idea was a natural one for him to form. He had grown up in an artist's home, but it was an Irish Protestant home. His father, John Butler Yeats, had found it impossible to become a Church of Ireland clergyman like his own father and grandfather, and he had transmitted his incapacity for Christian belief to his son. But John Butler Yeats was no bohemian. He wrote, very firmly,

---

[1] WBY, quoted in A. Norman Jeffares, *W. B. Yeats: Man and Poet*, rev. ed. (London, 1962) p. 57.

[2] See WBY, *Autobiographies* (London, 1956) pp. 152 f.

[3] WBY, quoted in Jeffares, p. 58.

'I think a man and a woman should choose each other for life, for the
simple reason that a long life with all its accidents is barely long enough
for a man and a woman to understand each other; and, in this case,
to understand is to love. The man who understands one woman is
qualified to understand pretty well everything.'[4] His influence on his
son was strong; his conduct of the life of his family and its habit of
much conversation (described in such brilliant generalisations in his
Essays Irish and American) no doubt created in his son's mind the
happier dreams, described later in 'What Then?' of 'wife, daughter,
son',[5] for, like his father, he was no bohemian.

Towards the end of his teens he was infatuated with a cousin, Laura
Johnson. But she was engaged, so he did not tell her he was in love
with her. He wrote her 'some bad poems' and had more than one sleep-
less night 'through anger with her betrothed'.[6] This was the period
when his father's influence on him was at its height, and from his
father's Pre-Raphaelite enthusiasms came, no doubt, two ways of dealing with the inclination of his mind 'towards women and love'.[7] One
way derived from his father's reading him a passage from Thoreau's
Walden: he would overcome bodily desire and live in search of wisdom
on a little island called Innisfree. Despite his writing in *Autobiographies*
that he gave up this particular dream when he was twenty-two or
twenty-three, it was a general idea to which he returned at intervals in
later life: Byzantium, for instance, symbolised a place where a search
for wisdom might be pursued as an escape, in part, from the conflicts
of sex, envy of 'The young / In one another's arms'.[8] The other way
was the idea of serving a mistress with the hopeless devotion of a
Rossetti or a Morris hero. Out of this idea came the cloudy beauty of
the love poetry of 'The Wanderings of Oisin' (1889), founded uodn
translations of Gaelic poems[9] which tell the love story of Oisin and
Niamh, who spend three hundred years in the Land of the Young. In
one version, they marry and have three children. However romantic,
they too were not bohemian; and in this they resembled Yeats, who was
dreaming, as he wrote the poem, of the goddess who would come and
inspire his ageless love. In Yeats's poem, Niamh seeks out Oisin; and,

4 J. B. Yeats, *Letters to his son W. B. Yeats and Others 1869–1922* (London, 1944) p. 236
5 WBY, *Collected Poems* (London, 1950) p. 347.
6 WBY, *Autobiographies*, p. 76.
7 Ibid., p. 72.
8 WBY, *Collected Poems*, p. 217.
9 These sources are discussed in Russell K. Alspach, 'Some Sources of Yeats's "The
Wanderings of Oisin"', *PMLA* (Sept 1943) pp. 849 ff., and in Jeffares, pp. 43–5.

in his old age, Yeats described Oisin as 'led by the nose' through the three enchanted islands by 'Man-picker' Niamh:

> But what cared I that set him on to ride,
> I, starved for the bosom of his faery bride?[10]

He was ready to fall in love. He knew the kind of woman he wanted to love, and he wanted to love her in 'the old high way of love'.[11] Everything was ready, and when he was twenty-three what he later described as the trouble of his life began. Maud Gonne drove up to the Yeats house in Bedford Park, that London suburb which harboured so many artists and writers:

> I had never thought . . . to see in a living woman so great beauty. It belonged to famous pictures, to poetry, to some legendary past. A complexion like the bloom of apples and yet face and body had the beauty of lineaments which Blake calls the highest beauty because it changes least from youth to age, and stature so great that she seemed of a divine race. Her movements were works of grace and I understood at last why the poets of antiquity, where we would but speak of face and form, sing, loving some lady, that she seemed like a goddess.[12]

He dined with her that evening. She disturbed his father by praising war; influenced by French Boulangists, she was ruthless and revolutionary. It seemed that he must commend himself to her by a public talent. He offered to write *The Countess Kathleen* for her, for she wanted a play that she could act in Dublin. He talked to her of his spiritual philosophy, his interest in the supernatural, his desire to find something in which he could believe. At first, he decided never to speak of his love; he was shy and penniless; she was beyond his reach. He would offer her devotion without a hope of reward. But, two years after their first meeting, he proposed to her:

> I remember a curious thing. I had come into the room with the purpose in my mind and hardly looked at her or thought of her beauty but sat there holding her hand and speaking vehemently. She did not take away her hand for a while and I ceased to speak and presently as we sat in silence I knew my confidence had gone and an instant later she drew her hand away. No, she could not marry, there were reasons that she could never marry. . . . Her words were not of a conventional ring; she asked for my friendship. We spent the next day upon the cliffs at Howth, we dined at a little cottage near the Baily lighthouse where her old nurse lived and I overheard the old nurse ask her if she were engaged to be married. At the day's end I found that I had spent ten shillings, which seemed to me a very great sum.[13]

---

[10] WBY, 'The Circus Animals' Desertion', *Collected Poems*, p. 391.
[11] WBY, 'Adam's Curse', *Collected Poems*, p. 88.
[12] WBY, quoted in Jeffares, p. 59.   [13] Ibid., p. 68.

The love poems which arose from his devotion were filled with melancholy and defeat. Some of their titles indicate his hopelessness and despair – 'When You are Old', 'The Pity of Love', 'The Sorrow of Love', 'A Dream of Death'. And yet, the poems have a haunting beauty and delicacy not always fully appreciated in an age when reserve and chivalry are out of fashion. He wanted to keep ugliness out of his poetry; he wanted to be concerned with beauty, separate from everything heterogeneous and casual. His father had suggested the idea of 'Unity of Being' to him, and he had the strong conviction that all art should be a centaur 'finding in the popular lore its back and strong legs'.[14] Out of this came his desire to create a deeper political passion, through rediscovery by the educated classes in Ireland of the mythology, the imaginative stories known and sung by the uneducated classes. Out of this passion should come unity. Despite his father's most important (and best-learned) precept, that a gentleman does not think of 'getting on' in the world, part of Yeats's mind ran 'on money cares and fears'.[15] Yet he knew what he was doing no less than the earlier, more obvious nationalist poets, Davis, Mangan, Ferguson: he was uniting patriotic poetry in the service of both Ireland and Maud Gonne. He was blending Christian and pagan material in his search for unity. When he wrote his poems of the 'Rose', they were highly symbolic.

> Far-off, most secret, and inviolate Rose,
> Enfold me in my hour of hours; where those
> Who sought thee in the Holy Sepulchre,
> Or in the wine-vat, dwell beyond the stir
> And tumult of defeated dreams; and deep
> Among pale eyelids, heavy with the sleep
> Men have named beauty. Thy great leaves enfold
> The ancient beards, the helms of ruby and gold
> Of the crowned Magi; and the king whose eyes
> Saw the Pierced Hands and Rood of elder rise
> In Druid vapour and make the torches dim;
> Till vain frenzy awoke and he died; and him
> Who met Fand walking among flaming dew
> By a grey shore where the wind never blew,
> And lost the world and Emer for a kiss;
> And him who drove the gods out of their liss,
> And till a hundred morns had flowered red
> Feasted, and wept the barrows of his dead;

---

[14] WBY, *Autobiographies*, p. 190.
[15] WBY, 'The Man who Dreamed of Faeryland', *Collected Poems*, p. 49.

And the proud dreaming king who flung the crown
And sorrow away, and calling bard and clown
Dwelt among wine-stained wanderers in deep woods;
And him who sold tillage, and house, and goods,
And sought through lands and islands numberless years,
Until he found, with laughter and with tears,
A woman of so shining loveliness
That men threshed corn at midnight by a tress,
A little stolen tress. I, too, await
The hour of thy great wind of love and hate.
When shall the stars be blown about the sky,
Like the sparks blown out of a smithy, and die?
Surely thine hour has come, thy great wind blows,
Far-off, most secret, and inviolate Rose?[16]

Here he is using the rose as a symbol of intellectual beauty; the lines
hint at the rose of Rosicrucian lore, but they echo Mangan's use of the
rose as a symbol for Ireland; and they are written to Maud Gonne. In
many ways she was Ireland for him. She was the Countess Kathleen
and, later, Cathleen ni Houlihan. And, like the poet Kevin in *The
Countess Kathleen*, he was driven crazy by love:

> She lived, as ever, surrounded by dogs and birds, and I became gradually
> aware of many charities – old women or old men past work were always seek-
> ing her out; and I began to notice a patience beyond my reach in handling
> birds or beasts. I could play with bird or beast half the day but I was not patient
> with its obstinacy. She seemed to understand every subtlety of my own art and
> especially all my spiritual philosophy and I was still full of William Blake and
> sometimes she would say I had saved her from despair. We worked much with
> symbols. . . . I heard much scandal about her but dismissed the grossest scandal
> at once, and one persistent story I put away with the thought 'She would have
> told me, if it were true'. It had come to seem as if the intimacy of our minds
> could not be greater and I explain the fact that marriage seemed to have slipped
> further away by my own immaturity and lack of achievement. One night
> when going to sleep I had seen suddenly a thimble, and a shapeless white mass
> that puzzled me. Next day on passing a tobacconist's I saw that it was a lump
> of meerschaum not yet made into a pipe. She was complete and I was not.[17]

Through 'The Rose of the World', she becomes a European symbol:
his mythologising goes back to Helen and to Deirdre of the Sorrows,
for he saw many sorrows in Maud Gonne's changing face:

> Who dreamed that beauty passes like a dream?
> For those red lips, with all their mournful pride,
> Mournful that no new wonder may betide,

---

[16] WBY, 'The Secret Rose', *Collected Poems*, p. 77.
[17] WBY, quoted in Jeffares, p. 88.

Troy passed away in one high funeral gleam,
And Usna's children died.[18]

This awareness of the passing of beauty may be basically close to a
carpe diem idea, but it looks forward in a different way, because of his
despair: 'What wife would she make, I thought, what share could she
have in the life of a student?'[19] But she would value his love for her
when she was old. His Muse was indeed old when he was young, and
the computer tells us that the word *old* occurs more frequently in his
poems, with 575 instances, than any other of the 10,666 words indexed,
except *all*, with its 1,019 instances.[20] Yeats saw their hearts as old, outworn in a time outworn. The end of the century was near: greyness
lay over the passion-dimmed Celtic land; Yeats's adjectives describe it
all as pale, paling, death-pale, pearl-pale, shadowy, glimmering, dim,
dream-dimmed, desolate, drowsy. And the spirit of the poems comes
from these adjectives: love-lorn, faint, piteous, rambling, vain, defeated, still. The poet was old with long wandering in the labyrinth of
unrequited love.

Yet not all the poems in *The Wind among the Reeds* (1899) were
written to Maud Gonne. He had been intellectually frustrated and
poetically ready to fall in love before he met Maud Gonne in 1889:
now he met, five years later, the woman he called Diana Vernon in his
unpublished autobiography:

Her beauty, dark and still, had the nobility of defeated things and how could
it help but wring my heart? I took a fortnight to decide what I should do. I was
poor and it would be a hard struggle if I asked her to come away and perhaps
after all I would be adding my tragedy to hers for she might return to the evil
life but after all if I could not get the woman I loved it would be a comfort,
even for a little while, to devote myself to another. No doubt my excited senses
had their share in this argument but it was an unconscious one. At the end of a
fortnight I asked her to leave home with me. She became very joyous and a few
days later praised me for what she called my beautiful tact in giving at the
moment but a brother's kiss. Doubtless at the moment I was exalted above the
senses and yet I do not think I knew any way of kissing for when on our first
railway journey together – we were to spend the day in Kent – she gave me the
long, passionate kiss of love, I was startled and a little shocked. Presently I told
something of my thoughts during that fortnight and she was perplexed and
ashamed that I should have had such imagination of her.[21]

18 WBY, 'The Rose of the World', *Collected Poems*, p. 41.
19 WBY, quoted in Jeffares, p. 60.
20 Stephen Manfield Parrish (ed.), *A Concordance to the Poems of W. B. Yeats* (Ithaca,
N.Y., 1963) p. 935.
21 WBY, quoted in Jeffares, p. 100.

Diana Vernon was unhappily married; she and Yeats decided to wait
until her mother, a very old woman, had died; but eventually a liaison
began in the middle of his thirtieth year. Yeats took his rooms in
Woburn Buildings, and found her the one woman to whom he could
say everything. But then his thoughts reverted to their irresistible
obsession with Maud Gonne again. Two poems, 'Michael Robartes
bids his Beloved be at Peace' and 'The Travail of Passion', are certainly
written to Diana Vernon, and there is, I believe, a haunting record of
that terrible morning when instead of reading love poetry to Diana
Vernon, Yeats found he could not speak to her and she left him. It is in
the poem 'The Lover mourns for the Loss of Love':

> Pale brows, still hands and dim hair,
> I had a beautiful friend
> And dreamed that the old despair
> Would end in love in the end:
> She looked in my heart one day
> And saw your image was there;
> She has gone weeping away.[22]

With all the kindness and ease and peace the affair had brought him,
the desperate hope of escaping from the frustration of his fascination
with Maud Gonne, it ended in remorse, and the old passion dominated
him more devastatingly than before:

> I saw now much of Maud Gonne and my hope renewed again. If I could go
> to her and prove by putting my hand in the fire till I had burnt it badly would
> not that make her understand that devotion like mine should [not] be thrown
> away lightly. Often as I went to see her I had this thought in mind and I do
> not think it was fear of pain that prevented me but fear of being mad. I
> wonder at moments if I was not really mad.[23]

The hopelessness continues to run through the sorrowful loveliness of
the poems of the late 1890s:

> Had I the heavens' embroidered cloths,
> Enwrought with golden and silver light,
> The blue and the dim and the dark cloths
> Of night and light and the half-light,
> I would spread the cloths under your feet:
> But I, being poor, have only my dreams;
> I have spread my dreams under your feet;
> Tread softly because you tread on my dreams.[24]

---

[22] WBY, *Collected Poems*, p. 68.   [23] WBY, quoted in Jeffares, p. 107.
[24] WBY, 'He wishes for the Cloths of Heaven', *Collected Poems*, p. 81.

There speaks the Pre-Raphaelite lover, full of self-abasement before the pedestal upon which he has placed his lady. Her face is an index to her soul. What happens if she does not possess the soul? These questions were asked by a character in one of the novels written by Yeats's friend Mrs Olivia Shakespear in 1896. (This character also commented on the role of the woman whose face does not attract, so that she is denied the soul forced on the beauty, which the beauty had never claimed to have!) Yeats had not come to consider this question, for he was as preoccupied as ever with Maud Gonne. He met Lady Gregory in 1896 and the following year he stayed at Coole Park, her house in the west of Ireland: later it seemed to him that a new scene was set, new actors appeared, in 1897. The scene was Coole, its seven woods and brimming lake:

> I wander by the edge
> Of this desolate lake
> Where wind cries in the sedge:
> *Until the axle break*
> *That keeps the stars in their round,*
> *And hands hurl in the deep*
> *The banners of East and West,*
> *And the girdle of light is unbound,*
> *Your breast will not lie by the breast*
> *Of your beloved in sleep.*[25]

The strain of his love for Maud Gonne he expressed in Gaelic mythology:

> I have drunk ale from the Country of the Young
> And weep because I know all things now:
> I have been a hazel tree, and they hung
> The Pilot Star and the Crooked Plough
> Among my leaves in times out of mind:
> I become a rush that horses tread:
> I became a man, a hater of the wind,
> Knowing one, out of all things, alone, that his head
> May not lie on the breast nor his lips on the hair
> Of the woman that he loves, until he dies,
> O beast of the wilderness, bird of the air,
> Must I endure your amorous cries?[26]

His unpublished autobiography is frank about it:

> It was a time of great personal strain and sorrow – since my mistress had left me no other woman had come into my life and for nearly seven years none did.

---

[25] WBY 'He hears the Cry of the Sedge', *Collected Poems*, p. 75.
[26] WBY, 'He thinks of his Past Greatness when a Part of the Constellations of Heaven', *Collected Poems*, p. 81.

> I was tortured with sexual desire and disappointed love. Often as I walked in
> the woods at Coole it would have been a relief to have screamed aloud.[27]

Lady Gregory created an ideal *ambiance* for him at Coole and her friendship was salutary:

> I was never before so sad and miserable as in the year that followed my first
> visit to Coole. In the second or during the first my nervous system was worn
> out. The toil of dressing in the morning exhausted me and Lady Gregory began
> to send me in cups of soup when I was called.[28]

She invited him to stay at Coole summer after summer; she invited
other writers and artists there too; she brought him on excursions to
collect folklore; and she helped him to create the Abbey Theatre. She
provided a perfect, ordered setting for his work:

> When I was in good health again, I found myself indolent, partly perhaps
> because I was affrighted by that impossible novel, and asked her to send me
> to my work every day at eleven, and at some other hour to my letters, rating
> me with idleness if need be, and I doubt if I should have done much with my
> life but for her firmness and her care. After a time, though not very quickly, I
> recovered tolerable industry, though it has only been of late years that I have
> found it possible to face an hour's verse without a preliminary struggle and
> much putting off.[29]

Poems recorded the passing of those seven years of celibacy – 'One
that is ever kind said yesterday:/ "Your well-belovèd's hair has threads
of grey."'[30] The old devotion remained: he aided Maud in her political
work. He joined in the '98 celebrations; but they showed him the
results of violence:

> It is eight or nine at night, and she and I have come from the City Hall,
> where the Convention has been sitting, that we may walk to the National
> Club in Rutland Square, and we find a great crowd in the street, who surround
> us and accompany us. Presently I hear a sound of breaking glass, the crowd has
> begun to stone the windows of decorated houses, and when I try to speak that
> I may restore order, I discover that I have lost my voice through much speaking
> at the Convention. I can only whisper and gesticulate, and as I am thus freed
> from responsibility, I share the emotion of the crowd, and perhaps even feel
> as they feel when the glass crashes. Maud Gonne has a look of exultation as she
> walks with her laughing head thrown back.
> Later that night Connolly carries in procession a coffin with the words
> 'British Empire' upon it, and police and mob fight for its ownership, and at
> last, that the police may not capture it, it is thrown into the Liffey. And there
> are fights between police and window-breakers, and I read in the morning

---

[27] WBY, quoted in Jeffares, p. 118.   [28] Ibid.   [29] Ibid., p. 120.
[30] WBY, 'The Folly of Being Comforted', *Collected Poems*, p. 86.

papers that many have been wounded; some two hundred heads have been dressed at the hospitals; an old woman killed by baton blows, or perhaps trampled under the feet of the crowd; and that two thousand pounds' worth of decorated plate-glass windows have been broken. I count the links in the chain of responsibility, run them across my fingers, and wonder if any link there is from my workshop.[31]

And the second play he wrote for her, *Cathleen ni Houlihan* (performed in 1902), in which she played the part of Cathleen, had an explosive effect that worried him ever afterwards: 'Did that play of mine send out / Certain men the English shot?'[32] He had given his heart – poured it out in poems like 'Red Hanrahan's Song about Ireland' (Maud Gonne's favourite poem, incidentally) and then suddenly the whole fabric of his love broke asunder when Maud Gonne married John MacBride in 1903. There was an unpublished reaction:

> My dear is angry, that of late
> I cry all base blood down,
> As if she had not taught me hate
> By kisses to a clown.

In Yeats's personality the claims of 'passion' and of 'wisdom' alternated. A much later poem put the idea in the mouth of a lady:

> I am in love
> And that is my shame.
> What hurts the soul
> My soul adores,
> No better than a beast
> Upon all fours[33]

But in his reaction to Maud's marriage the alternation is within one of the extremes. It is between love and hate, and passion is still dominant. Passion, but passion resigned, beats through a succession of very unusual and very moving love poems written over the next dozen years: poems about the past, about Maud's failure to understand his work. Here is the prose draft of one, taken from a diary entry for 22 January 1909:

Today the thought came to me that P.I.A.L. [Maud Gonne] never really understands my plans or notions or ideas. Then came the thought – what matter? – how much of the best that I have done and still do is but the attempt to explain myself to her? If she understood, I should lack a reason for writing and one can never have too many reasons for doing what is so laborious.

---

[31] WBY, *Autobiographies*, p. 367.
[32] WBY, 'The Man and the Echo', *Collected Poems*, p. 393.
[33] WBY, 'The Lady's First Song', *Collected Poems*, p. 343.

This prose entry is followed by the poem 'Words':

> I had this thought a while ago,
> 'My darling cannot understand
> What I have done, or what would do
> In this blind bitter land.'
>
> And I grew weary of the sun
> Until my thoughts cleared up again,
> Remembering that the best I have done
> Was done to make it plain;
>
> That every year I have cried 'At length
> My darling understands it all,
> Because I have come into my strength,
> And words obey my call.' . . .

The poems of *The Green Helmet* (1910) and *Responsibilities* (1916) celebrated her beauty in a new way. The twentieth century had begun: cold dawn light replaced the Celtic clouds. Maud Gonne is contrasted with the people she served and incited to rebellion. Yet she is above praise or blame. 'Friends' dismisses the idea of praise:

> How could I praise that one?
> When day begins to break
> I count my good and bad,
> Being wakeful for her sake,
> Remembering what she had,
> What eagle look still shows,
> While up from my heart's root
> So great a sweetness flows
> I shake from head to foot.

And 'No Second Troy' dismisses any idea of blame:

> Why should I blame her that she filled my days
> With misery, or that she would of late
> Have taught to ignorant men most violent ways,
> Or hurled the little streets upon the great,
> Had they but courage equal to desire?
> What could have made her peaceful with a mind
> That nobleness made simple as a fire,
> With beauty like a tightened bow, a kind
> That is not natural in an age like this,
> Being high and solitary and most stern?
> Why, what could she have done, being what she is?
> Was there another Troy for her to burn?[34]

---

[34] WBY, 'No Second Troy', *Collected Poems*, p. 101.

'Fallen Majesty'[35] records his continuous sense of her goddess-like movements, and 'The Cold Heaven' flares into memories of the hot blood of youth in one of Yeats's most evocative and memorable of poems:

> Suddenly I saw the cold and rook-delighting heaven
> That seemed as though ice burned and was but the more ice,
> And thereupon imagination and heart were driven
> So wild that every casual thought of that and this
> Vanished, and left but memories, that should be out of season
> With the hot blood of youth, of love crossed long ago;
> And I took all the blame out of all sense and reason,
> Until I cried and trembled and rocked to and fro,
> Riddled with light. Ah! when the ghost begins to quicken,
> Confusion of the death-bed over, is it sent
> Out naked on the roads, as the books say, and stricken
> By the injustice of the skies for punishment?[36]

These poems are the opposite of his earlier love poetry: they show him withering into truth. The decoration has gone, the clarity is there; because the past and the present have no future. Maud is married. When she sought separation from her husband it was contested. There was no question of a divorce, as she had become a Roman Catholic. *And* she was hissed when she appeared in a Dublin theatre, and Yeats was incensed with:

> . . . how what her dreaming gave
> Earned slander, ingratitude,
> From self-same dolt and knave;
> Aye, and worse wrong than these.[37]

The audience he had hoped for in Ireland actively disliked Synge's plays, his own verse plays were not popular, and the younger dramatists wrote realistic comedies; yet he fought on for his dream of a truly national theatre. During what is the middle period of his life – and his poetry – his former belief in the people shattered, he turned to an admiration of aristocracy. Lady Gregory's friendship had given him the experience of the dignified order of a large country house, the ideal of public service linked with patronage. His visit to Italy in 1907 with

35 WBY, 'Fallen Majesty', *Collected Poems*, p. 138.
36 WBY, 'The Cold Heaven', *Collected Poems*, p. 140.
37 WBY, 'Against Unworthy Praise', *Collected Poems*, p. 103. See B. L. Reid, *The Man from New York*, p. 35, for an account of how Yeats was shaken by the ugliness of the facts, writing on 14 Jan 1905 to describe the 'most painful affair of my life'. He brought John Quinn into the imbroglio for advice, and Quinn joined Yeats and Lady Gregory in helping Maud Gonne.

Lady Gregory and her son brought home to him the virtues of the Renaissance patrons. 'The People' is a poem which explains it all, the new values he had formed, the new allegiances he had made, and the constancy of Maud Gonne to her particular aim:

'What have I earned for all that work,' I said,
'For all that I have done at my own charge?
The daily spite of this unmannerly town,
Where who has served the most is most defamed,
The reputation of his lifetime lost
Between the night and morning. I might have lived,
And you know well how great the longing has been,
Where every day my footfall should have lit,
In the green shadow of Ferrara wall;
Or climbed among the images of the past –
The unperturbed and courtly images –
Evening and morning, the steep street of Urbino
To where the Duchess and her people talked
The stately midnight through until they stood
In their great window looking at the dawn;
I might have had no friend that could not mix
Courtesy and passion into one like those
That saw the wicks grow yellow in the dawn;
I might have used the one substantial right
My trade allows: chosen my company,
And chosen what scenery had pleased me best.'
Thereon my phoenix answered in reproof,
'The drunkards, pilferers of public funds,
All the dishonest crowd I had driven away,
When my luck changed and they dared meet my face,
Crawled from obscurity, and set upon me
Those I had served and some that I had fed;
Yet never have I, now nor any time,
Complained of the people.'
                           All I could reply
Was: 'You, that have not lived in thought but deed
Can have the purity of a natural force,
But I, whose virtues are the definitions
Of the analytic mind, can neither close
The eye of the mind nor keep my tongue from speech.'
And yet, because my heart leaped at her words,
I was abashed, and now they come to mind
After nine years, I sink my head abashed.[38]

Throughout this middle period, when politics came into his poetry – the title of one fiercely angry poem upon a contemporary event, the

[38] WBY, 'The People', *Collected Poems*, p. 169.

controversy over the Lane gallery, 'To a rich man who promised a
Bigger Subscription than his First to the Dublin Municipal Gallery
when the Amount collected proves that there is a Popular Demand
for the Pictures'[39] (which later became 'To a wealthy man who
promised a Second Subscription to the Dublin Municipal Gallery if it
were proved the People wanted Pictures'), is almost a political mani-
festo in its own right – when poems about beggars and rogues introduced ugliness, comedy, and sex into his range, and when all things
could keep him from his craft of verse, there were still the broken
dreams of Maud and her loveliness:

> Your beauty can but leave among us
> Vague memories, nothing but memories.
> A young man when the old men are done talking
> Will say to an old man, 'Tell me of that lady
> The poet stubborn with his passion sang us
> When age might well have chilled his blood.'[40]

The period after Maud Gonne's marriage in 1903 is not an easy one
for the biographer of Yeats to fill in.[41] The old tension between surrender to the senses and the pursuit of wisdom continued. His friendship with Lady Gregory lay on the side of wisdom – she remarked that
it was good for him to be at Coole among civilised people. But his
senses were no less demanding. The liaison with Diana Vernon was
renewed, and there were close associations with other women, the
possible consequences of one of which caused consternation when a
telegram arrived at Coole in 1910 to announce pregnancy. Even though
this proved to be a false alarm, Lady Gregory thought it high time
Yeats was married, and so did Diana Vernon. Various young women
were thought of. He himself wanted – as he had when young – like the
sardonic beggar of his poem, to

[39] WBY, *Collected Poems*, p. 119. The full title was 'The Gift J To a friend who promises
a bigger subscription than his first to the Dublin Municipal Gallery if the amount collected
proved that there is a considerable "popular demand" for the picture' in the *Irish Times*
version of 8 Jan 1913.

[40] WBY, 'Broken Dreams', *Collected Poems*, p. 172.

[41] Some of Yeats's letters to his friend Mabel Dickinson, to be included in a forthcoming
revised edition of the *Letters*, will expand our knowledge of his life around the 1908-11
period. For instance, he wrote to Miss Dickinson from Paris in 1908 describing his meetings with Maud Gonne, who seemed content and happy. They talked over old things but
with a sense of remoteness. These letters also give gossipy accounts of the perennial
problems of the Abbey Theatre and include comments on Florence Farr, Mrs Patrick
Campbell, Sarah Allgood and her sister Maire O'Neill, as well as on Shaw, Synge and
two old Galway beggar-women.

> '. . . get a comfortable wife and house
> To rid me of the devil in my shoes,'
> *Beggar to beggar cried, being frenzy-struck,*
> 'And the worse devil that is between my thighs.'[42]

George Moore had taunted him about his family. He had begun to take a great pride in his unusual ancestors. Writing his *Autobiographies* had, as the opening rhymes of *Responsibilities* informed his ancestors, sharpened his awareness that, because of his barren passion, he had, at the age of forty-nine, no child:

> *. . . nothing but a book,*
> *Nothing but that to prove your blood and mine.*[43]

After the 1916 rising, Maud's husband John MacBride was one of the leaders shot by the British. Yeats went to Normandy and yet again proposed to her, only to receive the usual reply, that the world would thank her for not marrying him. He had begun to fall in love with Iseult Gonne. Poems already written to her were 'To a Child Dancing in the Wind' and 'Two Years Later', which ended:

> O you will take whatever's offered
> And dream that all the world's a friend,
> Suffer as your mother suffered,
> Be as broken in the end.
> But I am old and you are young,
> And I speak a barbarous tongue.[44]

'To a Young Girl', 'Men Improve with the Years', 'The Living Beauty', 'To a Young Beauty', 'Memory', are probably all addressed to her; and she is the 'child' of 'Presences', her cat was Minnaloushe of 'The Cat and the Moon', and she is one of the speakers in *Michael Robartes and the Dancer*.

These poems have a tender affection for the young girl as well as an occasionally bitter awareness of the poet's own age. He had proposed to Iseult in 1916 and was answered neither yea nor nay. When he returned to Coole in the autumn he remembered the barren passion for Maud Gonne that had been torturing him nineteen years before. He looks at the swans whose hearts have not grown old:

> I have looked upon those brilliant creatures,
> And now my heart is sore.
> All's changed since I, hearing at twilight,

[42] WBY, 'Beggar to Beggar Cried', *Collected Poems*, p. 128.
[43] WBY, 'Introductory Rhymes', *Collected Poems*, p. 113.
[44] WBY, 'Two Years Later', *Collected Poems*, p. 137.

> The first time on this shore,
> The bell-beat of their wings above my head,
> Trod with a lighter tread.
>
> Unwearied still, lover by lover,
> They paddle in the cold　.
> Companionable streams or climb the air;
> Their hearts have not grown old;
> Passion or conquest, wander where they will,
> Attend upon them still.
>
> But now they drift on the still water,
> Mysterious, beautiful;
> Among what rushes will they build,
> By what lake's edge or pool
> Delight men's eyes when I awake some day
> To find they have flown away?[45]

The phrase 'All's changed' reminds us of the theme of 'Easter 1916', 'All changed, changed utterly: / A terrible beauty is born'. The Easter rising had disturbed Yeats profoundly by its unexpectedness. He had drawn away from nationalist, revolutionary politics. But he celebrated MacBride, among the other leaders, though he had done wrong 'to some who are near my heart'.

Iseult refused him in 1917, and on 21 October he married Miss Hyde Lees, whom he had known for some years. But after their marriage he was unhappy. A poem entitled 'Owen Aherne and His Dancers', not published until many years afterwards, describes his rage at age:

A strange thing surely that my Heart, when love had come unsought
Upon the Norman upland or in that poplar shade,
Should find no burden but itself and yet should be worn out.
It could not bear that burden and therefore it went mad.

The south wind brought it longing, and the east wind despair,
The west wind made it pitiful, and the north wind afraid.
It feared to give its love a hurt with all the tempest there;
It feared the hurt that she should give and therefore it went mad.

This part of the poem was written four days after he married. Three days after that he wrote the second part:

The Heart behind its rib laughed out. 'You have called me mad,' it said.
'Because I made you turn away and run from that young child;
How could she mate with fifty years that was so wildly bred?
Let the cage bird and the cage bird mate and the wild bird mate in the wild.'

[45] WBY, 'The Wild Swans at Coole', *Collected Poems*, p. 147.

'You but imagine lies all day, O murderer,' I replied.
'And all those lies have but one end, poor wretches to betray;
I did not find in any cage the woman at my side.
O but her heart would break to learn my thoughts are far away.'

'Speak all your mind,' my Heart sang out, 'speak all your mind; who cares,
Now that your tongue cannot persuade the child till she mistake
Her childish gratitude for love and match your fifty years?
O let her choose a young man now and all for his wild sake.'[46]

Then began the automatic writing, which in turn produced *A Vision*, and Yeats's feelings towards Iseult became less intense. The poem 'Two Songs of a Fool', where the speckled cat symbolises Mrs Yeats, the tame hare Iseult Gonne, sums up his attitude.[47] He wrote to Lady Gregory that his wife was 'a perfect wife, kind, wise and unselfish'. She had made his life 'serene and full of order'.[48]

At last he had found some tranquillity: the pursuit of love and wisdom seemed at last to coincide. The Solomon poems, 'Solomon and Sheba' and 'Solomon and the Witch', written to Mrs Yeats assert this:

'There's not a man or woman
Born under the skies
Dare match in learning with us two,
And all day long we have found
There's not a thing but love can make
The world a narrow pound.'[49]

In 'An Image from a Past Life' and 'Towards Break of Day' he records some of the dialogue of husband and wife. And when his daughter was born, the prayer he wrote conveys his appreciation of the wisdom and the content his marriage has brought him:

Yet many, that have played the fool
For beauty's very self, has charm made wise,
And many a poor man that has roved,
Loved and thought himself beloved,
From a glad kindness cannot take his eyes.[50]

[46] WBY, 'Owen Aherne and his Dancers', *Collected Poems*, p. 247.
[47] WBY, 'Two Songs of a Fool', *Collected Poems*, p. 101.
[48] WBY, quoted in J. M. Hone, *W. B. Yeats 1865–1939* (London, 1942) p. 307. See B. L. Reid, *The Man from New York: John Quinn and his friends* (New York, 1968) p. 308, for Lily Yeats's comments on some reactions to the marriage: 'Lady Gregory and Maud both, I believe are pleased. And why shouldn't they be? They have both, so to speak, had their "whack" – the latter a very considerable "whack" of her own choosing, but she will live for ever in Willy's verse, which is a fine crown and tribute to her beauty. Lady Gregory would, I expect, have liked to choose the bride, but Willie liked in this to be his own master.' The Yeats sisters thought Yeats and his wife 'most happy together'.
[49] WBY, *Collected Poems*, p. 155.
[50] WBY, 'A Prayer for my Daughter', *Collected Poems*, p. 211.

The present was with Mrs Yeats, the future with his daughter Anne. Just as 'Easter 1916' recorded the decline of Constance Markievicz from being young and beautiful into a state of shrill-voiced argument, and recorded how hearts grow stony with overlong sacrifice, so Maud Gonne's beauty, too, was in the past.

> Have I not seen the loveliest woman born
> Out of the mouth of Plenty's horn,
> Because of her opinionated mind
> Barter that horn and every good
> By quiet natures understood
> For an old bellows full of angry wind?[51]

Yeats had begun the great period of his poetry – and his life. He settled into his tower in Galway

> And decked and altered it for a girl's love[52]

and there his two children, Anne and Michael, played, and there he studied his Anglo-Irish literary forebears, read deeply in history and philosophy, and wrote poetry. The erstwhile revolutionary was a Senator now; and the man who had ceaselessly sought belief created his own system of it in *A Vision*.

Out of this new certainty and poise of his life came the brilliantly assured poetry of 'The Tower', heralded by the earlier brilliant poems of *Michael Robartes and the Dancer*, 'Easter 1916', 'The Second Coming', and 'A Prayer for My Daughter'. These poems showed how he could unite truth and beauty, idealism and realism into a new magniloquence.

Now his own situation came into sharper focus. 'Easter 1916' had dealt with an Irish event; 'The Second Coming' with the state of the world, a perception sharpened by his experience of the bitter fighting in Ireland; and 'A Prayer for My Daughter' had speculated in part on the devastation caused by hatred and the need for ceremony. The 'murderous innocence' of this poem and its insistence on ceremony link it with 'The Second Coming', where 'The ceremony of innocence'[53] is drowned. But he was faced with that earlier situation of his youth, where he sought to escape from his senses into the pursuit of wisdom

---

[51] Ibid., p. 213. After Maud Gonne returned from France to England in 1917 Yeats had placed his rooms in Woburn Buildings at her disposal in 1918; she in turn rented Yeats and his wife her house in Dublin for a nominal rent. But when Maud Gonne arrived unexpectedly Yeats refused to take her in, as Mrs Yeats was seriously ill with influenza. The scene, the strong letters are described in J. Hone, *W. B. Yeats 1865–1939*, p. 314.

[52] WBY, 'Meditations in Time of Civil War, IV', *Collected Poems*, p. 228.

[53] WBY, 'The Second Coming', *Collected Poems*, p. 211.

CA D 2

on Innisfree. Because of his decrepit age, despite the fact that he never
had a more excited, passionate, fantastical imagination:

> It seems that I must bid the Muse go pack,
> Choose Plato and Plotinus for a friend . . .[54]

Thus the theme of 'The Tower': his savage query, as he reviews in his
mind the people associated with the neighbourhood – Mrs French,
Mary Hynes the peasant girl celebrated by the blind Irish poet Raftery,
his own character Hanrahan, and the bankrupt owner of the tower –
as to whether they, too, raged as he did against the coming of age. Out
of this comes the devastating memory of Maud Gonne:

> Does the imagination dwell the most
> Upon a woman won or woman lost?
> If on the lost, admit you turned aside
> From a great labyrinth out of pride,
> Cowardice, some silly over-subtle thought
> Or anything called conscience once;
> And that if memory recur, the sun's
> Under eclipse and the day blotted out.[55]

He faces what age means, the need to make his soul, studying in a
learned school as the body declines, and friends die. Out of this mood,
too, came 'Sailing to Byzantium'. It seems to have come out of
thoughts of Maud as well as of making his soul. 'When Irishmen', he
wrote in a draft for a broadcast, 'were illuminating the Book of Kells
and making the jewelled croziers in the National Museum, Byzantium
was the centre of European civilization and the source of its spiritual
philosophy, so I symbolise the search for the spiritual life by a journey
to that city.'[56] There were some magnificent draft stanzas, like this one:

> I therefore travel towards Byzantium
> Among these sun-browned pleasant mariners
> Another dozen days & we shall come
> Under the jetty & the marble stairs
> Already I have learned by spout of foam,
> Creak of the sail's tackle, or of the oars,
> Can wake from the slumber where it lies
> That fish whereon souls ride to paradise.[57]

But the poem, as Mr Stallworthy has argued in *Between the Lines*, probably began with a prose fragment of which I shall quote the first part:

[54] WBY, 'The Tower', *Collected Poems*, p. 218.   [55] Ibid., p. 222.
[56] WBY, quoted in Jon Stallworthy, *Between the Lines: Yeats's Poetry in the Making*
(Oxford, 1963) p. 96.
[57] Ibid., p. 93. I have selected from Stallworthy's versions of the drafts.

Now the day has come I will speak on of those
Loves I have had in play
That my soul loved
That I loved in my first youth
For many loves have I taken off my clothes
For some I threw them off in haste, for some slowly and indifferently
And laid on my bed that I might be
                    but now I will take off my body[58]

'Sailing to Byzantium' in its final form is a rejection of the sensual music
of Ireland, of the young, of love. The poem is a taking off of body, for
it is no country, Ireland, for old men, and the poet has therefore sailed
the seas to Byzantium to be gathered into the artifice of eternity.

The interference of love with wisdom was always a possibility. One
of the most poignant expressions of this occurs, of course, in 'Among
School Children', set so quietly in the schoolroom of a school run on
Montessori principles in Waterford, the poet visiting as a Senator interested in education,[59] 'a sixty-year smiling public man' into whose
thoughts bursts the idea of Maud Gonne and the memory of how she
had once told him of some childish day turning into tragedy:

And thinking of that fit of grief or rage
I look upon one child or t'other there
And wonder if she stood so at that age –
For even daughters of the swan can share
Something of every paddler's heritage –
And had that colour upon cheek or hair,
And thereupon my heart is driven wild:
She stands before me as a living child.[60]

Before proceeding to the great philosophical question of the poem, he
views her present image and his own with sardonic savagery:

Her present image floats into the mind –
Did Quattrocento finger fashion it
Hollow of cheek as though it drank the wind
And took a mess of shadows for its meat?
And I though never of Ledaean kind
Had pretty plumage once – enough of that,
Better to smile on all that smile, and show
There is a comfortable kind of old scarecrow.[61]

[58] Ibid., p. 89. Further discussion of the poem is contained in A. Norman Jeffares,
'The Byzantine Poems of W. B. Yeats', *RES*, XXII 144–52; in Curtis Bradford, 'Yeats's
Byzantine Poems', *PMLA*, LXXV (1) 110–25; and in E. Schanzer, ' "Sailing to Byzantium",
Keats and Andersen', *English Studies*, XLI (1960) 376–80.
[59] See Donald T. Torchiana, ' "Among School Children" and the Education of the
Irish Spirit', in Jeffares and Cross (eds) *In Excited Reverie* (London, 1965) pp. 123 f.
[60] WBY, *Collected Poems*, p. 242.   [61] Ibid., p. 243.

Love was constantly in his thoughts in 1926: he was at the tower in May of that year and wrote to his friend Mrs Shakespear:

> I am writing poetry as I always do here, and as always happens, no matter how I begin, it becomes love poetry before I am finished with it. I have lots of subjects in my head including a play about Christ meeting the worshippers of Dionysos on the mountain side – no doubt this will somehow become love poetry too. . . . One feels at moments as if one could with a touch convey a vision – that the mystic vision and sexual love use the same means, opposed yet parallel existence. . . .[62]

In *A Man Young and Old* he was writing the regrets of an old man for youth and love, some of them reminders of Maud's intractable, stone-like heart in 'First Love' and 'Human Dignity' (though another poem, not in the series, 'Quarrel in old age', paid tribute once again to her youthful beauty). His poems on love gained even greater exuberance, however, after his first serious illness in 1927. After this illness, he began his winter visits to the south in search of sunshine; and in the spring of 1929 a burst of creative activity produced poems in 'all praise of joyous life', full of emotion of an impersonal kind. They included the superb 'Lullaby', celebrating the loves of Helen, Iseult, and Leda. Yeats was mingling the graphic speech of Galway peasants with memories and some of the esoteric ideas of *A Vision* (first published privately in 1926) in the 'Crazy Jane' poems of *Words for Music, Perhaps*. These were founded upon the acidulous conversation of Cracked Mary, an old countrywoman who lived at Gort near Ballylee. Crazy Jane remembers her youth, and talks with the Bishop, on the theme of desecration and the lover's night.

In the autumn of this year Yeats saw his old friend Mrs Shakespear; and a poem refers to the conflict of the senses and wisdom in another manner:

> Speech after long silence; it is right
> All other lovers being estranged or dead,
> Unfriendly lamplight hid under its shade,
> The curtains drawn upon unfriendly night,
> That we descant and yet again descant
> Upon the supreme theme of Art and Song:
> Bodily decreptitude is wisdom; young
> We loved each other and were ignorant.[63]

---

[62] WBY, letter to Olivia Shakespear, 25 May 1926, quoted in Jeffares, *W. B. Yeats*, p. 214.

[63] WBY, 'After Long Silence', *Collected Poems*, p. 301.

Then followed the poems of *A Woman Young and Old*, with their emphasis on the body; a witty emphasis in 'Consolation', and in 'A Last Confession', with its renewed metaphysical soul–body conflict:

> What lively lad most pleasured me
> Of all that with me lay?
> I answer that I gave my soul
> And loved in misery,
> But had great pleasure with a lad
> That I loved bodily.
>
> Flinging from his arms I laughed
> To think his passion such
> He fancied that I gave a soul
> Did but our bodies touch,
> And laughed upon his breast to think
> Beast gave beast as much.
>
> I gave what other women gave
> That stepped out of their clothes,
> But when this soul, its body off,
> Naked to naked goes,
> He it has found shall find therein
> What none other knows,
>
> And give his own and take his own
> And rule in his own right;
> And though it loved in misery
> Close and cling so tight,
> There's not a bird of day that dare
> Extinguish that delight.[64]

Here again is the idea of shedding the body which occurred in the drafts for 'Sailing to Byzantium'. As Yeats remarked, he spent his life saying the same thing in different ways. His thoughts continued in this metaphysical vein. The girl who was looking for the face she had before the world was made, the woman who proclaimed 'The lot of love is chosen' are now generalised in the thought of 'whence had they come?'

> Eternity is passion, girl or boy
> Cry at the onset of their sexual joy
> 'For ever and for ever'; then awake
> Ignorant what Dramatis Personae spake . . .[65]

---

64 WBY, 'A Last Confession', *Collected Poems*, p. 313.
65 WBY, 'Whence had they come?' *Collected Poems*, p. 332.

These metaphysical poems may have reflected the effect of the Steinach operation he underwent in 1934,[66] but it is possible that his friendship with Oliver St John Gogarty had encouraged him in the ribaldry he enjoyed – the simple, bucolic, Rabelaisian strain in his work described by F. R. Higgins, with whom he greatly enjoyed discussing women. As he wrote in an unpublished letter to Ethel Mannin:

> We poets would die of loneliness but for women, and we choose our men friends that we may have somebody to talk about women with; Higgins is full of fine discourse about loves of Connaught women and Dublin typists. I don't think women choose their women friends to talk of men – I don't know.[67]

But, as ever, he was changeable in mood. In 1931 he had wanted, he wrote to his wife, to exorcise that slut Crazy Jane:[68] the result was a long and splendid poem, 'Vacillation', significantly entitled 'Wisdom' in its first draft. The conflict between wisdom and the senses continued as ever and indeed its echoes continued through some of his friendships with women in the thirties. Among his new friendships were those with Lady Gerald Wellesley (the course of this friendship is charted in their correspondence, first published in 1940 as *Letters on Poetry from W. B. Yeats to Dorothy Wellesley*), with Edith Shackleton Heald, a journalist, with Ethel Mannin, an authoress, and, not least interesting, with Margot Collis [or Ruddock; she used both names]. She was a beautiful young married woman, an actress, dancer and poetess. Yeats's interest in and kindness to her is again revealed in his letters:[69] they show how Yeats insisted upon disciplined work – 'our plough is difficulty' he wrote to her in one letter – and found her romantic spontaneity distressingly inadequate. The difficulties of this friendship are amply illustrated in a letter he wrote to Olivia Shakespear on 22 May 1936:

> The girl who is quite a beautiful person came here [Mallorca] seven or eight days ago. She walked in at 6.30, her luggage in her hand and, when she had

---

[66] Part of a letter to Shri Purohit Swami, of 21 Mar 1937, may bear this out. The relevant passage reads as follows: 'I told him that though I longed for India, there was a practical difficulty of a very personal kind; this made it impossible. You are with him; please tell him of the operation I went through in London and say also that though it revived my creative power it revived also my sexual desire; and that in all likelihood will last me until I die. I believe that if I repressed this for any long period I would break down under the strain as did the great Ruskin.'

[67] WBY, letter to Ethel Mannin, 15 Nov 1936, quoted by permission of Miss Nora Niland, Librarian, Sligo County Library.   [68] Cf. Jeffares, *W. B. Yeats*, p. 272.

[69] What survives of their correspondence will be edited by Professor Roger McHugh in *Ah, Sweet Dancer* (1970).

been given breakfast, said she had come to find out if her verse was any good. I had known her for some years and had told her to stop writing as her technique was getting worse. I was amazed by the tragic magnificence of some fragments and said so. She went out in pouring rain, thought, as she said afterwards, that if she killed herself her verse would live instead of her. Went to the shore to jump in, then thought that she loved life and began to dance. She went to the lodging house where Shri Purohit Swami was, to sleep. She was wet through, so Swami gave her some of his clothes; she had no money, he gave her some. Next day she went to Barcelona and there went mad, climbing out of a window, falling through a baker's roof, breaking a kneecap, hiding in a ship's hold, singing her own poems most of the time. The British Consul in Barcelona appealed to me, so George and I went there, found her with recovered sanity sitting up in bed at a clinic writing an account of her madness. It was impossible to get adequate money out of her family, so I accepted financial responsibility and she was despatched to England and now I won't be able to afford new clothes for a year. When her husband wrote it had not been to send money, but to congratulate her on the magnificent publicity. The paragraph you saw is certainly his work. Will she stay sane? It is impossible to know.

When I am in London I shall probably hide because the husband may send me journalists and because I want to keep at a distance from a tragedy where I can be no further help.[70]

The published poems which record aspects of this friendship are 'Sweet Dancer'[71] and 'A Crazed Girl'.[72] They have something of the strain of protectiveness Yeats felt earlier for Iseult Gonne as she danced upon the shore; and they also praise the attractions created by a young woman's physical beauty.

Another strain of poetry continued, that of the great celebratory poems on Coole and Lady Gregory continued on into his last volume, the *Last Poems*, into 'The Municipal Gallery Revisited' and into 'A Bronze Head', where a bronze head of Maud Gonne reminds him she was no dark tomb haunter (a reference to her wearing long black clothes in old age):

> But even at the starting-post, all sleek and new,
> I saw the wildness in her and I thought
> A vision of terror that it must live through
> Had shattered her soul. Propinquity had brought
> Imagination to that pitch where it casts out
> All that is not itself: I had grown wild
> And wandered murmuring everywhere, 'My child, my child!'[73]

[70] WBY, *Letters*, ed. Allan Wade, 1954, p. 856.
[71] WBY, *Collected Poems*, p. 340.
[72] WBY, *Collected Poems*, p. 348.
[73] WBY, *Collected Poems*, p. 382.

He had spent his last years in the foul rag-and-bone shop of the
heart, but it is well to remember his realistic humour. In the trouble
of his middle age he had found time to describe the scholars coughing
in ink:

> Lord, what would they say,
> Did their Catullus walk that way?[74]

And in old age, too, that sardonic note could permeate his attitude
towards politics and even his passionate contemplation of beauty:

> There is no release
> In a bodkin or disease,
> Nor can there be work so great
> As that which cleans man's dirty slate.
> While man can still his body keep
> Wine or love drug him to sleep,
> Waking he thanks the Lord that he
> Has body and its stupidity,
> But body gone he sleeps no more,
> And till his intellect grows sure
> That all's arranged in one clear view,
> Pursues the thoughts that I pursue,
> Then stands in judgment on his soul,
> And, all work done, dismisses all
> Out of intellect and sight
> And sinks at last into the night.[75]

---

[74] WBY, 'The Scholars', *Collected Poems*, p. 158.
[75] WBY, 'The Man and the Echo', *Collected Poems*, p. 393.

Gyres in Yeats's Poetry

THE word 'gyre' is used by writers, especially poets, to describe any whirling, spiral or circular motion. Its appearance in Spenser, Jonson, Fletcher, Drayton, Mrs Browning and Rossetti as a noun, and in Southey, Drayton, Fletcher, Barlow, Meredith, Hall and Carroll as a verb, need not cause any difficulty. It is an unusual word, but its meaning is clear, and it obviously corresponds to the commonplace 'gyration'.

In Yeats's poetry the word first[1] appears in *Michael Robartes and the Dancer*. Since it occurs in two poems in that volume[2] which are based on the thought of *A Vision* we can discover there what Yeats meant by the word. He gives his sources for it in a section headed *The Gyre*; and it obviously derives not only from his reading but from his talking to Irish countrymen:

> Flaubert talked much of writing a story called 'La Spirale' and died before he began it, but since his death an editor has collected the scheme from various sources. It would have concerned a man whose dreams during sleep grew in magnificence as his life became more and more unlucky.[3] He dreamt of marriage with a princess when all went wrong with his own love adventure

---

[1] The use of the word in 'The Two Trees' which appears in *Collected Poems*, p. 54, may mislead the reader who has not seen that this poem did not contain the word when published in *The Rose* (1893) nor when it appeared in *The Poems* (1927).

[2] WBY, 'Demon and Beast', *Collected Poems*, p. 209, and 'The Second Coming', ibid. p. 210.

[3] Mrs Daphne Fullwood, who has worked with Patrick Lyons on Yeats's literary relations with the French symbolists, remarks that Yeats's comment suggests a second hand acquaintance with the story, since he speaks of what were notes or a plan in manuscript as talk about the project, and that Yeats's remark that Flaubert died before he began it ('La Spirale') might seem to suggest that Flaubert died before he could begin it, whereas the project seems to have been finally shelved seventeen years before his death. In Yeats's second mention of the story – in his Introduction to the Macmillan edition of Dorothy Wellesley's poems he spells it as *L'Aspirail*, which suggests that he had heard of it in conversation – or else forgot it. Mrs Fullwood further remarks that Flaubert was set off on this project by Balzac's *Louis Lambert*, itself one of Yeats's 'sacred books'; and she thinks that Yeats may have heard of Flaubert's story through T. Sturge Moore, who mentions in his *Art and Life* (1910) that E. W. Fischer published a study of Flaubert's unfinished projects in 1908. Fischer records that his hero's mind soared up to 'une spirale qui monte à l'infini'.

Swedenborg wrote occasionally of gyrations, especially in his 'Spiritual Diary', and in 'The Principia' where the physical universe is described as built up by the spiral movement of points, and by vortices which were combinations of these; but very obscurely except where describing the physical universe; perhaps because he was compelled as he thought to keep silent on all that concerned Fate. I remember that certain Irish country men whom I questioned some twenty years ago had seen Spirits departing from them in an ascending gyre; and there is that gyrating 'tangle of world lines in a fourth dimensional space' of later discoverers, and of course, Descartes and his Vortex, Boehme and his gyre, and perhaps, were I learned enough to discover it, allusions to many writers back to antiquity. Arrived there I am attracted to a passage in Heraclitus which I can, I think, explain more clearly than his English commentators.[4]

He discusses Blake's use of the Gyres in Book Two, Section III of *A Vision*:

Blake, in the 'Mental Traveller', describes a struggle, a struggle perpetually repeated between a man and a woman, and as the one ages, the other grows young. A child is given to an old woman and . . .

> She lives upon his shrieks and cries
> And she grows young as he grows old.
> Till he becomes a bleeding youth
> And she becomes a virgin bright;
> Then he rends up his manacles
> And bends her down to his delight.

Then he in turn becomes 'an aged shadow' and is driven from his door, where 'From the fire on the hearth a little female babe doth spring'. He must wander 'until he can a maiden win' and then all is repeated for

> . . . The wild game of her roving eye
> Does him to infancy beguile . . .
> . . . .
> Till he becomes a wayward babe
> And she a weeping woman old . . .

The woman and the man are two competing gyres growing at one another's expense . . . (p. 133).

Yeats did not owe much to the Swedenborgian gyres which are described in the *Diarium Maius*,[5] and, more explicitly, in the *Principia*:

For since they [particles] are not only most highly prone but also most highly suited to a common or vortical motion; since the figure of each particle respectively conspires to this and to no other motion, as will subsequently be shown; it follows that merely in virtue of the origin of their motion, whatever that origin may be, they tend to no other than a vortical motion; just as the least sound, the least commencement of motion in the air, puts a volume of its

---

[4] WBY, *A Vision* (1926) pp. 128 ff. All quotations in this essay are from this first edition.
[5] See E. Swedenborg, *Diarium Spirituale* (1845), § 2920 (entry for 24 Aug 1748).

parts into a motion undulating from the centre to the circumference and on every side circularly; as we see also in water and in every element whose phenomena come within the cognizance of the senses. This tendency is more particularly observable in the present case; in which one particle, as it were, assists another into the performance of the same gyre with its own; a gyre into which in consequence of their elasticity all must readily and similarly flow; so that upon the slightest origination of motion they flow spontaneously into a vortex.[6]

The conclusions of the earlier parts of the *Principia* are summed up in the second volume as follows:

In our first and second parts we have abundantly shown that the first and second elementaries can move only in a spiral and vortical direction; that they cannot for instance be put into any other motion than such as accords with their mechanism and figure; that they are then in their veriest and most natural situation when they assume a vortical arrangement; that they so dispose themselves as to adapt even their very figure to their distance and motion; or that when compressed they tend to a more rapid gyration than when dilated, more rapid at a smaller distance from the sun than at a longer; that they cannot be quiescent unless there be no centre around which they can gyrate; that the perpetual active vivifies, renews, and as it were preserves the perennial action of the particles of the element; not to mention other particulars which we have above mentioned.[7]

Gyres as forming part of the spiritual progress of the soul are described in the *Diarium Maius*:

There are gyres into which the newly arrived spirits are obliged to be inaugurated to the extent that they may be initiated into fellowship with others, so as both to speak and think together with them.[8]

This idea is also dealt with in *Arcana Coelestia*,[9] and these gyres are quite unlike the Yeatsian:

It has been given to apperceive the gyres of those who belong to the province of the liver. . . . The gyres were gentle, flowing about according to the operation of that entrail . . . and affected me with much delight; their operation is diverse but it is commonly orbicular.[10]

in that one gyre permits of access to another, and there is no implication of any inevitable contrariety of gyres.

These quotations from Swedenborg have been made to demonstrate that Yeats did not owe much to Swedenborgian sources, for these

---

[6] E. Swedenborg, *The Principia* (1845), § 38, p. 160. Cf. also § 39, p. 162.

[7] Ibid., ch. VI, p. 345.

[8] Swedenborg, *Diarium Spirituale*, § 1015. Cf. §§ 1015$\frac{1}{2}$, 1016, 1017, 2921.

[9] See Swedenborg, *Arcana Coelestia*, §§ 5171, 5173, 5181, 5182, 5183 (§ 5182 is identical with § 1015 of the *Diarium Maius*).

[10] E. Swedenborg, *Arcana Coelestia*, § 5183.

concepts are concerned either with the physical basis of matter, in which Yeats was not profoundly interested, or with a view of the soul's evolution different to that which Yeats imagined, as will be shown when Yeats's own descriptions of gyres are dealt with later.

The theory of Descartes with regard to vortices was summed up by Mahaffy:

> There are produced an innumerable series of vortices of matter of various volume and various regularity of form, in which are carried along the grosser bodies situated in them. Our solar system is such a vortex and the earth though in one sense moving along with the matter of its vortex, in another is at rest, as the passenger is at rest in a moving ship. The easier and quicker motion of the subtler matter in each vortex causes the grosser to deflect towards the centre, and this is the principle by which he explains weight and gravity – a hypothesis regarded with admiration by his followers. Solidity he explains as nothing but an absence of motion in the particles of a body and he can conceive no stronger 'cement' which would hold them together.[11]

This theory is not connected with Yeatsian gyres except that there is a whirling motion implied. There are, however, several ideas in Boehme's writings which are echoed in *A Vision*, the most indisputable being that of the 'tinctures',[12] which are an essential part of the system of *A Vision*. We find in Boehme that the 'will fashions itself a mirror' and 'in this union of the joy of contemplation and of desire, of imagination and desire, the eternal nature hidden in God is aroused, and now comes forward as the contrarium of the idea'.[13] This doctrine can be found in the section of *A Vision* dealing with The Four Faculties, if we realise that Boehme's 'mirror' corresponds to the 'mask' in Yeats. These obvious parallels justify an examination of the belief in contraries which Boehme professed – 'All existing things in nature are encircled by a magical band; they influence one another by attraction and repulsion, sympathy and antipathy'[14] – and the inevitability of change,[15] which he stressed in the *40 Questions*:

> If the will has nothing of the divine power of true humility there can be no entering of it within itself into the life by means of death; but the soul is then like a furiously turning wheel, seeking continually to rise and continually sinking down on the other side. . . . There is in that state surely a kind of fire but not a combustion for there rules the severe harshness and bitterness. The

---

[11] J. P. Mahaffy, *Descartes*, p. 159.
[12] Boehme, in his turn, had derived these from Paracelsus. Cf. H. L. Martensen, *Jacob Boehme*, p. 31: 'Boehme was influenced not only by his [Paracelsus'] ideas but by his certainly barbarous terminology. From him Boehme also derives the term "tinctures".'
[13] Ibid., p. 33.   [14] Ibid., p. 62.   [15] Ibid., p. 258.

bitterness seeks the fire and wants to increase it; but the acridity keeps it imprisoned and thus results in a terrible anxiety and resembles a turning wheel, turning perpetually around itself.[16]

These conceptions are similar to the views put forward in *A Vision*. One of Yeats's diagrams to illustrate the gyres was that of the two opposing triangles

Their connection with Boehme's semi-episodic explanation of the history of the universe becomes apparent, for Boehme's tenth figure uses triangles to illustrate this principle:

Here Adam by that word of grace treasured up in his heart, whose name is Jesus, is raised so far, that he can stand above the Earthly globe, upon the basis of a fiery triangle which is an excellent emblem of his own soul, and the holy names Jesus above him upon the top of a watery triangle ▽. And these two triangles which in Adam's fall were divorced from each other, do now touch each other again though (in this beginning) but in one point, that the Soul's desire may draw down into itself the △ and that the holy name may draw up into itself more and more the △ till these two make up a complete ⟨⟩, the most significant figure in all the universe; for only then the work of Repentance and Reunion with Sophia will be absolved. And although, during this mortal life, no such perfection of the whole man can be wrought out, yet is it attainable in the inward part, and whatsoever seems to be an obstruction (even sin not excepted) must, for this very end, work together for good to them that love God.[17]

The idea of catastrophic change which comes at the end of each era of history in *A Vision* can also be found in Boehme:

'Centrum naturale' is thus, in Boehme, the first thing in nature, that original variance and conflict between opposing forces with which life begins, and which cannot lead it further than anguish, a tension, vibration, or gyration of the forces which is designated now as an apprehensive darkness, now as a fire which is not yet kindled, but smoulders in the depth, which only the lightning is able to bring out of this restlessness into subordination to the higher principle.[18]

---

[16] Jacob Boehme, *40 Questions*, ed. Franz Hartmann.
[17] See Rev. W. Law's *An illustration of the Deep Principles of Jacob Boehme the Teutonic Philosopher in thirteen figures*. Proof that Yeats was acquainted with this work can be found in a reference in *A Packet for Ezra Pound*, p. 31, where Yeats writes that 'One remembers the diagrams in Law's Boehme where one lifts a flap to discover both the human entrails and the starry heavens, and that William Blake thought them worthy of Michael Angelo, but remains almost unintelligible because he never drew the like.'
[18] H. L. Martensen, op. cit., p. 77.

These are the sources which Yeats gives us, but he modifies their application:

> Swedenborg and Blake and many before them knew that all things had their gyres; but Swedenborg and Blake preferred to explain them figuratively, and so I am the first to substitute for Biblical or mythological figures historical movements and actual men and women. (*A Vision*, p. xi.)

What he does mean by a gyre can be gathered from *A Vision*:

> A line is the symbol of time and it expresses a movement . . . [it] symbolises the emotional subjective mind. . . . A plane cutting the line at right angles constitutes, in combination with the moving line, a space of three or more dimensions, and is the symbol of all that is objective, and so . . . of intellect as opposed to emotion. Line and plane are combined in a gyre, and as one tendency or the other must always be the stronger, the gyre is always expanding or contracting. For simplicity of representation the gyre is drawn as a cone. Sometimes this cone represents the individual soul . . . sometimes general life . . . understanding that neither the soul of man nor the soul of nature can be suppressed without conflict . . . we substitute for this cone two cones. (*A Vision*, p. 129.)

There are then four gyres, two expanding, two narrowing, the apex of each cone coinciding with the base of the other:

> when, however, a narrowing and widening gyre reach their limit, the one the utmost contraction, the other the utmost expansion, they change places, point to circle, circle to point, for this system conceives the world as catastrophic, and continue as before, one always narrowing, one always expanding, and yet bound for ever to one another. (*A Vision*, p. 183.)

Here Yeats asserts that much of Parmenides, Empedocles and especially Heraclitus can be explained. He quotes Heraclitus:

> 'When Strife was fallen to the lowest depth of the vortex.' (Not as might be supposed,' Birkett explains, 'the centre, but the extreme bound') 'and love has reached the centre of the whirl, in it do all things come together so as to be one only . . . For of a truth they (Love & Strife) were afore time and shall be, nor ever can (?) boundless time be emptied of the pair, and they prevail in turn as the circle comes round, and pass away before one another and increase in their appointed time.' (*A Vision*, p. 132.)

The single cone, he writes, whose extreme limits are described as *anima hominis* and *anima mundi*, is formed by the whirling of a sphere which moves onward leaving an empty coil behind it; and the double cones by the separating of two whirling spheres that have been one. Later parts of *A Vision* illustrate the connection between the gyres and the cones:

> Each age unwinds the thread another age had wound, and it amuses one to remember that before Phidias, and his westward moving art, Persia fell, and that

when full moon came round again, amid eastward moving thought, and
brought Byzantine glory, Rome fell; and that at the outset of our westward
moving Renaissance Byzantium fell; all things dying each other's death.[19]

The gyres are touching the sides of the cones and are the horizontal
movement. There is a continuous oscillation at work, symbolised by
'the King and Queen who are sun and moon also, and whirl round
and round as they mount up through a Round Tower'.[20]

The symbolic meaning of gyres in the poems of Yeats is best illustrated in 'The Second Coming':[21]

> Turning and turning in the widening gyre
> The falcon cannot leave the falconer;
> Things fall apart; the centre cannot hold;
> Mere anarchy is loosed upon the world.

These lines are explained when we realise that in the Yeatsian system
modern civilisation had its initial impulse in the teaching of Christ. He
may, in this poem, be the falconer who began an era of history which
has almost reached its conclusion:

> In pity for man's darkening thought
> He walked that room and issued thence
> In Galilean turbulence. , . .[22]

The falcon is man, losing touch with Christianity at the time the poem
is written. The civilisation of the poem's period began with Christ at
the point of the cone, and the gyre which then began has almost reached
its fullest expansion. When it reaches this fullest expansion there will
be a revolution, a catastrophic change 'from circle to point', the point
being the apex of an historical period beginning its course in an opposite direction to the previous age as 'The Second Coming' predicts:

> The darkness drops again; but now I know
> That twenty centuries of stony sleep
> Were vexed to nightmare by a rocking cradle,
> And what rough beast, its hour come round at last,
> Slouches towards Bethlehem to be born?

The imagery of this poem, couched in the idiom of *A Vision* and to
be understood in reference to that work, may not be indebted only to
the literary sources Yeats enumerated. In addition to his memory of
the talk of the Irish country people he may also be remembering a
visual image. There is a passage in Dante where the image of a falcon
is used in the same manner as that of 'The Second Coming'. Dante

[19] WBY, *A Vision*, p. 183.   [20] Cf. WBY, *Collected Poems*. p. 154.
[21] Ibid., p. 210.   [22] 'Two Songs from a Play,' ibid., p. 239.

and Virgil reach the eighth circle of Hell seated on Geryon's back, much to Dante's terror:

> But he whose succour then not first I proved,
> Soon as I mounted, in his arms aloft,
> Embracing, held me up; and thus he spake:
> 'Geryon I now move thee: be thy wheeling gyres
> Of ample circuit, easy thy descent . . .
> As falcon that hath long been on the wing
> But lure nor bird hath seen, while in despair
> The falconer cries, 'Ah me! thou stoop'st to earth,'
> Wearied descends whence nimbly he arose
> In many an airy wheel and lighting sits
> At distance from his lord in angry mood. . . .[23]

The similarity between this passage and Yeats's 'The Second Coming' is obvious. Geryon's gyres are described by the 'many an airy wheel' of the falcon. Yeats's falcon also travels in gyres. Mrs Francis Stuart ('a girl that knew all Dante once'[24]) told the present writer that Yeats was extremely fond of the Doré illustrated edition of Dante which she possessed. This edition contains two pictures of Geryon emerging from the abyss with his body shaped like the path of a gyre on a cone. The shape of this monster is unusual and could have impressed Yeats by its peculiarity. If he thought of gyres in connection with a poem to be written on cycles of history the shape of Geryon might have come into his mind, and from that to the image of the falcon is but a small step in the path Dante had made. That Yeats was interested in the mere movement of gyration from a much earlier period than that in which gyres appear in his poetry can be seen from his allusion to an old countrywoman's description of spirits ascending in what is, to all intents and purposes, a gyre. An essay, 'The Friends of the People of Faery', shows that he records the movement as delicate and graceful; there is as yet no particular idea that this twirling upwards of the spirits has any symbolic significance, beyond the fact that it was unusual and important because of its use by the fairies. His description of the 'wee woman's' disappearance illustrates the movement thus:

> With that she gave a swirl round on her feet and raises up in the air and round and round she goes, and up and up, as if it was a winding stairs she went up, only far swifter. She went up and up, till she was no bigger than a bird up against the clouds, singing and singing the whole time the loveliest music I ever heard in my life from that day to this.[25]

---

[23] Dante, *The Vision of Hell*, canto XVII. Cary's translation.
[24] WBY, *Last Poems and Plays*, p. 76.   [25] WBY, *The Celtic Twilight* (1902) p. 205.

Since it seems likely that Yeats drew from other sources than those which he listed in *A Vision*, and since Yeats's interest in some of these other sources depends upon a visual concept of a mere movement, we can question whether all the uses of 'gyres' in his poetry depend on the material of *A Vision*, or whether the word is sometimes employed merely because it represents a movement pleasing to the poet. The word is used in its two senses in 'Demon and Beast'.[26] The first line of this poem must be explained by *A Vision*'s thought and terminology[27] if we are to extract from it the associations which it represented for Yeats and if we are not to be arrested by the unusual appearance of the line:

> Though I had long perned in the gyre.

In the third verse –

> For aimless joy had made me stop
> Beside the little lake
> To watch a white gull take
> A bit of bread thrown up into the air;
> Now gyring down and perning there
> He splashed where an absurd
> Portly green-pated bird
> Shook off the water from his back.

which is a description of a scene in St. Stephen's Green, Dublin, the poet appears to use the word in a normal manner without any reference to the system of *A Vision*. The seagull's 'gyring down' is merely a description of its graceful movement[28] (implicitly contrasted with that of the 'absurd' duck?)

There may have been a touch of humour in this second use of the word, a mockery of its more serious and esoteric meanings. We find that Yeats altered these lines of an early poem:

> There, through bewildered branches, go
> Winged loves borne on in gentle strife,

---

[26] WBY, *Collected Poems*, p. 209.

[27] The gyre is between hatred and desire, an antithesis to which Yeats often refers in *A Vision* and other writings.

[28] There is nothing unusual in such a use of the word to indicate movement. Cf. Southey, *Poems*, 'Roderick', I 216:

> . . . The eagle's cry
> Who far above them, at her highest flight
> A speck scarce visible, gyred round and round.

Spenser (*The Faerie Queene*, II v 8, and III i 23) and Rossetti (*House of Life*, Sonnet 'Cloud and Wind') both use the word for simple description. Yeats read these poets, and therefore had knowledge of the simple description of movement indicated by 'gyres', simple, that is, in the sense that no symbolic meaning was attached to the word as in Swedenborg and Boehme.

> Tossing and tossing to and fro
> The flaming circle of our life.

to

> There the Loves a circle go,
> The flaming circle of our days,
> Gyring, spiring to and fro
> In those great ignorant leafy ways.[29]

This alteration seems to have been made through a delight in the movement of the Loves (there is no need to consult *A Vision* for the meaning of the second version of the poem, for its basic thought of 'the circle of our life' remains unchanged) as well as the usefulness of achieving an internal rhyme[30] in the revised version by the introduction of the word 'gyring'.

The association of 'perning' with 'gyres' which occurs in 'Demon and Beast' requires explanation in 'Sailing to Byzantium'.[31] Gwendolen Murphy seems to have misinterpreted the phrase 'perne in a gyre' when she wrote:

> Gyre, a spiral, here seems to represent the twisting twirling flames, the perne, the core of stillness. (Cf. Yeats' *Collected Poems*, p. 445, pern = spool) perne is usually spelt *pirn*, a Scots word meaning spool or bobbin also spinning top: often used in proverbial phrases e.g. I shall have a fine ravelled pirn to unwind. (R. L. Stevenson *Catriona*, ch. XXIII.)[32]

This gyre does not represent flames, for if Yeats is being symbolic the word implies an abstract diagram; if not, it signifies the path of some moving body. Flames do not trace out a gyre, which is a deliberate movement. 'Gyre' could not describe both the movement of a sea-gull (as in 'The Demon and the Beast') and the 'twisting twirling flames' as Miss Murphy stated. The gyre is chosen in 'Sailing to Byzantium'

---

[29] WBY, *Collected Poems*, p. 54.

[30] This is illustrated by a comparison of the lines from the second verse of the early version:

> There through the broken branches, go
> The ravens of unresting thought:
> Peering and flying to and fro
> To see men's souls bartered and bought.

with the corresponding lines of the revised version:

> There through the broken branches, go
> The ravens of unresting thought
> Flying crying to and fro
> Cruel claw and hungry throat.

[31] WBY, *Collected Poems*, p. 217.

[32] Gwendolen Murphy, *The Modern Poet*, p. 153.

because it is a motion which pleased the poet. It had some supernatural significance; because it suggested a supreme design for all things, it possessed a hint of the 'Artifice of eternity' into which the Sages were to lead the poet:

> O sages standing in God's holy fire
> As in the gold mosaic of a wall,
> Come from the holy fire, perne in a gyre,
> And be the singing-masters of my soul.

Once the Sages have come from the holy fire they have obviously left it, and therefore are no longer in the flames, but are tracing out the movement which interested Yeats so much. 'Perne', according to Miss Murphy, is the 'core of stillness'. This assumption that 'perne' is a noun in the poem in question is not reinforced by argument, and, as Yeats used the verbal 'perning' at least as frequently as the noun 'pern', we need to examine the passage in 'Sailing to Byzantium' in the light of the word's meanings and Yeats's use of them.

He describes the word 'pern' in a note:[33]

> When I was a little child at Sligo I could see above my grandfather's trees a little column of smoke from 'the pern mill' and was told that 'pern' was another name for the spool as I was accustomed to call it, on which the thread was wound. One could not see the chimney for the trees, and one day a foreign sea-captain asked me if that was a smoking mountain.

Yeats ignored the other dictionary meaning[34] of pern, viz. hawk or buzzard (the possibility of taking 'perne' in 'Sailing to Byzantium' as a memory of 'The Second Coming's' falcon in a gyre is too far fetched). 'Pern', meaning to change one's opinions for some ulterior object, will not suit the line 'Though I had long perned in the gyre'[35] without straining the sense, because Yeats was in this troubled condition neither by his own volition nor for some ulterior purpose. 'Pern', meaning to spin or turn, however, suits both the metaphorical[36] and literal[37] senses of the word which we find in Yeats. 'Pernyng' (O.E.D.) is part of an obsolete verb prene/preen, and so does not suit the mood of Yeats's intense symbolic poems (e.g. it would be ridiculous to think of the sages preening themselves in a gyre) nor does it give the associations

[33] WBY, *Collected Poems*, p. 445.
[34] Cf. relevant portions, *Oxford English Dictionary*.
[35] WBY, *Collected Poems*, p. 209.
[36] Ibid., p. 163:
> 'He unpacks the loaded pern
> Of all 'twas pain or joy to learn.'
[37] Ibid., p. 209: 'Gyring down and perning there.'

which 'perne' coined from 'pern' (= a spool) conveyed to Yeats. 'Perne',
meaning to spin, suggests at once connections with the twisted threads
of Yeatsian spindle imagery; 'pirn' can mean, as well as a spool, a
weaver's bobbin or reel.[38] In Yeats's poetry a bobbin often symbolises a
spirit; there are references to Plato's spindle; and 'The Fool by the
Roadside' has in it a suggestion of Clotho, Lachesis and Atropos:

> When all works that have
> From cradle run to grave
> From grave to cradle run instead;
> When thoughts that a fool
> Has wound upon a spool
> Are but loose thread, are but loose thread.

In 'Crazy Jane and Jack the Journeyman' Yeats again plays with the
image:

> For love is but a skein unwound
> Between the dark and dawn.[39]

In view of these examples it seems clear that Yeats used 'perne' as an
imperative in 'Sailing to Byzantium'. 'Perne in a gyre', then, is for him,
a phrase loaded with symbolic meaning ranging from Plato's philosophy to his own, from personal to impersonal fate, with beauty of
movement and strangeness of language; a typical antithesis by which
the poignantly remembered local dialect of his youth is chosen to hold
the mystery and permanence of the sophisticated seers of cosmopolitan
Byzantium.

[38] Cf. 'Hades' bobbin' in 'Byzantium' (*Collected Poems*, p. 280) and the present writer's
article on 'The Byzantine Poems of W. B. Yeats', *Review of English Studies*, Jan 1946.
[39] Cf. Sir Walter Scott, *The Antiquary*, Border edn, ed. A. Lang (Edinburgh, 1892–4)
ch. 39:

' "The human mind . . . [said the Antiquary] is to be treated like a skein of ravelled
silk, where you must cautiously secure one free end before you can make any progress
in disentangling it."

"I ken naething about that," said the Gaberlunzie, "but an my auld acquaintance
be hersell, or anything like hersell, she may come to wind us a pirn. . . .'

PART TWO

John Butler Yeats, Anglo-Irishman

I am a genuine Irish Protestant and believe with Christ that the law was made for man and not man for the law.[1]

A debonair man, buoyant and cheerful, with the sense of gaiety and love of life that the French have.[2]

JOHN BUTLER YEATS, barrister, artist, essayist, letter-writer and conversationalist, was representative of the best of Victorian life. He belonged to the heyday of a great civilisation and yet was detached from it: as artist, as thinker, as Anglo-Irishman. Yet his virtues were its virtues: his capacity for work, his refusal to specialise, his fundamentally serious-minded approach to poetry and painting, his devotion to his family and his friends, and his firm belief in the gentler qualities of life.

He was born in 1839 at Tullylish, Co. Down, where his father, 'an Irish gentleman of the old school and not at all thrifty', was Rector. From him he inherited a spacious disregard of time and finance, and a certain optimism and gaiety. Though he was lonely as a child (for he was older than his brothers) he was perfectly happy. He was taught to read by a village schoolmaster, after which he read *Robinson Crusoe* diligently:

> In the evening after dinner my father would sit beside his candle reading, and my mother would sit by her candle sewing, and I would nestle beside her reading *Robinson Crusoe*, and I can remember that at certain critical passages in this history I would tremble with anxiety, and I was most careful lest my elders should discover my excitement and laugh at me.[3]

He was sent to a school at Liverpool, after education by his impatient father seemed unlikely to succeed. This school was kept by three maiden ladies:

> My father was evangelical as was then fashionable in the best intellectual circles. He must have said something about hell in my hearing, yet I did not make any real acquaintance with that dismal and absurd doctrine till I went to Miss Davenport's school. The school was managed upon the highest principles of

---

[1] J. B. Yeats, *Early Memories: Some Chapters of Autobiography* (Dublin, 1923) p. 15. Henceforth referred to as *Early Memories*.

[2] John Quinn, quoted in B. L. Reid, *The Man from New York: John Quinn and his Friends* (New York, 1968) p. 543. Henceforth referred to as *The Man from New York*.

[3] J. B. Yeats ibid., p. 4.

duty, no prizes were ever given for all must work from sake of duty, and we
slept with our Bibles under our pillows with directions to read them as soon
as we awoke in the morning; but hell was the driving force. Miss Emma
Davenport, who was the chief of the school, often spoke of it.[4]

At twelve he went to a school in the Isle of Man. Here the terrors
imposed by a flogging headmaster were alleviated in part by the
presence of George Pollexfen, a boy from Sligo, very unlike the English
boys in the school, whom Yeats disliked, and yet unlike Yeats himself.
Indeed there was an attraction of opposites: George Pollexfen was
melancholy, John Butler Yeats cheerful and perennially hopeful. Their
families were very different. The Pollexfens were well-to-do mer-
chants; the Yeats family intellectual and not much concerned about
money. In later years Yeats regarded his friend as tied up in puritanism.
Though he himself distrusted and disliked puritanism, he said he didn't
think he would like it 'to be entirely removed from the world, unless
it be the Belfast variety, which like the East wind is good for neither
man nor beast'.[5] Like Dr Johnson, J. B. Yeats took good care that the
Whig dogs should not get the best of the argument. Remarking once
that there were more things in heaven and earth than were dreamed of
in George Russell's[6] philosophy, he added, 'I used to tell him he was
still a *Portadown* boy'.[7]

Owing to the difficulties and expense of travel Yeats and his brothers
stayed at the school in the Isle of Man all the year except for a precious
six weeks in summer. It was during these holidays that he learned to
appreciate his father, who constantly read Shelley and Charles Lamb,
was an enthralling conversationalist and had within him an artist who

incessantly arranged and rearranged life, so that he lived in fairyland. Sometimes my father's and another man's account of the same incident would widely
differ; but I always preferred what my father said. William Morris told my son
that Kipling when a boy would come home from a day's walk with stories of
the day's adventures which were all fiction. I wonder if Shakespeare would
always cleave to the truth in the common matters of every day. At no time
did I lose respect for my father, I knew with him it was only the gentle sport
of 'make believe' without which life would be intolerable to men who live
by their affections. Saints and lovers and men governed by affection, poets and

[4] J. B. Yeats, *Early Memories*, p. 6.   [5] Ibid., p. 15.
[6] George Russell (1867–1937) a poet, dramatist, essayist and mystic, and active member
of the Irish literary renaissance, who edited the *Irish Statesman*. He became a friend of
W. B. Yeats when both were students at the Dublin Metropolitan School of Art. He
used the pen-name AE, the shortening of 'Aeon'.
[7] J. B. Yeats, *Letters to his son W. B. Yeats and Others, 1869–1922*, ed. J. Hone (London,
1944) p. 232. Henceforth referred to as *Letters*.

artists, all live in phantasy, its falsehood truer than any reality. By such false-hood we got nearer to truth. His charm to me was his veracious intellect. He would lie neither to please the sentimentalists nor the moralists. What talent I have for honest thinking I learned from him.[8]

Fear of the cane forced Latin and Greek into John Butler Yeats at his school, so that when he arrived, like his father and grandfather before him, at Trinity College, Dublin, the ordinary college examina-tions gave him no trouble. An attack of rheumatic fever, however, laid him low in his final year just as he was to sit an Honours examination in Metaphysics and Logic.

He spent most of his college years at Sandymount Castle, which belonged to his uncle, Robert Corbet. The household included his grandmother, two great-aunts as well as his bachelor uncle, a wealthy man who was stockbroker to the Court of Chancery.[9] John Butler Yeats took life easily there, toyed with the idea of the Church, and walked frequently to Lough Dan to admire its beauties and fish in its dark waters:

> All through my College days I lived the Sandymount Castle life. It was my Capua and only too welcome after my school life. I had been braced too tight, now I was braced too lightly: self-abandoned to a complete relaxation. I left that school, weakened morally by its constant discipline and vigilance, to live all my College days in that pleasant Capua. I did not think, I did not work, I had no ambition, I dreamed. Week after week went by, and no one criticised. As far as the demands of that sympathetic circle went, I satisfied everybody, and was well-behaved. The only thing that ever troubled my uncle was my habit of going long walks in the mountains, all by myself. His old-fashioned, eighteenth century gregarious worldliness was shocked that I should walk all by myself, it seemed to him abnormal and he distrusted the abnormal.[10]

After taking his degree John Butler Yeats began to study law. He read Butler's *Analogy* and lost his orthodoxy:

> I suddenly amazed myself by coming to the conclusion that revealed religion was myth and fable. My father had himself pushed me into the way of thinking for myself; and my Scotch schoolmaster, who had lived on his own resources since he was twelve years old, acquiring thereby a bold and independent spirit, had unconsciously assisted in the process. Thus it came about that I had the courage to reject the Bishop's teachings, drawing an entirely different con-clusion from the premises he placed before his reader, and with it went also my worldly-minded uncle's hope that some day I should be a respectable, Episco-palian clergyman. Everything now was gone, my mind a contented negation.

---

[8] J. B. Yeats, *Early Memories*, p. 38.
[9] He eventually lost his money and drowned himself.
[10] J. B. Yeats, *Early Memories*, p. 56.

CA E

At school my ethics had been based on fear of the school-master and now was gone fear of God and God's justice. I went to Church when I couldn't help it, that is once every Sunday. I do not know how it is now-a-days, but at that time Churches were so crowded that young men, unable to find a seat, remained the whole service through standing in the aisle. This exactly suited my inclinations, especially in one of the Kingstown churches down by the sea, for there I could stand all the two hours at the front door, half within and half without, so that while listening to the clergyman I could at the same time comfort my eye and soothe my spirit by looking toward the sea and sky. The Reverend Hugh Hamilton, Dean of Dromore, reckoned the most learned man in the Diocese, had determined that my father should, on presenting himself for ordination, be rejected because of his love for hunting, shooting and fishing and I may add, dancing, but was so impressed by his profound knowledge and understanding of Butler's Analogy that he became and continued from that hour on his constant friend. Yet this book that made my father a proudly orthodox man had shattered all my orthodoxy, so that I preferred sea & sky and floating clouds to the finest pulpit oratory of the Reverend Richard Brooke, father of the brilliantly successful Stopford. Yet I dared not say so, poetic and artistic intuitions not having reached at that time the dignity of any sort of opinion, theory, or doctrine. The finest feelings are nothing if you cannot bulwark them with opinions about which men wrangle and fight.[11]

He became a disciple of John Stuart Mill. He was attracted by his writings 'on behalf of rationality and for progress'; he remained firm in his new conviction that revealed religion was 'myth and fable'. The idea of his becoming a respectable clergyman was abandoned in favour of the law. He returned to Trinity as a graduate and won a ten-pound prize for political economy. This he spent on a holiday in Sligo with the Pollexfens. His grandfather had been rector of the parish of Drumcliffe, Co. Sligo, until he died there in 1846.[12] This was a significant visit, recorded with warm memory in his autobiographical fragment. It sharpened a dialogue which was to run continuously through his mind for the rest of his life:

At Sligo, I was the social man where it was the individual man that counted. It is a curious fact that entering this sombre house of stern preoccupation with business I for the first time in my life felt myself to be a free man, and that I was invited by the example of everyone around me to be my very self, thereby receiving the most important lesson in my life.[13]

---

[11] J. B. Yeats, *Early Memories*, p. 72.
[12] Cf. WBY, 'Under Ben Bulben', *Collected Poems*, p. 400:
      Under bare Ben Bulben's head
      In Drumcliff churchard Yeats is laid.
      An ancestor was rector there
      Long years ago . . .
[13] J. B. Yeats, *Early Memories*, p. 89.

To live among his people, he wrote, was pleasanter, but to live among the Pollexfens was good training. His preoccupation with the Pollexfens ran deep. When his father died suddenly in 1862, he inherited the family property in Co. Kildare. This brought in a few hundreds a year: enough to marry on; and he had already fallen in love with George's sister, Susan Pollexfen. They married on 10 September 1863, took a semi-detached house, 'Georgeville', in Sandymount, not far from Robert Corbet's Sandymount Castle, and there in 1865 William Butler Yeats was born. By marriage with a Pollexfen, said John Butler Yeats, '. . . I have given a tongue to the sea-cliffs.'[14]

The next year Yeats was called to the Irish Bar: he never practised but devilled for Isaac Butt, whom he greatly admired and of whom he made an admirable portrait. (There is a superb copy in chalks in the Irish National Portrait Gallery.) Professor William M. Murphy has described this part of his life with skill and humour:

> He was fully prepared to become a lawyer, and he set to work diligently enough:
>
>> I became a law student and read quantities of very big books, the names of which have perished from my memory, even tho' I filled reams of foolscap with notes. . . . I meant to succeed. My will was in it, that is my conscious will.
>
> But after serving his terms and being admitted he had no stomach for what he saw, and more and more the prospect depressed him. He wanted to make more money, and he observed that all too many barristers waited in vain for assignments. He saw them gathered in the Law Library, 'old and young, busy and idle'. There,
>
>> round the fire with their backs pressed up against the mantelpieces are the men who have nothing to do, and these are by no means mostly only the newly arrived with young faces, and fresh wigs . . . They shout and cry out at each other saying the wittiest things and by no means sparing anyone's feelings. . . . I listened to it for a whole year. The Law Library is a depressing place if you are at all troubled with despondent doubts of yourself and your prospects, and it is an accentuated depression when some one is kind enough to point out to you a bewigged gentleman wandering about by himself, and tells you that he knows for a certainty that man has never had a brief for twenty years.
>
> His break with the law, however, was not brought on by doubts and fears alone. His own characteristic disregard of the amenities, a congenital incautiousness, assisted the inevitable.

---

[14] Ibid., p. 20. See also p. 92: 'Inarticulate as the sea-cliffs were the Pollexfen heart and brain, lying buried under mountains of silence. They were released from bondage by contact with the joyous amiability of my family, and of my bringing up, and so all my four children are articulate, and yet with the Pollexfen force.'

Down in the unconscious part of me was another will. . . . At school I had picked up a bad habit of making pencil portraits of both boys and masters. In those days there were no photographers so I was in much request. . . . Thus I acquired a facility which pursued me everywhere, even when sitting in court clothed in the quaint dignity of wig and gown. It was vain for my friends to warn me that I would ruin myself with the attorneys. . . . I could not refrain. . . . I sketched everybody, the judges, the lawyers, the witnesses, the jury men.

One day he sketched a pompous QC, but the sketch was 'a little too effective, being indeed malignant'. While the Q.C. was in the middle of a long plea at the Bar one of his colleagues handed him the offending sketch. Thinking it a memorandum on a point of law bearing on the case he put on his glasses to look at what was handed him. His infuriated disgust was counterbalanced by the suppressed laughter of his colleagues; but that was just about the end. 'Afterwards various things happened', J.B.Y. commented cryptically. A short time later he accepted an offer to go to London and show his sketches.[15]

Yeats's views of Trinity varied. He was to regret that his son did not enter college, even though he wrote in his autobiographical fragment:

Trinity College Dublin did very little for me, which is entirely my own fault, neither did Trinity College Dublin inspire me with affection, and that was the fault of Trinity College Dublin. One night, in the College park, walking under the stars with that brilliant scientist George Fitzgerald, I saw him look round at some new buildings just erected and with a snap of satisfaction he said, 'No ornament, that is one good thing.' I made the obvious retort 'How is Trinity College Dublin to inspire affection, if it is not made beautiful in its buildings, its quadrangle, its trees and its park.' He gave a grunting assent. Had he not been in a controversial mood, and ascetic for severe science, he would have responded generously; for he was a true scientist, that is, a poet as well. Trinity College inspires no love; outside what it has done for learning and mathematics and things purely intellectual it has a lean history. Still youth is youth, and the time of youth is pleasant to look back upon.[16]

---

[15] William M. Murphy, 'Father and Son: the Early Education of William Butler Yeats', *A Review of English Literature*, VIII 4 (Oct 1967) pp. 82–3. Cf. a passage in his *Memoirs*, I, f. 17 (quoted by Murphy, op. cit., p. 79):

Instead of entering Trinity I am persuaded it would have been better for me to have become an art student at once and not waited until I was ten years older. I was born to observe and paint what I saw. With a man of my type curiosity is a passion, not malignant, which is the soul of gossip and scandal, nor yet that of the scientist who wants to know things, but that of the artist. If I go into the woods to find a flower, it is not that I want a flower important to the botanist or the doctor. I merely desire a flower to my taste as a young man finds his sweetheart – like his, my choice a mystery, and in his case a miracle of success or failure. An artist has the vagrant mind, and to such Trinity College is not congenial. Always at the back of Trinity College, drawing it on, are hungry parents and the hungry offspring of a poor country. Trinity flourishes by pleasing these people.

[16] *Early Memories*, p. 68.

His own youth appeared to have ended when in 1867 he took the decisive step of giving up the law for art. He moved to London, leased 23 Fitzroy Road, Regent's Park, and attended Heatherley's School until 1868. He met Samuel Butler there and thought him, though polite and ceremonious, 'ready to sneer, in a manner the more palpable because so veiled'. He regretted that work kept him from seeing more of Butler, for he liked his look of 'helpful kindness in a moving face'. He continued to work at art, next at the Academy School with Poynter.

It was five years before he received a commission – a long apprenticeship when there were five children to support: W. B., Robert (b. 27 March 1870), who died of croup in March 1873, John Butler (Jack, the artist), Elizabeth Corbet (known as Lolly) and Susan Mary (known as Lily). During these years Mrs Yeats and the children lived largely in Sligo with the Pollexfens, who disapproved of Yeats's impracticability: his preoccupation with the matter of how to live rather than that of how to make a living, his belief that a gentleman was not concerned with getting on in the world. It seemed to Yeats, however, that he had cut his apprenticeship short, too short, in order to please the Pollexfens, who were prosperous, owning a shipping line – their ships ran between Sligo and Liverpool[17] – and a grain company. They were also, however, inclined to melancholia and Yeats was well aware of this nervous weakness. He wrote to his brother Isaac that he sometimes thought all the Pollexfens were mad[18] and later commented to him[19] on the Pollexfen traits, 'a distant tendency to what the doctors call depressive mania'. His wife suffered from her relatives' comments on her husband; her mother thought he had no common sense and he wrote, probably from 23 Fitzroy Road, to his wife when she was in Merville, her father's house in Sligo: 'I fancy she [Mrs Yeats's mother] can't understand my reading so much or occupying myself with ideas.[20] She of course cannot know that these are the materials with which I work.'[21]

The financial position was difficult in the extreme. He wrote to his wife saying he could foresee when he would have enough for her to

[17] Cf. WBY, *Autobiographies*, pp. 49–50, for a brief vignette of voyages on the s.s. *Sligo* and the s.s. *Liverpool*.

[18] Letter of 5 Aug 1911, quoted by Murphy, op. cit., pp. 85–6.

[19] Letter of 11 July 1912, quoted by Murphy, op. cit., p. 81.

[20] His uncle, Robert Corbet, had looked on ideas 'as a species of contraband' and had often quarrelled with him because of his propensity for them.

[21] Undated letter, probably 1871 or 1872. Text from Lily Yeats's scrapbook, now in the possession of Senator M. B. Yeats.

come to London; he had to acquire skill – 'possess skill and you possess money'.[22] The strains upon the young couple were severe, yet Yeats saw that living in London was doing him good:

> I shall have more 'morale' – and get over my weaknesses and foibles. I shall be more worth your liking when we next live together. The wearing anxiety of the last few years has told on us both, injuring our characters as our physical strength.[23]

He was worried about his eldest son and wrote to Susan Yeats in November 1872

> I am continually anxious about Willy. He is almost never out of my thoughts. I believe him to be intensely affectionate, but from shyness, sensitiveness, and nervousness very difficult to win, and yet he is worth winning. I should of course like to see him made do what was right, but he will only develop by kindness and affection and gentleness. Bobby is robust and hardy, and does not mind rebuffs, but Willy is sensitive, intellectual and emotional, very easily rebuffed and continually afraid of being rebuffed, so that with him one has to use great – sensitiveness sensitiveness which is so rare in Merville.[24]

He was perturbed by her own agitated state and in 1873 wrote to warn her not to become hysterical through fruitless anxiety.[25]

In 1874 the Yeats family moved to 14 Edith Villas, West Kensington,[26] until 1876, when they moved to 8 Woodstock Road, Bedford Park.[27] Here Yeats's chief friends were J. T. Nettleship, a Pre-Raphaelite water-colourist (whose daughter Augustus John married) who had

---

[22] Ibid.   [23] Ibid.

[24] See J. Hone, *W. B. Yeats 1865–1939* (1942) pp. 15–31, and A. Norman Jeffares, *W. B. Yeats: Man and Poet* (1962) pp. 9–18, for accounts of Yeats's youth in Sligo.

[25] In a letter of 17 Feb 1873, quoted by Murphy, op. cit., p. 84.

[26] Murphy, op. cit., p. 86, rightly remarks that it is not easy to pin down the movements of all the members of the family during the London years. He gives 1875 as the date for the move to Edith Villas on the evidence of Lily Yeats's scrapbook. Before her death she told me in conversation that she then thought 1874 was more correct.

[27] See A. Norman Jeffares, op. cit., pp. 13–21, for an account of these London years and holidays in Sligo. On one occasion J. B. Yeats was visiting his family in Sligo. He never went to church and W. B. therefore refused to go, 'though often devout'. J. B. Yeats said if he would not go to church he would teach him to read; he was, however, an impatient and angry teacher, flinging the book at his son's head, who decided the next Sunday that he would go to church. Cf. WBY, *Autobiographies*, p. 29. J. B. Yeats remarked in his *Memoirs* that he had read in Herbert Spencer:

> that to educate a child too early is bad, since a too early development stops growth, so that he did not even learn his letters till he was more than seven years old, and by that time he had found out so many things to occupy his mind, imaginative and busy, that it was with the greatest difficulty he mastered the English alphabet. His teachers, which consisted of the whole household, said he would never learn it. And afterwards we had to teach him to read, and though I retained a hopeful belief, most thought he would never read, that is, properly.

(*Memoirs*, 1, f. 49, quoted by Murphy, op. cit., pp. 86–7.)

begun to turn his attention to symbolic paintings in the sixties, and
thence to realistic studies of animals; George Wilson, a Scot, who died
in 1890; and Edwin J. Ellis, a poet and painter, who later collaborated
with W. B. Yeats in an edition of Blake which contains an elaborate
commentary on Blake's symbolism. These four friends formed the
'Brotherhood': they were befriended by John Todhunter (a fellow
undergraduate of Yeats at Trinity), then practising medicine in London,
writing plays, and acting as patron of these artists. They shared views
on the union of the arts and were admirers of Blake and Rossetti:
indeed Rossetti himself admired a drawing by Yeats so much that he
invited him to Cheyne Walk. But during this period Yeats was so
filled with indecision and doubt that he did not accept the invitation.
In *Reveries over Childhood and Youth* W. B. Yeats remembers his father
at work on a painting of a pond – he began this in spring and continued
to work on it throughout the year, abandoning it when he found
himself painting snow on its banks.

The Land War meant the disappearance of rents from the unmort-
gaged part of the Kildare lands, and so at the beginning of the eighties
Yeats took his family back to Ireland, where living was cheaper. They
lived at Howth from 1881 to 1883 – first at Balscadden Cottage, then
at Island View – and then, in 1884, at Ashfield Terrace, Rathgar. Yeats
had a studio in York Street and later one in St Stephen's Green.

During this period in Dublin Yeats educated his eldest son. They
travelled to Dublin by train from Howth in the mornings; they break-
fasted in the painter's studio in York Street (before W. B. went on to
the High School in Harcourt Street) and there the father read aloud
Shakespeare, Balzac and Blake. He spoke often of the idea of the
solitary man. He was radical in his views, a Home-Ruler, a questioner
of accepted values. He enjoyed discussion; he encouraged his son to
write poetry;[28] he introduced him to his old friends, among them

[28] There is an interesting passage in his *Memoirs* where he describes his eldest son's
methods of composing verse:

At that time for the sake of a necessary thrift we gathered every evening in one
room round the single lamp, and my son would be quiet over his lesson. These
finished, he betook himself to the study of verse, murmuring over to himself the
lines as he made them, at first quietly so as to disturb no one – only his voice would
grow louder and louder till at last it filled the room. Then his sisters would call out
to him, 'Now Willie, stop composing!' And he would meekly lower his voice.
Alas, the murmuring would again become a shout. My daughters would again object,
the evening always ending in his finding another lamp and retiring with it into the
kitchen where he would murmur verses in any voice he liked to his heart's content.
(*Memoirs*, I, ff. 63–4, quoted in Murphy, op. cit., p. 92.)

Edward Dowden, then the first Professor of English Literature at Trinity College. It was a period of great domestic liveliness which is reflected in an essay:

> The typical Irish family is poor, ambitious, and intellectual; and all have the national habit, once indigenous in 'Merry England', of much conversation. In modern England they like a dull man and so they like a dull boy. We like bright men and bright boys. When there is a dull boy we send him to England and put him into business where he may sink or swim; but a bright boy is a different story. Quickly he becomes the family confidant, learning all about the family necessities; with so much frank conversation it cannot be otherwise. He knows every detail in the school bills and what it will cost to put him through the university, and how that cost can be reduced by winning scholarships and prizes. As he grows older he watches, like an expert, the younger brothers coming on, and is eager to advise in his young wisdom as to their prospects. He studies constantly, perhaps overworks himself while his mother and sisters keep watch; and yet he is too serious, and they on their side are too anxious for compliments. It is indeed characteristic of the Irish mother that, unlike the flattering mothers of England, she loves too anxiously to admire her children; with her intimate knowledge there goes a cautious judgment. The family habit of conversation into which he enters with the arrogance of his tender years gives him the chance of vitalizing his newly acquired knowledge. Father, Mother, brothers and sisters are all on his mind; and the family fortunes are a responsibility. He is not dull-witted, as are those who go into business to exercise the will in plodding along some prescribed path; on the contrary, his intellect is in constant exercise. He is full of intellectual curiosity, so much conversation keeping it alive, and therein is unlike the English or the American boy. Indeed, he experiences a constant temptation to spend in varied reading the time that should be given to restricted study. He is at once sceptical and credulous, but, provided his opinions are expressed gaily and frankly, no one minds. With us intellect takes the place which in the English home is occupied by the business faculty. We love the valour of the free intellect; so that, the more audacious his opinion, the higher rise the family hopes. He and all his family approve of amusement – to do so is an Irish tradition unbroken from the days before St. Patrick; but they have none. They are too poor and too busy; or rather they have a great deal, but it is found in boyish friendships and in the bonds of the strongest family affection, inevitable because they are Irish and because they have hopes that make them dependent upon one another. The long family talks over the fire, the long talks between clever boys on country walks – these are not the least exciting amusements – even though they bear no resemblance to what is called 'sport'.[29]

J. B. Yeats hoped his eldest son would follow family tradition and attend Trinity College, but W. B. decided not to go there, and entered the Dublin Metropolitan School of Art. The father had worried over his son's interest in science; soon, however, he bothered over his deter-

[29] J. B. Yeats, *Essays Irish and American* (1918) p. 30.

mination to be a poet, but with an uneasy tolerance, a sense, almost, of complicity:

> It is impossible for a rich man's son to enter the heaven of poetry, yet a poor man's son should avoid poetry, because it is impossible to make money by the writing of poetry. My son and myself both saw this to be true. Nevertheless he abided by poetry and I encouraged him. It was a secret between us.[30]

This was a period of strain. Yeats did not succeed in establishing himself in Dublin as a highly successful painter. He charged too little and perhaps he talked too well and too much. And so in 1887 he returned to London, to Bedford Park. There his wife had two strokes, in 1887 and 1889, from which she never fully recovered. She was, according to her daughter Lily, 'quite unable for the care and anxiety of life in London, on an incertain income'. The question of finance loomed large. W. B. Yeats thought that 'her sense of personality, her desire of any life of her own, had disappeared in her care for us and in much anxiety about money'.[31] Lily was more forthright; she described her as 'grim and austere'. This comment is borne out by a somewhat baffled comment on her character made by her husband:

> There is a good deal of his mother in Willie. I often said to her these words: 'You know I have to take your affection for granted,' for I never saw the slightest sign of it, except once, and here was the manner of that 'once': I had left the house and been gone a few moments when, remembering something, I returned and found her where I left her, and she showed so much pleasure that I was surprised and gratified – that was the 'once'. I knew and never doubted that, more than most wives, she was 'wrapt up' in her unworthy husband. She was not sympathetic. The feelings of people about her did not concern her. She was not aware of them. She was always in an island of her own. Yet had you penetrated to her inner mind you would have found it all occupied with thoughts of other people and of how to help them. She was much liked by simple people – the poor and uneducated – for these people, knowing nothing of sympathetic discourse and its courteous ways, did not miss what others looked for and so were able to see her as she really was. *They* knew that she was not thinking of herself. . . . I used to tell her that if I had been lost for years and then suddenly presented myself she would have merely asked, 'Have you had your dinner?' All this is very like Willie.[32]

After her strokes Mrs Yeats took to her bed and suffered all in silence. 'She asked no sympathy', wrote Lily in her scrapbook, 'and gave none.' She died in 1900. During these years Yeats renewed his friendships with Nettleship and Ellis, and he found in York Powell, Professor of Modern

---

[30] *Memoirs*, I, f. 51, quoted by Murphy, op. cit., p. 93.
[31] WBY, *Autobiographies*, p. 31.
[32] Quoted in Reid, *The Man from New York*, pp. 425–6.

History at Oxford, who lived at Bedford Park, and Oliver Elton, who left Bedford Park in 1890 for the Chair of English in Liverpool, the kind of academic minds he valued. These men were more appreciative of his originality than most of the Dublin dons, with the notable exception of Dowden:

> The late Dr. Salmon was a great man and a great mathematician but it was well known that tho' he was an infallible judge of every kind of investment he paid no attention to what is called the artistic values being exclusively a man of science and therefore a philistine. Mathematicians are as a rule philistines and are apt to think that there is nothing in life valuable except the utilities, and that what is called efficiency is the chief of human faculties. A friend of mine, a fine classical scholar, told me that in his experience, mathematicians could only talk of the price of things – tell them, he said, what you pay for your boots. I once met Dr. Salmon at dinner and was much flattered by his taking me aside and asking me what I paid for my lodgings – I thought that the great man was interested in me. Professor Dowden, his relation and my friend, undeceived me. He said it was only Salmon's way. All his long life Dr. Salmon sought for scientific and practical truth and has left a distinguished name. Yet at that dinner table had he listened to me I could have told him things that would have opened his eyes to a world of which he had never dreamed and perhaps he would have acknowledged that the tangible is valuable only for the sake of the intangible. There are whole streets in London, whole districts where the people inhabiting the houses are prisoners each in his cell and to walk through them is to breathe prison air since their houses have no grace, no architectural charm, no artistic decoration, nothing to remind or to suggest that there is anything in life except this and that utility – houses everywhere but nowhere a home, nowhere an asylum for the affections – amid such surroundings humanity is withered. Artists exist that these places be destroyed – a kind of prison reform much needed in great cities.[33]

After his wife's death John Butler Yeats returned to Dublin in 1900. His sons had established themselves; his daughters took a house in Dundrum and there they conducted the handpress and embroidery department of the Dun Emer Industries, later conducted under the name Cuala Industries. Yeats walked every day to his studio in Dublin; first at Harrington Street and then in St Stephen's Green. During this period he painted some of his best-known work: portraits of Synge, Lady Gregory, Miss Horniman, George Moore, Padraic Colum, Standish O'Grady, W. G. Fay. His previous stay in Ireland had seen the beginning of the Irish literary movement. This period from 1900 to 1907 covered its flowering, and Yeats became a lively figure in Dublin's life. He enjoyed the liveliness of the city which would become, he though in 1902, the most wide-awake city in the world:

[33] J. B. Yeats, *Letters*, p. 200.

perhaps we shall be wide awake in *ideas literature philosophy drama.* – I hope all
sides will stand up & fight their guns well – the church included. *One's best
helper is a good opponent.* . . .[34]

He was fortunate himself in finding a helper who was not an opponent but a generous patron, 'the nearest approach to an angel in my
experience', as he described him in his early enthusiasm. This paragon
was John Quinn, the Irish-American lawyer, who had been reading
W. B. Yeats and the new Irish writing with enthusiasm and had
corresponded with Jack Yeats before his first visit to Europe in the
early autumn of 1902. Quinn, having found there were two Yeats
painters, and bought ten of Jack's paintings, found John Butler Yeats's
conversation equally delightful, and bought a portrait of W. B. from
him, as well as commissioning other paintings, of John O'Leary,
Douglas Hyde and AE, at twenty pounds each. He also realised the
merits of the artist's sketches and commissioned a series of pencil
drawings of Irish men and women from him. The notebook with these
arrived in November 1902 and another was promptly commissioned –
the second, on which J. B. Yeats was working in 1903, contained
sketches of Susan Mitchell, Katharine Tynan and Kuno Meyer. Quinn
was lucky to get his portraits finished: that of AE was completed
quickly. With the usual burst of family optimism-after-creation, the
artist described it as by far the best thing he had done; he then launched
into the portrait of John O'Leary while also working on one of Father
Dineen, and when Quinn arrived in August 1903 he agreed to attempt
a portrait of Quinn's mother from photographs. Quinn commissioned
a painting of Standish O'Grady, and on Quinn's visit to Dublin in
1904 a sketch was made of O'Grady talking to Quinn. The sitting next
day for O'Grady's portrait is amusingly described by Professor B. L.
Reid:

> O'Grady was wearing a light blue shirt and a blue tie, but J. B. Yeats had
> already painted in a red tie. Quinn left the studio, bought a white satin tie
> which O'Grady put on, and Mr. Yeats painted out the red tie and painted in
> the white one.[35]

This was on a Wednesday morning – and it was an achievement to
have got O'Grady to come to the studio – but on the Friday Quinn,
afraid that the portrait might be ruined – for J. B. Yeats often went on
painting far too long – managed to stop him working further on it;

---

[34] Quoted in Reid, *The Man from New York*, p. 11. Letter to John Quinn, 23 Oct 1902.
[35] Reid, *The Man from New York*, p. 26. I am greatly indebted to this book for information on the relationship between Quinn and J. B. Yeats.

the next day he came to the studio to find the artist working at the hands in this portrait but from an oversize model. Padraic Colum was there but his hands proved too small, so Quinn himself then posed for the hands.[36]

Quinn obviously enjoyed these visits to Yeats's studio. John Butler Yeats had written to him at the beginning of their friendship that Ireland was like ancient Athens where all were such talkers and disputants, England like ancient Rome 'with its religions and cohorts and dull business of conquering the world'.[37] The Yeats family had brought him into touch with such talkers and disputants as John O'Leary, Standish O'Grady, Douglas Hyde, Lady Gregory, J. M. Synge, George Moore, T. W. Rolleston, James Joyce, Nathaniel Hone, Sarah Purser, Susan Mitchell, Maud Gonne, the Count and Countess Markievicz, Oliver St John Gogarty, the Fays, and many other figures of Dublin's literary and artistic world. Quinn's days in Dublin were crowded with gay social life and spiced with Dublin's malice. He had discovered, however, as he told some Dublin friends, that all those who were denounced turned out to be very charming people.[38]

John Butler Yeats dispensed conversation freely as he paced out the long distance he kept between his easel and his subject; generalising happily; savouring, enjoying and explaining Dublin's vitality as he worked on. Progress on the Hyde portrait was slow in 1905, but he then began a portrait of George Moore, and Quinn wrote to Lily Yeats early in 1906 to ask her to persuade her father to finish it. Next Quinn commissioned a new portrait of W. B. Yeats to illustrate his new and powerful appearance as man of action rather than dreamer. In the midst of conversing and painting the artist also played his part in controversy. His speech at the famous debate on Synge's *The Playboy of the Western World* in 1907 is immortalised in his son's poem, 'Beautiful Lofty Things':

> My father upon the Abbey stage, before him a raging crowd:
> 'This Land of Saints', and then as the applause died out,
> 'Of plaster Saints'; his beautiful mischievous head thrown back.[39]

His own account of the incident is no less vivid; he wrote to a friend:

> Of course I did not make a speech in favour of patricide. How could I? Here is what I said. I began with some information about Synge which interested my listeners and then: 'Of course I know Ireland is an island of Saints, but

[36] Reid, *The Man from New York*, p. 29.   [37] Ibid., p. 8.   [38] Ibid., p. 31.
[39] WBY, *Collected Poems* (1950) p. 348.

thank God it is also an island of sinners – only unfortunately in this Country people cannot live or die except behind a curtain of deceit.' At this point the Chairman and my son both called out, 'Time's up, Time's up'. I saw the lifted sign and like the devil in *Paradise Lost* I fled. The papers next morning said I was howled down. It was worse, I was pulled down. . . . The sentence about the curtain of deceit flashed on my mind at the moment, and was a good sentence, but manifestly a blunder, although I did enjoy it. . . .[40]

In 1908 John Butler Yeats went on a visit to New York which was financed by Andrew Jameson, Hugh Lane and other Dublin friends. He was accompanied by his daughter Lily, who was showing her embroidery there. Lily left after six months and the artist promised to return after she had left, and, as Hone remarks, would sometimes even fix the date of his sailing. But he stayed. He had found work – mainly commissions (especially pencil sketches) that Quinn had arranged for him – and he was curious about American life, which in its rich variety gave added hope to his Micawberish belief that something would turn up. There was another factor, too, and a very human one. He once remarked that he did not care to play the role of father to an illustrious son. He 'wrote to Willie some time ago and said it was as bad to be a poet's father as the intimate friend of George Moore'. Indeed in a sombre mood in 1904, when his eldest son was in fact financing him, he wrote that he wished Willie did not sometimes treat him as if he were a black beetle. In New York his capacity for talking was highly appreciated – there was perhaps less competition than in Dublin – and he gave various lectures.

His relationship with Quinn, so admirably treated in Professor Reid's recent biography of Quinn, was close. Quinn had been taking an increasingly disillusioned view of Irishmen and Irish Catholicism (in a bad mood in 1909 he characterised Irishmen as 'suspicious, vindictive, uncertain in temper, ungrateful, and lying'), and he had been deeply depressed by Irish behaviour over Synge's *Playboy*. The artist now found him "the crossest man in the world' as well as 'the kindest'.[41] Quinn's kindness continued, despite the tensions created by his telling John Butler Yeats how to paint. Professor Reid describes one incident:

J. B. Yeats had promised to paint Quinn in two or at most three sittings. After 'eight solid Sundays' of painting and repainting, Quinn rebelled and issued an

---

40 J. B. Yeats, *Letters*, p. 214.
41 See Hone, *W. B. Yeats, 1865–1939*, p. 243. See also J. B. Yeats, *Letters*, p. 108, where he wrote on 1 July 1908 to W. B. Yeats that Quinn was 'the crossest man I ever met and the most affectionate'.

ultimatum: he would allow one more hour for the eyes, one hour for the hair, and so on. Mr Yeats promised, but soon started painting out again. Quinn exploded and threatened to stick a knife through the picture. After further promises, mutual apologies, and cigars, the picture was 'finished', though a friend said of it, 'It has a rather worried look'.[42]

More serious, however, was their row over a painting of Quinn's mistress, Dorothy Coates (curiously enough, Quinn's long quarrel with W. B. Yeats, which lasted from 1909 to 1914, was over her). This went deeper, and the artist rebuked the patron with dignity; it would after a while dawn on Quinn, he told him, that only a Goth or Philistine, or a man blinded by too much friendship would deprive an artist of his right to paint his own way: it would soon be revealed to him that 'the right is *inalienable* and that he *cannot be contracted* out of it'.[43] J. B. Yeats had been very upset, hands trembling not from anger but nervousness, as he wrote.

Quinn and the old man got on extremely well, and perhaps the better for such direct exchanges; their friendship developed, with frequent letters from J. B. Yeats to the lawyer. In 1909 Quinn offered to pay his fare to Ireland if he would go back with him when he went there on a brief holiday; he found the old man delightful but a responsibility. Lady Gregory admired Yeats but 'at a distance' (she regarded him as the most trying visitor possible in a house) and her views of him were akin to Quinn's. 'Space and time', she wrote, 'mean nothing to him; he goes his own way, spoiling portraits as hopefully as he begins them and always on the verge of a great future!'[44] She wrote of him with loving exasperation, finding it wonderful 'how hopeful, how cheerful, how impossible he is': and Quinn thought the same when J. B. Yeats refused the fare. The artist had tried various hotels, and then settled in the Petipas sisters' boarding-house in West 29th Street. This was run by three Breton women, and it suited his style of life well, though at times he would, he thought, have liked to escape from New York and all it stood for – except the one thing

that New York always holds with bountiful hands held out towards me – and that is a chance of work – of employment. Anything may turn up here – a lecture, an article, a portrait. It is a high gaming table where the poorest has a welcome and a chance.[45]

[42] Reid, *The Man from New York*, p. 58.

[43] Ibid., p. 59.

[44] In 1904 she predicted that the paintings of J. B. Yeats and AE would be interesting in thirty years' time. See Reid, *The Men from New York*, p. 30.

[45] J. B. Yeats, *Letters*, pp. 272–3.

He had many friends, especially the painter John Sloan and the other members of a group known as 'The Eight'. He had some Irish friendships, with Charles Johnston (W. B.'s friend of the High School days in Dublin) and his wife, Padraic and Mary Colum, and E. A. Boyd; and there were many other friendships, with Van Wyck Brooks, Alan Seeger, Zelinski and Zimmern, Eric Bell and Mr and Mrs Simeon Ford. He saw Quinn frequently, and there were occasional outings – to Sheepshead, to Fisher's Island, and elsewhere, once to Oak Ridge in Virginia. Ezra Pound remembered an excursion in 1910, and had a very clear recollection of 'Yeats père on an elephant' where he was smiling 'like Elijah in the beatific vision'.[46]

Something of his personality emerges in the famous self-portrait commissioned by Quinn, on which he began work in 1911 and on which he worked intermittently till his death. He did two sketches of Synge; he drew eight members of the Abbey Theatre who came to the United States in 1912. In 1914 Quinn arranged to buy W. B. Yeats's manuscripts, some of which Lily Yeats had saved, and the money involved was to be paid as an allowance to the painter, who was still making some money from portraits, drawings, journalism and occasional lectures. And he survived being knocked down by a car in 1915: 'as usual, strolling through the traffic of New York like an emperor in his garden', as Quinn put it. There was the pleasure of his first book in 1917, the selection of letters made by Ezra Pound, whom he described as 'a powerful astringent'; he was beginning, however, to feel his seventy-eight years a little, and found he didn't like going out in the evening. He regarded himself as a radiant youth of promise in the morning, a virile man at midday and in the afternoon, but in the evening a depressed old fellow.[47] By 1918 he was working on the autobiography which W. B. had suggested in a letter of 21 November 1912, 'a great project' which might lead to 'a wonderful book'. It would tell people 'about those things that are not old enough to be in the histories or new enough to be in the reader's mind, and these are always the things that are least known'.[48] Now Quinn was to pay J. B. Yeats a pound (from cash sent by W. B. Yeats or from the money gained by the sale of his manuscripts to Quinn) for every thousand words that J. B. Yeats wrote. He went on developing his ideas as usual, the flow of letters to Quinn unabated, but an attack of pneumonia in November 1918 raised the perpetual question of his returning to

---

[46] Quoted in Reid, *The Man from New York*, p. 86.
[47] See ibid., p. 316.   [48] See WBY, *Letters*, p. 571.

Ireland. Lily Yeats was perhaps the member of his family most anxious that he should return: she missed her father's friendship, and she realised, as the artist in his modesty did not, 'what a success he is, how fine his work is, what a big man he is'.[49] In his first year in New York AE had suggested that he should be sent a cable from Dublin, 'Family all dying. Come to receive last messages', but nobody then thought this would bring him back and, despite his family's worries and hopes for his return, he went on writing letters to them, filling them with moving messages full of hope. A wit called him the old man who ran away from home and made good. He said to his friend Padraic Colum, when discussing the idea of returning, some day, to Dublin, 'When we get to Dublin we'll paint the town red'. 'An old man', he wrote to his son Jack, 'should think of the past, but I am all interested in the future.' He was equally interested in the present, chiding Quinn on a very serious matter, his corrupt American use of 'ass' rather than 'arse' – this, however, was the fault of Englishmen too debilitated to pronounce an 'R'. An Englishman had to call that 'intelligent but much misunderstood animal with the handsome ears' a donkey lest he embarrass the ladies, whereas an Irishman spoke of him as an ass: in Ireland ladies know the difference between arse and ass.[50]

In January 1919 Quinn yet again tried to get John Butler Yeats back to Ireland, and wrote to W. B. about this; both men failed to persuade him, and W. B. decided to separate his sales of manuscripts from his arrangements about an allowance for his father. He then paid his father's outstanding bill at the Petipas's. Quinn gave the old man advice on his health, about keeping warm and dry, and going easy on wine and spirits; and at the end of the year he paid a bill for a new set of false teeth for him: their correspondence continued, and while he continued to try to collect the autobiographical writings for the Yeats family he also tried to get the artist to continue his self-portrait on a fresh canvas.

The next attempt to persuade him to return to Ireland took place in January of 1920, when W. B. Yeats and his wife were in New York. This was the first time J. B. had met his son's wife and he 'beamed upon both of them, and was evidently pleased and delighted with the wife'.[51] But again he could not be persuaded to return: it seemed to Mrs Yeats that he was worried about becoming a nuisance to his children, while Quinn thought he might return to Dublin if his

[49] Reid, *The Man from New York*, p. 310.   [50] See ibid., p. 265.
[51] Ibid., p. 418.

children promised him a studio in Dublin. He gave as his excuse that
he had not yet finished his self-portrait. In fact, he enjoyed his life in
New York, and it was Quinn – not his children – who had, as he put
it in January 1921, 'old man Yeats on my back' as far as close worry
about his health went.

At eighty-two the old man was as full of ideas as ever; in May he
was full of generalisations about Irish Protestants, the people who were
Dowden's and Mahaffy's friends, who now seemed to him the most
conceited and self-complacent men in the world. By October he was
writing on Joyce's *Ulysses*. He had reacted to *Dubliners* with a South
Dublin Protestant's *hauteur*, with the remark:

> Good God, how depressing! One always knew there were such persons and
> places in Dublin but one never wished to see them.[52]

The *Portrait of an Artist* pleased him more; he realised Joyce was a
student, and recognised his vitality. On a second reading in 1917 he
told Quinn that the book could 'live forever, preserved like a fly in
amber by its incomparable style'.[53] *Ulysses* reeked of the cynicism of
the slums, but he saw it as the work of a man of genius working to
dispel false sentiment, with a feeling for what was true. He wrote a
long letter (fifteen pages of typescript) about the problem of Joyce
and censorship, and some of this was used by Quinn when he was
defending *The Little Review* for publishing *Ulysses*. Yeats regarded
Joyce as an artist of the middle way – and the greatest of these artists
was Shakespeare:

> I do not say that Joyce's books would make a man happy. I am not sure that
> Shakespeare makes a man happy.[54]

He continued that he was none the less certain that a man was wiser
'and therefore stronger who has read deeply in such books as Joyce's'.[54]

His critical judgements flowed on but the picture remained unfinished, and Quinn kept on worrying about him. But in February
1922 he suddenly fell ill, exhausted after a walk in a blizzard and was
in severe pain. Quinn picked up Dr Likely and Mrs Foster, a friend
whom J. B. Yeats had earlier introduced to Quinn, and rushed to
Petipas's (now run by a Mme Jais, who was as kind to the painter as the
Petipas sisters had been); by the next morning he was as cheerful as
ever, full of jests and anecdotes: 'no decrepitude in him', as Quinn
wrote, his body was 'fine and straight and slim, with none of the

[52] Reid, *The Man from New York*, pp. 310–11.   [53] Ibid., p. 311.
[54] Ibid., p. 428.

coarseness or feebleness or repulsiveness of old age'.[55] He died quietly on the morning of 3 February 1922. His last words, to Mrs Foster, who was sitting at his bedside, were 'Remember you have promised me a sitting in the morning.' As his son wrote to Olivia Shakespear, 'a good death'.[56]

What did he achieve in his eighty-three years? He was a painter whose sketches and drawings have more attraction for us than his finished portraits in oils. These portraits convey a likeness well, sometimes the better for J. B. Yeats's belief that a portrait should illustrate the flaw or weakness that goes to the making of beauty. But, as Professor Bodkin remarked, 'he was not strikingly accomplished in the mere technique of painting'. What interested him was the essential nature of the sitter: from his penetrating portraits of, say, John O'Leary or Lady Gregory or John Synge there radiates some of the individual quality, the dominating desire and mood, the essential character, of the sitter. His own self-portrait, painted at eighty, conveys the curiosity and vitality, even the speculative and sympathetic interest in others that underpinned his whole life. The eyes, those large bright eyes that Oliver Elton described as changeful and ever-watchful, dominate the rendering of the head, as in most of his portraits, where, indeed, the head dominates the rest of the painting. (They are themselves sometimes dominated by his clever painting of spectacles.) This concentration on the intelligence of his sitters is what we might expect; it is explained in Bodkin's remark, 'his bent was intellectual rather than sensuous'; it emerged clearly in his discerning paintings of children.

J. B. Yeats produced some superb pencil drawings, and he used his pencil ceaselessly to capture character. There is a sureness and economy of execution in his drawings which evaded much of his portraiture, despite his valiant and unceasing hopes that he would achieve success. A few weeks before he died he saw portraits by Laszlo and wrote gaily to John Quinn:

> That shining cohort of fashionable horrors was amusing. I got from them one good thing. My self-portrait has been facing me for a long time lying against the wall of my room and filling me with despondency. I now see that it is the making of a masterpiece. To know good you must have seen evil. I have seen Laszlo and now I appreciate Yeats.[57]

In an earlier letter he summed up the same painting with characteristic insight: 'It is an honest portrait.'[58]

[55] Reid, The Man from New York p. 523. [56] WBY, Letters, p. 677.
[57] J. B. Yeats, Letters, p. 287. [58] Ibid., p. 258.

This insight and honesty pervaded the work of his pen. He wrote very many letters. Selections from some of them were made by Ezra Pound in 1917, and by Lennox Robinson in 1920, both published by the Cuala Press in limited editions. Joseph Hone edited a larger selection which was published by Faber & Faber in 1944, now, alas, out of print. And there are many unpublished letters which many of us would like to see in print. A small volume of *Essays Irish and American* was published in Dublin and London in 1918, and the Cuala Press issued *Early Memories: Some Chapters of Autobiography* in 1923. From these brief collections we can discover much of the temper of Yeats's mind; we can recognise the liveliness and quick, imaginative, paradoxical wit that made a success of what was regarded by many of his contemporaries as his main art, his conversation.

Like many Anglo-Irish writers he had an instinct for finding himself an object of amusement. In part this sprang from what he regarded as an Irish characteristic – 'a perfectly disinterested, an absolutely unselfish love of making mischief, mischief for its own dear sake':[59] in part it was based upon a dislike of self-importance:

> Aristocracies and pessimists are malign, and the whole of Nietzsche is malign; so are college dons and their retinue, but so were not Shakespeare and Shelley. Wordsworth was malign, so was Byron and so is Swinburne. These people could not get away from their self-importance.[60]

This dislike of self-importance arose out of the good manners which made him such a good correspondent – *in writing a letter*, he said, *one generally escapes it* [an indulged facility], *because one is so interested in the person who is to receive the letter*. When writing of himself he could, therefore, use irony with casual ease. Here, for instance, is a typical example from a letter in which he is telling Susan Mitchell of his relationship with the *New Republic*. The account builds up from a statement into an ironic contrast before it crystallises itself into an arrestingly witty generalisation:

> The *New Republic* is edited by a group of young writers, all supposed to be awfully clever. They are having a fine time, and their magazine is greatly lauded – all the superior people take it in. I might think more highly of it but they without a moment's delay refused some articles and stories I did them the honour to submit. It is reported that the magazine is financed for three years by a rich American woman. I think all American magazine writing far too frightfully clever. It is as if a man had by mistake hired an acrobat for a

59 *Passages from the Letters of John Butler Yeats*, selected by Ezra Pound (Dublin, 1917) p. 60.
60 Ibid., p. 54.

footman, so that when he asked for a glass of water it was handed to him by a man standing on his head.[61]

His letters are lively because they are able to shift their viewpoint with the ease of a good conversation. He carried serious thoughts with lightness; his levity was usually exercised in conjunction with a deep sense of the seriousness of art. A letter written to his son in 1917 illustrates this range of tone:

> I have always maintained that every man of sense should keep in his library a box of strong cigars, saturate each cigar with some drug soporific, so that if anyone said such a sentence as 'Excuse me, Sir, but what you are saying now is quite inconsistent with what you said earlier in the evening, etc.', you might reply: 'Sir, your views are very interesting. May I offer you a cigar? It is of a special brand that I only give to my most valued friends.' Ah! with what pleasure one would watch the gradual lowering of the eyelids and the falling away of the mouth and the paling of the lip as one waited for the blessed silence.[62]

Having invented his comic situation he continues the letter on a serious note, defending his own approach to poetry:

> Oriental philosophy is like that cigar. That is why we turn to it. Sir Philip Sidney wrote that poetry cannot lie because it affirms nothing, and if you affirm nothing, what becomes of the fighting intellect? Either it conceals its instincts, or is converted, like a heathen king listening to the preaching of St. Augustine. – The man with the logical mind does not – for he cannot – read poetry.[63]

The role of the poet and the artist were themes which ran through his letters, especially after his stay in New York. He believed that the world of art was a dreamland. The moment a poet meddled with ethics, moral uplift or thinking scientifically he left dreamland, lost his music and ceased to be a poet. He regarded Shakespeare as never quitting this realm:

> We all live when at our best, that is when we are most ourselves, in dreamland. A man with his wife or child and loving them, a man in grief and yielding to it, girls and boys dancing together, children at play – it is all dreams, dreams, dreams. A student over his books, soldiers at the war, friends talking together – it is still dreamland – actual life on a far away horizon which becomes more and more distant. When the essential sap of life is arrested by anger or hatred we suddenly are aware of the actual, and music dies out of our hearts and voices – the *anger subtly present* in ethical thought – as it is also in most kinds of argument; how many poems has it laid low? . . .
> The poet is a magician – his vocation to incessantly evoke dreams and do his

---

[61] *Letters*, p. 209.   [62] Ibid., p. 241.   [63] Ibid. p. 242.

work so well, because of natural gifts and acquired skill, that his dreams shall
have a potency to defeat the actual at every point. Yet here is a curious thing,
the poet and we his dupes know tha tthey are only dreams – otherwise we lose
them. With our eyes open, using our will and powers of selection, we, together in friendship and brotherly love, create this dreamland. Pronounce it to
be actual life and you summon logic and mechanical sense and reason and all
the other powers of prose to find yourself hailed back to the prison house, and
dreamland vanishes – a shrieking ghost.[64]

This continued emphasis on the importance of the dream reminds
us of his effect on his famous son. Continually he insisted that the real
contest was not against material things but between those who want
to get on and those who don't want to get on, having more important
things to attend to. When York Powell offered to recommend W. B.
Yeats for the sub-editorship of a provincial paper, and the young man
told his father he could not accept the offer, J. B. Yeats replied, though
the family was badly short of funds, 'You have taken a great weight
off my mind.' He believed

> A gentleman is such, simply because he has not the doctrine of getting on and
> the habit of it. For this reason a poor peasant and a true artist are gentlemen,
> but people talk as if the doctrine of getting on was greater than all the law and
> the prophets.[65]

Here was the idea his son developed after his disillusionment with
nationalist politics, the belief stated in his poems praising the virtues of
aristocratic life, 'At Galway Races' and 'To a Wealthy Man . . .', and
brought to its final assertion in 'The Municipal Gallery Revisited' where
he sees the work of John Synge, Augusta Gregory and himself as coming from contact with the soil:

> We three alone in modern times had brought
> Everything down to that sole test again,
> Dream of the noble and the beggar-man.[66]

There are many correspondences between the ideas of father and son.
Indeed the first part of W. B. Yeats's *Autobiographies*, *Reveries over
Childhood and Youth*, bears ample witness to the early influence of John
Butler Yeats on his son's development.[67] They argued incessantly and
Elizabeth Yeats's diary entry for 9 September 1888, when W. B.

[64] Ibid., p. 198.
[65] *Passages from the Letters of John Butler Yeats*, p. 52.
[66] WBY, *Collected Poems*, p. 368.
[67] WBY wrote to his father (J. B. Yeats, *Letters to his son W. B. Yeats and Others*, p. 203):
'Some one to whom I read the book said to me the other day, "If Gosse had not taken the
title you should call it 'Father and Son'".'

Yeats was twenty-three, gives a sensible explanation of the relationship:

> I can hear a murmur of talk from the dining-room where Papa and Willie
> are arguing something or other. Sometimes they raise their voices so high that
> a stranger might fancy that they were both in a rage, not at all, it is only their
> way of arguing because they are natives of the Emerald Isle.[68]

It is a commonplace that the painter's influence over his poet son
ceased when the latter began to develop his interest in mysticism – a
mystic, incidentally, was defined by John Butler Yeats as 'a man who
believes what he likes to believe and makes a system of it and plumes
himself on doing so'.[69] He thought Blake's mysticism was 'never the
substance of his poetry, only its machinery',[70] and during the period of the
First World War his letters to his son insisted that 'the poet is not
primarily a thinker but incidentally he is a thinker and a stern thinker
since the source of his magic is his personal sincerity'.[71] Again, he
wrote, 'Let poets by all means touch on ideas, but let it only be a
"touching" and a tentative groping with the poetical fingers. It is bad
poetry which proclaims a definite belief – because it is a sin against
sincerity.'[72] These views probably had their effect upon W. B., who
wrote to his father describing his own *Anima Hominis* and *Anima Mundi*
as philosophical and 'a kind of prose backing' to his poetry.[73]

The question of John Butler Yeats's influence on his son needs fresh
exploration. It extended further than the early period of W. B. Yeats's
life, though less directly.[74] The printed works of John Butler Yeats, as

---

[68] Cf. J. Hone, 'A Scattered Fair', *The Wind and the Rain*, III 3 (Autumn 1946), and
J. B. Yeats, *Letters*, p. 291.   [69] *Passages from the Letters of John Butler Yeats*, p. 16.
[70] Ibid., p. 19.   [71] *Letters*, p. 210.   [72] Ibid., p. 221.
[73] Ibid., p. 238. Cf. Murphy, 'Father and Son', loc. cit., pp. 76–7:

> John Butler Yeats could not stand Willie's forays into magic because the magic was
> of Willie's choosing and not his. When the son was twenty-seven years old, a respected
> writer among the literary men of England and Ireland, the father was still urging
> him to abandon the magic in favour of the rational, even going so far as to have
> John O'Leary, the venerable and admired Fenian, write to him about the question-
> ability of the course he was pursuing.'

[74] No doubt remembering the poet's comments on Professor Dowden's view of
Shakespeare in the essay 'At Stratford-on-Avon' of 1901 (WBY, *Essays and Introductions*,
pp. 104 ff.) and the very differing views of poet and professor on the Irish literary revival
and on politics, John Butler Yeats wrote very directly indeed on 11 Dec 1913 to W. B.,
when Dowden's poems were in question: 'I would ask you, indeed beg of you, to remember that he not only was a very old friend, but the best of friends.' He reminded him how
Dowden had been helpful when there was a possibility of W. B., succeeding Dowden in
the Chair of English at Trinity College, Dublin. He saw in Dowden's poetry a bourgeois
point of view about marriage, comfortable, sentimental and affectionate, and ended his
letter, 'merely a word to the wise', with a plea for caution and the avoidance of giving
pain 'even to your Dublin enemies, which is after all a poor kind of fun – tho' I admit it
is tempting'. (J. B. Yeats, *Letters*, pp. 168–9.)

well as the references to his conversations in W. B. Yeats's prose, show
that father and son shared very many ideas – for instance, J. B. Yeats
writes to W. B. in 1916[75] that Stendhal said a novel should be like a
looking-glass dawdling along the road, and W. B. writes in his *Pages
from a Diary Written in 1930*: 'Because freedom is gone we have
Stendhal's "mirror dawdling down a lane".' This is but a small echo,
like the interest they shared in the hermits of the desert;[76] the larger,
longer echoes are more significant. The most important idea they
shared was probably that of the role of the lonely man. 'The poet is
always solitary',[77] wrote J. B. Yeats; again he commented:

> The individual man of entire sincerity has to wrestle with himself, unless
> transported by rage or passion; he has so much mind to make up, with none to
> help him and no guide except his conscience; and conscience after all, is but a
> feeble glimmer in a labyrinthine cavern of darkness.[78]

Or again,

> Outside mathematics and science, there is no such thing as belief positive;
> yet there is a certain intensity of feeling whether of love, hope or sorrow or fear
> which we label belief; with the solitary man this remains a feeling and is some-
> thing presonal, and therefore the very substance of poetry.[79]

These are ideas we find W. B. Yeats carrying on in the poem 'My
House' – he describes how 'two men have founded' in the ancient
tower: the original man-at-arms and his score of horse:

> And I, that after me
> My bodily heirs may find,
> To exalt a lonely mind,
> Befitting emblems of adversity.[80]

On 10 June 1918 John Butler Yeats wrote to his son quite simply,
'The way to be happy is to forget yourself. That is why Robert Gregory
was happy. . . .'[81] He distinguished two ways of achieving self-
forgetfulness, as in the war, or in a movement for reform, or in games;
or again through art and beauty. He saw war as so overwhelmingly
gregarious that 'while it lasts it suspends all the movements and the

---

[75] See J. B. Yeats, *Letters*, p. 157, where he writes to his son on 8 Mar 1913: 'I began
this letter in order to suggest that you read Stendhal's *Red and White* (you can get it in
English). It has enlarged my imagination: it is a tragedy. You read it in a sort of high
seriousness in which there is no pain.'

[76] See *Letters*, p. 207, and W. B. Yeats's reference to the monks of the Thebaid in
'Demon and Beast', *Collected Poems*, p. 209.

[77] *Early Memories*, p. 23.   [78] Ibid., p. 90.

[79] He also remarked that 'solitude is food for the intellect but a drain on the spirits'.

[80] WBY, *Collected Poems*, p. 226.   [81] *Letters*, p. 247.

susceptibilities of the solitary man'.[82] The same idea runs through one
of W. B.'s poems on Robert Gregory, 'An Irish Airman Foresees his
Death', written in 1918:

> Nor law, nor duty bade me fight,
> Nor public men, nor cheering crowds,
> A lonely impulse of delight
> Drove to this tumult in the clouds;
> I balanced all, brought all to mind,
> The years to come seemed waste of breath,
> A waste of breath the years behind
> In balance with this life, this death.[83]

This belief in the necessity of solitude led him to believe also in the
detachment needed by a poet. Emotionalism, he thought, was bad
because it lacked seriousness – 'Walt Whitman did not believe half what
he said' – emotionalism was spectacular. The true poet seemed to him
to be like the statesman, and to possess a cold heart, notwithstanding its
abiding ecstasy, and therefore to be more serious than any statesman.[84]
This emphasis on the cold heart is echoed in W. B. Yeats's 'Cast a cold
eye on death'.[85] It is a peculiarly Anglo–Irish fusion of coldness and
passion that found expression in the poet's ideal audience for whom
he wished to write:

> . . . one
> Poem may be as cold
> And passionate as the dawn.[86]

When John Quinn thought J. B. Yeats sentimental about women
and marriage he did not fully realise how aware Yeats was of the
dangers of sentimental thinking.[87] It is probable that W. B.'s long-

---

[82] On, 14 June 1918 WBY had finished his long poem 'In Memory of Major Robert
Gregory, *Collected Poems*, p. 148.   [83] Ibid, p. 152.
[84] J. B. Yeats, *Letters*, p. 237.   [85] WBY, 'Under Ben Bulben', *Collected Poems*, p. 401.
[86] WBY, 'The Fisherman', *Collected Poems*, p. 166. I owe this idea to Professor Brendan
Kennelly.
[87] See J. B. Yeats, *Letters*, pp. 226–7. He wrote an interesting letter to John Quinn on
27 Oct 1912 (quoted in Reid, *The Man from New York*, p. 137):

> 'When people marry it is not as the vulgar vainly imagine, that they may bring
> strength into union with strength. Marriage of that sort is not a marriage at all, no
> tenderness on either side. Marriage means that two people are bringing into the
> common stock all their weaknesses, and there are two comparisons possible. Marriage
> is sometimes like two drunken men seeing each other home. Neither can reproach
> the other or refuse sympathy or help. The other comparison is this: Marriage is like
> two mortal enemies (the sexes are enemies) meeting on the scaffold and reconciled
> by the imminence of the great enemy of both.'

There is a strong supposition that he did consider a second marriage some time after
his wife's death.

frustrated dreams which eventually came true of 'wife, daughter, son' were formed early and upon his father's belief in the virtues of marriage. J. B. Yeats was attractive to women and enjoyed their company, while holding firm, conservative views on marriage:

> Marriage is the earliest fruit of civilization and it will be the latest. I think a man and a woman should choose each other for life, for the simple reason that a long life with all its accidents is barely enough for a man and a woman to understand each other; and in this case to understand is to love. The man who understands one woman is qualified to understand pretty well everything.[88]

The poet must, he thought, have self-control and allow no single feeling to remain single, forcing it into harmony with all the other feelings, an idea shared by his son, who saw that in life courtesy and self-possession and in the arts style arose out of deliberate shaping of all things.[89]

Both men were instinctively aristocratic ('Every day I see some new analogy between the long-established life of the well-born and the artists' life', wrote W. B. Yeats in 1909);[90] both valued manners greatly. 'Damn nervous energy', wrote the father, 'and damn efficiency. They have killed good manners as they have killed conversation, for the sake of which good manners exist, and they have killed art and literature.'[91] This is a sentiment echoed in W. B. Yeats's 1909 diary where he develops the idea of the mask. Father and son shared a dislike of logic; they shared a dislike of the English character which arose from their experiences of English schoolboys, from whom they felt essentially different.[92] John Butler Yeats built up an image of the 'Englishman': Tory, class-conscious, self-centred, dull, official: 'Someone who

[88] *Letters*, p. 236. He could see the difference between his ideal and the reality of some situations, however, remarking, 'I think lots of men die of their wives and thousands of women die of their husbands. But not an American. Here, if there is a little trouble over a hand glass or a tooth brush, they shake hands and part, unless of course, there is a lot of money, when the lawyers take a hand.' (*Letters*, p. 275.) The question of his own contemplation of a second marriage, however, will probably not be understood until some letters – at present placed under a long embargo – can be read.

[89] WBY, *Essays and Introductions* (1961) p. 253.

[90] WBY, *Autobiographies* (1961) p. 473.

[91] *Passages from the Letters of John Butler Yeats*, p. 1.

[92] J. B. Yeats, *Letters*, p. 108: 'John Bull's pre-eminence is slipping away so that these airs are becoming a little ridiculous – to me they always have been so – since I had been at school with so many English boys.' WBY, *Autobiographies*, p. 35: 'I was divided from all those boys [at the Godolphin School, Hammersmith] not merely by the anecdotes that are everywhere perhaps a chief expression of the distrust of races but because our mental images were different', and on p. 33: 'I did not think English people intelligent or well behaved unless they were artists.'

enjoys liberty and believes in it – for himself alone,'[93] and in England
'character means a man in whom the will power is predominant, it is
in fact the bureaucratic mind, and is as interesting as Berlin governed
by its police'.[94] There were, of course, exceptions. 'It is a few Englishmen like Paget and York Powell and Oliver Elton that prevent the
Almighty from destroying England.'[95] He became mellower. In 1917
he wrote to Oliver Elton that he would do the Englishman full justice:
'he does not lose his head, even now (in the war) he ceases neither to
love his children nor his wife nor his garden nor his poetry.' He liked
ordinary English people; in 1915 he anticipated a social movement
coming after the First World War and in this the Irish, he thought,
'must help *their English brothers* – who certainly won't be the middle
class their old enemies'.[96]

He could generalise about the Irish as easily. Ireland was accused of a
lack of seriousness by England; this, he said, was because Ireland lacks
the collective mind. The Irish have the charm of being natural; 'the
Irish peasant mind is not common but is stored with rich enjoyment'.[97]
He could also enjoy being epigrammatic about differences: 'The Irish
spurn convention and are called cynical, and the English make of it a
religion and for their pains are called hypocrites.'[98] The Americans
searched for joy and happiness – talk only fit for athletes and football
players – a shallow vulgar paradise, easily come at, he thought, by
anyone except the true artist and poet. He mixed up his reflections
with anecdotes and gossip: they are often discerning, and always interesting. On democracy he had mixed feelings:

> There are no proud girls in America. Feminine beauty has not that *touch-me-
> not-quality* which is half the charm of the well-bred girl (of other countries).
> It is the pride of the democracies and the Amreicans to have no pride, and it
> does make life pleasant and easy, but it leaves the American girl naked and
> defenceless against all these false ideas that are so abundant among socialists.[99]

He dwelt long upon the characters of his relatives and friends and
continued to find the 'joyous amiability' of the Yeats family a source
of comfort, as the orderliness of the Pollexfens was a perpetual challenge. His reflections on dreams and death, on Protestantism and literature, on women, on art, all have a zest and vitality, which though often
lacking polish, have a gnomic quality, a casualness which comes from
a consciousness of more to come. '*Genius is personality*', he remarks

---

[93] J. B. Yeats, *Letters*, p. 41.   [94] Ibid., p. 124.   [95] Ibid., p. 96.
[96] Ibid., p. 211.   [97] Ibid., p. 255.   [98] *Early Memories*, p. 68.
[99] *Letters*, p. 274.

and adds, impishly, 'I always say that had Shakespeare a strong will he would have read for a Fellowship in T.C.D. [Trinity College, Dublin] and there would have been no Shakespeare.'[100]

He was a man of modesty. Many of the letters to his son contained excellent criticism, sometimes of the poet as poet and also as man: always there were phrases – 'I hope I don't weary you' or 'Don't trouble to answer this letter, which is merely a word to the wise'. He thought the only sincerity in a practical world was that of the artist; he knew when discussing 'real' matters with 'real' people he irritated them by producing phrases or ideas that were expressive, while they sought a practical result.[101] He looked back on his life, lived as a social life on social principles:

> we lived pleasantly, but falsely, and yet we did believe in human nature, at least in *our* human nature, in parental affection and in conjugal faith and loyalty between friends. On this matter we had a trustfulness that was at once romantic and robust. Parents and children and husbands and wives and friends and comrades, at least in our circles, would have stood by each other to the death.[102]

He shared the best virtues of his age, then, and in a remarkable letter to his son showed how his apparent failure was really a magnificent demonstration of the proper defence of art: the distinction of his own enjoyment of life speaks through every sentence:

> To find out what was the mind of Shakespeare is valuable, but the real thing is to find out what is my own mind when I read Shakespeare or any other poem. If I know the mind of Shakespeare and in order that I may know it better, am made acquainted with the period in which he lived, it is good because thereby I may come more quickly to know my own mind – for I study him and all other poets exclusively that I may find myself. It is the same with nature itself. As artist, as man, seeking what I have called dreamland I am concerned still to find myself and my own mind, and only incidentally am I concerned with the intentions of Nature and her mind. Herein I am the reverse of the historical and the scientific student. They are concerned with what is other than themselves, whereas the artist in us and in all men seeks to find himself. Science exists that man may discover and control nature and build up for

---

100 Ibid., p. 98.

101 Ibid., p. 275. WBY wrote, on 30 Sept 1921, that it was 'infirmity of will which has prevented him from finishing his pictures and ruined his career. He even hates the sign of will in others. It used to cause quarrels between me and him, for the qualities which I thought necessary to success in art or in life seemed to him "egotism" or "selfishness' or "brutality". I had to escape this family drifting, innocent and helpless. . . .' (Quoted in Reid, *The Man from New York*, p. 493.) J. B. Yeats would have defended a concept of 'weakness' – 'all those vulnerabilities and sensibilities which cannot be exposed, being by their nature unintelligible except in closest intimacy.' (See Reid, op. cit., p. 137.)

102 *Early Memories*, p. 88.

himself habitations in which to live in ease and comfort. Art exists that man cutting himself away from nature may build in his free consciousness buildings vaster and more sumptuous than these, furnished too with all manner of winding passages and closets and boudoirs and encircled with gardens well shaded and with everything that he can desire – and we build all out of our spiritual pain – for if the bricks be not cemented and mortised by actual suffering, they will not hold together. Those others live on another plane where if there is less joy there is much less pain. Like day labourers they work, with honest sweat to earn their wages, and mother nature smiles on them and calls them her good children who study her wishes and seek always to please her and rewards them with many gifts. The artist has not the gift for this assiduity, these servile labours – so falling out of favour with his great mother he withdraws himself and lives in disgrace, and then out of his pain and humiliations constructs for himself habitations, and if she sweeps them away with a blow of her hand he only builds them afresh, and as his joy is chiefly in the act of building he does not mind how often he has to do it. The men of science hate us and revile us, being angry with impotent rage because we seem to them to live in profitless idleness, and though we have sad faces we are yet of such invincible obstinacy that nothing can induce us to join their ranks. There are other things about us which perplex and offend them. They always work in gangs, many minds engaged on one task, whereas we live and work singly, each man building for himself accepting no fellowship – for we say it is only thus we can build our habitations. So it follows that they charge us with selfish egotism and insolence and pride, and it is vain for us to say that we work in the spirit of the utmost humility, not being strong enough for their tasks, and suffering many pains because of the anger of our offended and beloved mother. They are mighty men with strong wills. We are weak as water, our weakness is our raison d'être, and now and again when the strong man is broken he comes to us that we may comfort him. We even may make merry together, for we love our fellow men more than we do ourselves.[103]

---

[103] *Letters*, pp. 199–200.

Oliver St John Gogarty, Irishman

MAURICE HEADLAM in his *Irish Reminiscences* remarked that though Lord Dunsany had said there is no 'typical Irishman' he himself thought Gogarty [1] 'a type of contradictory qualities',[2] which is as far as the civil service caution of Headlam's book would allow him to go in the direction of saying that Gogarty seemed to him a typical Irishman. The reasons he gives for this are not very satisfactory: 'his fluent witty speech, his stories good, bad and indifferent, his brilliant professional reputation, his wide knowledge of literature and the classics.' All that Headlam said of Gogarty is true: the fluency and wit, the brilliant professional reputation, the wide knowledge of literature and the classics, all are there at work in his poetry;[1] but these are not exclusively Irish qualities, they are the kind of qualities we might equally well posit in, say, an Elizabethan Englishman. They would fit Sir Walter Raleigh, would they not? Provided, of course, that we remember that both Sir Walter Raleigh and Gogarty had also an abundant appetency for life, for beauty and bravery.[3] Or, if we look for another parallel we might say the terms fit another poet known for fluency and wit, Herrick, a man with wide knowledge of literature and the classics, but less known, perhaps, for a brilliant professional reputation: for Herrick was a man after Gogarty's poetic heart, though he did not have the worldly good fortune of the Irish poet in his (perhaps perforce) unworldly role in the Church. No, wit and fluency, brilliant professional reputation, and knowledge of the classics and

[1] Gogarty's name does not appear in the *Cambridge Bibliography of English Literature*; his work is not mentioned in the histories of recent literature; he has not afforded New Critics opportunity for pedantry; and he has been avoided by the anthologists with the notable exceptions of Lennox Robinson, *A Golden Treasury of Irish Verse* (1925) (3 poems); Sir Arthur Quiller-Couch, *The Oxford Book of English Verse* (rev. ed. 1927) (2 poems); W. B. Yeats, *The Oxford Book of Modern Verse* (1936) (17 poems); D. MacDonogh and Lennox Robinson, *The Oxford Book of Irish Verse* (1958) (5 poems); and Brendan Kennelly, *The Penguin Book of Irish Verse* (1970) (1 poem).

[2] Maurice Headlam, *Irish Reminiscences* (1947) p. 54.

[3] Since writing this I noticed, W. B. Yeats, *Letters on Poetry to Dorothy Wellesley* (1940) p. 151, a comment on Gogarty's *As I Was Going Down Sackville Street*: 'One can say much of it, as somebody said I think of Raleigh, it is "high insolent and passionate".'

literature are not necessarily typically Irish qualities (nor indeed are
they necessarily recognised as typically poetic qualities any more).

What then are the Irish elements? Perhaps we can approach these
through knowing something of the man behind the poems: an ear,
nose, and throat specialist with an ear for melody, a nose for the
ridiculous, and a throat unashamed of emotional speech and song.
Born in 1878, the son and grandson of doctors, he was taught at his
English school[4] to compose Latin verses

> like jigsaw puzzles irrespective of ear. We used a gradus to check the quantities
> of the vowels. The result of our work was futility. Hexameters meant nothing
> to the teacher; there was no appeal to the ear, for he was deaf to 'The stateliest
> measure ever moulded by the lips of man'.[5]

He read Xenophon in Greek but by the time he was ripe for ' "the
sweet and pleasant reading of old authors" the sparks of fervent desire
for learning were extinct with the burden of grammar'.[6] He had,
however, by this time realised that words can be selected and bent to
very different purposes; he had also begaun to stock his memory with
a vast repertoire of poetry; and he had been inducted into the classical
tradition of imitation. When he left school he had two years at the
old Royal University in Dublin before the prospect of entering the
University of Dublin seemed more attractive. He was admitted to
Trinity College, Dublin, and thus began the tension which made him
uneasily amphibious between the heady airs of Ascendancy and Castle
Society and the troubled waters of the Sinn Féin movement.

Trinity, however, set its mark firmly on Gogarty: he was there in a
golden period of scholarship and late in life he wrote:

> Often the thought strikes me, Have I ever left Dublin University? Certainly
> I have never sought to improve on the universal outlook on life. With Lachesis
> I sang of the Past, with Clotho of the Present and, thus equipped, I can look,
> as I do now, at the Future with assurance.[7]

Trinity believed that its medical students should not study merely
medicine, and so Gogarty took his compulsory Bachelor of Arts degree
in the midst of his work for a medical one. Of the dons, he admired
and especially liked Macran, the Hegelian philosopher, and Yelverton
Tyrrell, the classic, 'that gowned man who loved to foster / My

---

[4] He went initially to the Christian Brothers' School at Richmond Street, then to a
boarding-school on the Shannon, next to Stonyhurst, and finally to Clongowes Wood
College.
[5] O. St J. Gogarty, *It Isn't This Time Of Year At All!: An Unpremeditated Autobiography*
(1954) p. 27.   [6] Ibid.   [7] Ibid., p. 221.

waking wits',[8] to whom he said he owed 'all of the little acquaintance
I have of the classics and all my love of the plangent word or un-
alterable line'.[9] Gogarty liked to praise his friends, and his 'Elegy on
the Archpoet William Butler Yeats Lately Dead' is a good example of
this genre:

> We might as well just save our breath,
> There's not a good word to be said for Death
> Except for the great change it brings:
> For who could bear the loveliest Springs
> Touched by the thought that he must keep
> A watch eternal without sleep?
> But yet within the ends
> Of human, not eternal things,
> We all resent the change it brings:
> Chiefly the loss of friends:
> Tyrrell, Mahaffy and Macran,
> The last the gentlest gentleman, . . .[10]

However, it was a generous pupil's praise which he sang in memory
of Tyrrell in 'Aeternae Lucis Redditor':

> Too seldom on this world of ours
> Unwrackt the eternal radiance pours.
> Again we shall not see it pour
> As in the days and nights before
> We lost the wide Virgilian calm;
> Days when we sought to earn the palm –
> Through the endowment of a wit
> Which made us eligible for it –
> From you who were Wit's arbiter,
> Aeternae lucis Redditor.[11]

The endowment of a wit made his early reactions to Mahaffy less appreciative. While Mahaffy's wit (Gogarty particularly valued his reply
to a lady who asked him for the definition of an Irish bull: 'a male
animal, Madam, that is always pregnant') and scholarship were recognised in Dublin for their brilliance and breadth, he himself was also
renowned for his travels and king-hunting, and was on one occasion
given a dog by the niece of the King of Greece which died on its way
to Ireland. Gogarty parodied Swinburne's *Atalanta in Calydon* and

8 Gogarty, 'Perennial', *Collected Poems* (1951) p. 56.
9 Gogarty, *It Isn't This Time Of Year At All!*, p. 131.
10 Gogarty, *Collected Poems*, p. 205.
11 Ibid., p. 199.

Mahaffy's lisp together in *The Death of Diogenes, the Doctor's Dog*. The
Doctor [Mahaffy] laments the death:

> When I wambled awound
> In the gwound that was Gweece
> I was given that hound
> By the King's little niece,
> And had rather be fined e'er I found
>   him to gaze on
> His saddest surcease.

The Chorus of Scholars of the House adds its deadpan deadly comment:

> He was given that hound
>   By the seed of a King
> For the wisdom profound
>   Of his wide wandering.
> But was it the owner, or donor, or dog
>   that was led by a string?[12]

Mahaffy, who richly deserves a biography himself,[13] set Gogarty, and
probably Oscar Wilde before him, an example of intellectual arrog-
ance,[14] which was fed by Gogarty's own skill in parody. This developed in competition with an even greater parodist. Three years
after leaving the Royal University he had become friendly with Joyce
(who, four years younger, had also been a pupil at Clongowes Wood
College and had entered the Royal University 1898–99). He frequently met Joyce at the National Library in Kildare Street (and
other students, such as John Elwood, celebrated in their different ways
in *A Portrait of the Artist as a Young Man* and *Ulysses* and in Gogarty's
poems).[15] §There was an Oxford interlude during Gogarty's Trinity
days (1898–1907) – two terms at Worcester in 1904 where the high-
lights were failing the Newdigate, buying an Indian motor-bicycle
from William Morris, meeting Compton Mackenzie, successfully

[12] Text from 'Threnody on the Death of Diogenes, the Doctor's Dog', *Secret Springs
of Dublin Song* (1918) p. 40. The poem originally appeared in *Dublin University Magazine*.
[13] Two Fellows of Trinity College, Dublin, Professor W. B. Stanford and Dr R. B.
McDowell, are at present engaged in writing one.
[14] In an 'Ode on the Bicentenary' Gogarty wrote for *The Festival of the Bicentenary of
the School of Physic* (Dublin, 1912) he included his expression of this: 'Before this public
rape began / And Peasant grew to Overman.'
[15] By Gogarty in 'To Citizen Elwood in South America', *Secret Springs of Dublin Song*,
p. 11. I am indebted to Mr Ulick O'Connor, who told me of this volume's existence and
to Mr Walsh of Hodges Figgis, Dublin, who supplied a copy of it with identifications of
the authors which were confirmed by M. J. MacManus and Seamus O'Sullivan; these
attributions were originally made by Gogarty himself at his son's request.

drinking a sconce, and realising conduct was more in demand than scholarship – but when he returned to Dublin Joyce lived with him in the famous Martello tower he rented at Sandycove, outside Dublin. Here there was a good deal of rivalry:

> We quoted and parodied *all* the poets. Joyce could parody every prose style and get an equivalent sound for every word.[16]

This desire for parody was perhaps particularly strong in the heyday of classical studies in Dublin and the Trinity classical dons themselves produced many brilliant parodies in their Greek and Latin verses.[17]

Of Gogarty's parodies, however, Dublin still remembers English versions, particularly that witty echo of Keats's 'On first looking into Chapman's Homer' in his sonnet 'On first looking through Kraft Ebbing's[18] *Psychopathia Sexualis*':

> Much have I travelled in those realms of old
> Where many a whore in hall-doors could be seen
> Of many a bonnie brothel or sheebeen
> Which bawds connived at by policemen hold.
> I too have listened when the Quay was coaled
> But never did I taste the Pure obscene –
> Much less imagine that my past was clean –
> Till this Kraft Ebbing[18] out his story told.
> Then felt I rather taken by surprise
> As on the evening when I met Macran
> And retrospective thoughts and doubts did rise,
> Was I quite normal when my life began
> With love that leans towards rural sympathies
> Potent behind a cart with Mary Ann?

And this bawdy element, which began with his writing Rabelaisian verse while still a pupil at Clongowes Wood, and continued with limericks[19] and ballades written as an undergraduate, must not be

---

[16] Gogarty, *It Isn't This Time Of Year At All!*, p. 70.
[17] See, for instance, the various volumes of *Kottabos* published in 1874, 1877 and 1881. A second series began in 1888 and ended in 1895.
[18] Krafft-Ebing is spelt Kraft Ebbing consistently by Gogarty.
[19] One of these which is sometimes attributed to him is quoted in Ulick O'Connor, *Oliver St John Gogarty* (1964) p. 20:

> There was a young man from St. Johns
> Who wanted to Roger the swans.
> 'Oh no,' said the porter,
> 'Oblige with my daughter,
> But the birds are reserved for the dons.'

Mr O'Connor also quotes Gogarty's variant of the established classic 'Then out spoke the King of Siam' and mentions (pp. 22–3) another gay indelicacy. This was Gogarty's

CA F

glossed over. His medical-student days were set in a Dublin of slums, of tough conditions, in the tradition of ribaldry which often acts as a safety-valve for the sensitive. But Gogarty had a zest for getting to know men and women of all classes. His family had frowned upon his prowess in bicycle-racing, which was regarded as 'low', his friends from his Royal University days were considered vulgar, and he was regarded as keeping 'low company' at a restaurant and public-house called the Bailey; but then he relished the lively speech which characterised 'low' Dublin pub life as much as it did, in different, more refined vocabulary, the dining- and drawing-rooms of Dublin society. As a medical student and doctor Gogarty was automatically thrust face to face with appalling social conditions in the Dublin slums and formed in the process an outlook on life not unlike that of another Trinity medical graduate, Goldsmith. While extracting what fun he could

---

'Ode of Welcome', included under the initials J. R. S. in *Irish Society*, a snobbish society magazine, when the Irish regiments returned to Ireland after the Boer War in 1900 to a tumultuous reception:

> The gallant Irish yeoman
> Home from the war has come,
> Each victory gained o'er foeman,
> Why should our bards be dumb?
>
> How shall we sing their praises
> Or glory in their deeds,
> Renowned their worth amazes,
> Empire their prowess needs.
>
> So to Old Ireland's hearts and homes
> We welcome now our own brave boys
> In cot and hall; 'neath lordly domes
> Love's heroes share once more our joys.
>
> Love is the Lord of all just now,
> Be he the husband, lover, son,
> Each dauntless soul recalls the vow
> By which not fame, but love was won.
>
> United now in fond embrace
> Salute with joy each well-loved face.
> Yeoman, in women's hearts you hold the place.

Gogarty, who had written articles in *Sinn Féin* opposing the recruitment of Irishmen for the British Army in the Boer War, intended the initial letters of each line to be read downwards in succession, as a comment on the likely increase of custom in Dublin's Night-town now these regiments had returned. The joke went down well in Dublin, where his authorship was soon known.

from the ignoble crowding 'That leads to the Commune' he denounced it too:

> Break down the tenement
> Walls that surround them;
> Lead out from festering
> Lane and back garden
> The Heirs to the Kingdom,
> To sunlight, to highland,
> To winds blowing over
> Green fields; and restore to
> The sons of a City,
> By seafarers founded,
> The sight of white clouds on
> An open horizon.[20]

And so he recorded in unpublished verses (some of these are still remembered and recited at convivial students' parties in Dublin, perhaps
much as Goldsmith's ballads were sung in the streets when Goldsmith
was still an undergraduate) the affairs of fresh Nellie, of Mrs Mack,
and other lively ladies of Dublin's Night-town. Several long poems,
limericks, parodies, and prose anecdotes have passed into medical and
other Dublin folklore, the most absurdly Aristophanic an account of
how a king's detective was pursued by one of these intoxicated ladies
and fled before her advances.[21] Like the Australian poet A. D. Hope
in our time, his reputation as a wit and writer of Rabelaisian verses was
created through oral tradition long before he emerged more respect-
ably in print.[22] All that there is in print to hint at these wildly boisterous
fits of comic invention[23] are poems like 'To a Cock'[24] or a Villonesque
poem from the Irish, 'The Old Woman of Beare'[25] with its introduction of how

> . . . some old Abbey's shelf
> Kept the record of herself,
> Telling to men who disapprove
> Of Love, the long regrets of Love.

or the sophisticated poem 'Ringsend', written after reading Tolstoy:

> I will live in Ringsend
> With a red-headed whore,

---

[20] Gogarty, 'Angels', *Collected Poems*, p. 64.
[21] W. B. Yeats mentions this in an unpublished letter to Mrs Shakespear which was in
the possession of the late Mrs W. B. Yeats.
[22] Cf. M. Bryn Davies, 'The Verse of A. D. Hope', *Australian Letters*, II 2 (Aug 1959)
p. 42. See also in the same issue 'Literary Criticism. A. D. Hope'.
[23] A very late poem continues the strain, 'To his friends . . .', *Contemporary Poetry*
(Spring 1943) III i, p. 10.   [24] Gogarty, *Collected Poems*, p. 16.   [25] Ibid., p. 120.

And the fan-light gone in
Where it lights the hall-door;
And listen each night
For her querulous shout,
As at last she streels in
And the pubs empty out.
To soothe that wild breast
With my old-fangled songs,
Till she feels it redressed
From inordinate wrongs,
Imagined, outrageous,
Preposterous wrongs,
Till peace at last comes,
Shall be all I will do,
Where the little lamp blooms
Like a rose in the stew;
And up the back-garden
The sound comes to me
Of the lapsing, unsoilable,
Whispering sea.[26]

Gogarty was, as he frequently remarked, an accessory before the fact of *Ulysses*:[27] but he was also a Dubliner who knew more than the aspect Joyce presented of the city: Gogarty was able to move within an established society, to have friends who were wealthy and cultured as well as friends who were poor and bitterly clever. He was himself sophisticated and cosmopolitan. After his marriage on 10 August 1906[28] came a period of work in Vienna, which was to assist his medical reputation when he returned to Dublin in 1908 to put up his plate and to live beside George Moore in Ely Place:

George Moore kept the garden and I gazed out on its greenery and composed verses while I waited for patients.[29]

---

[26] Gogarty, *Collected Poems*, p. 102. See O'Connor, op. cit., pp. 56–8 for 'The Hay Hotel', a poem describing some of the wilder elements in Dublin's night life, and the Hay Hotel (so called because hay was kept in the windows for cabbies' horses) run by the Gogartys' former butler and cook, which survived the Kips (which vanished in 1924). Mr O'Connor also quotes, op. cit., p. 55, Gogarty's limerick on Joyce's visits to Night-town:

There was a young fellow called Joyce
Who possesseth a sweet tenor voice.
He goes to the Kips
With a psalm on his lips
And biddeth the harlots rejoice.

[27] Gogarty, 'James Augustine Joyce', *The Times Herald* (Dallas, Texas), 3 Apr 1949.
[28] His son Oliver was born on 23 July 1907.
[29] Gogarty, *It Isn't This Time Of Year At All!*, p. 83.

What these verses were it is hard to discover. They may have continued the whimsical note struck by 'To the Maids not to Walk in
the Wind'

> When the wind blows walk not abroad,
>   For maids, you may not know
> The mad, quaint thoughts that incommode
>   Me, when the winds do blow.
>
> What though the tresses of the treen
>   In double beauty move,
> With silver added to their green,
>   They were not made for love.
>
> But when your clothes reveal your thighs,
>   And surge around your knees,
> Until from foam you seem to rise
>   Like Venus from the seas . . .
>
> Though ye are fair, it is not fair!
>   Unless ye will be kind,
> Till I am dead *and changed to air*,
>   O walk not in the wind![30]

and 'The Ship',[31] a Fleckeresque poem ending with a characteristic
piece of self-mockery:

> A ship from Valparaiso came
>   And in the Bay her sails were furled;
> She brought the wonder of her name,
>   And tidings from a sunnier world.
>
> O you must voyage far if you
>   Would sail away from gloom and wet,
> And see beneath the Andes blue
>   Our white, umbrageous city set.
>
> But I was young and would not go;
>   For I believed when I was young
> That somehow life in time would show
>   All that was ever said or sung.

---

[30] *Secret Springs of Dublin Song*, p. 35. The poem was composed in 1904 (information
from Mr Ulick O'Connor).

[31] Neither poem appeared in print until 1918, but some of the poems written by
Gogarty about George Moore in *Secret Springs of Dublin Song* dealt with Moore's departure from Dublin in February 1911, so that there is precedent for assuming that the poems
in Gogarty's *The Ship and Other Poems* (1918) and *Secret Springs of Dublin Song* were
written over the period of twenty years before 1918, that is, from his entry into Trinity
College onwards.

CA G

Over the golden pools of sleep
  She went long since with gilded spars;
Into the night-empurpled deep,
  And traced her legend on the stars.

But she will come for me once more,
  And I shall see that city set,
The mountainous, Pacific shore –
  By God, I half believe it yet![32]

Mockery was not reserved for himself, however: there is a witty
'Lament for George Moore' written at the time of Moore's departure
from Dublin to London:

Lonely, O Moore, your old friends are;
  We miss you; and, forgive the banter,
We miss the generous cigar,
  The coy decanter.

We miss the nights when you were here –
  All Ely Place a catacomb,
Where we sat solemn and severe
  Denouncing Rome.

We were the Stellar Zodiac
  You took your part in:
Virgo Magee, Leo AE,
  And Edward Martyn,

Who hailed your firstlings as they grew
  Chapter by chapter;
And when we showed our Muse to you
  You did adapt her!

Guidance from thoughts thus crowding thick
  Was what you needed
You were the grandest Catholic
  That e'er seceded.

Thus through a window shines your ray
  All polychrome,
For 'still the light that led astray
  Was light from' Rome.

We miss Les Dames aux Temps jadis,
  And all whose Christian names would fall so
Ingenuously of living ladies –
  We miss them also.

---

[32] Gogarty, *Collected Poems*, p. 96.

> Now Yeats suggests (with Goethe) here
>   The likeliest measure of a mind
> Is – what we can't find anywhere –
>   The girls it leaves behind.
>
> O bad gray head good women knew,
>   There comes a thought unmixed with sadness,
> In that the worst that you could do
>   Was hardly badness!
>
> O hazardous and harmless lover,
>   Come back to Ireland, come back and bring
> (What though your writings are all passed over)
>   In your person a Playboy unguessed at by Synge![33]

Gogarty did not have long to wait for patients. And hospital appointments followed. He was able to indulge good taste in motor-cars, an Argyll was followed by a Daimler; then he bought a Rolls-Royce 'Silver Ghost' in 1909, 'to drive himself into a practice'[34] and later he acquired a Mercedes-Benz to indicate the speed with which he achieved the success at which he had aimed. As well as contributing to his dashing reputation these cars were a means of reaching rapidly into the countryside: just to be in it, to look at it, to get out of the man-made city, for to shoot, to ride, and to fish (with unbaited hook) were merely occasional and luxuriously unnecessary pretexts for enjoying its changing beauty. His poetry records exuberantly the emotional fullness of this life, records the moments of intense perception that charged his batteries for facing the solemnities of life and death as cavalierly as possible.[35]

Many of his poems praise the seasonal return of blossom:

> I thank the gods who gave to me
> The yearly privilege to see,
> Under the orchards' galaxy,
> April reveal her new-drenched skin;
> And for the timeless touch within
> Whereby I recognise my kin.[36]

But this is a more classically restrained note than is common in these

---

[33] Gogarty, *Secret Springs of Dublin Song*, p. 47.

[34] A phrase used by Gogarty, which I owe to Mr Ulick O'Connor.

[35] An interesting poem, 'At the Abbaye la Trappe, on hearing the cry Memento homo quia pulvis es', quoted by O'Connor, op. cit., pp. 135–6, and formerly included in *Hyperthuleana*, blends his theological speculations or free will with a witty Rabelaisian conclusion.

[36] Gogarty, 'The Eternal Recurrence', *Collected Poems*, p. 54.

poems. 'Perennial' conveys the energy and gusto of the poet. When
Mr Eliot was watching

> The grimy scraps
> Of withered leaves about your feet,
> And newspapers from vacant lots[37]

Gogarty watched

> By an old lot a cherry tree,
> An old wild cherry blooming brightly,
> A sight of joy in the unsightly.
> It sprayed the air with April snow
> As merrily as long ago
> When every little wind that blew
> Could bend it, and with blossoms strew
> The garden or the shaven lawn.
> The lot was bare, the house was gone;
> And yet the brave old tree bloomed on.

and his conclusion has no metropolitan misery about it:

> You'd think that Orpheus found his girl;
> Or that this old daft heart of mine
> Improved, as it grew old, like wine.
> I feel the soul within me sing:
> By God, I'm grateful for the Spring
> That makes all fading seem illusion;
> The foam, the fullness, the profusion;
> For every lovely thing misplaced;
> The bloom, the brightness and the waste![38]

There were other interests besides attending to private and hospital
patients, besides writing verse,[39] and enjoying the country. Gogarty
made public speeches against recruiting in the early 1900s and from as
early as 1905, when he received a reproof from Mahaffy for these
activities, Gogarty was a member of the Sinn Féin movement.[40] He
was not a believer in physical violence: that is to say, he carried no gun.
He did, however, on one occasion assist prisoners to escape from

---

[37] T. S. Eliot, 'Preludes', *Collected Poems 1909–1935* (1958) p. 21.
[38] Gogarty, *Collected Poems*, pp. 56–7.
[39] See O'Connor, op. cit., pp. 113–14, for some of his medically based poems. 'To his
friends when his prostate shall have become enlarged' may well have affected some of
Yeats's later poems on 'lust and rage' with its stanza:

> When I am contemplating rape
> And growing careless of escape
> And Lust not art engrosses me –
> For who writes old men's poetry?

[40] I owe to Mr Ulick O'Connor my information about Gogarty's political activities.

Mountjoy jail. During the First World War he did not approve of
John Redmond's recruiting campaign (though he also did much on
behalf of wounded soldiers). His great friend in the Sinn Féin movement was Arthur Griffith and his later dislike of Mr de Valéra was
probably originally caused by the late entry of de Valéra into the independence movement, late, that is, in comparison with Griffith's
earlier 'labouring in a grey dawn when the sun seemed distant'. This
dislike was not unnaturally exacerbated by the civil war which occurred
after the Treaty of 1922. Whatever the complexities of Gogarty's
political career between 1916 and 1923, there is no doubt that his interest in politics (and possibly his ambitions) eventually waned. He
was a member of the first Senate of the Irish Free State (from 1923 to
1936): but his seventeenth-century country-house – 'a sea-gray house,
whereby the blackbird sings' – at Renvyle in Connemara, which he
bought in 1917, was burnt down in the troubles; he very narrowly
escaped death at the hands of an execution squad of gunmen in the
civil war; and he was not, perhaps, as effective as he had hoped to be
as a Senator. Like Yeats he disliked the murderous mob, and he found
it difficult to take politicians seriously. Perhaps, as Yeats had found
Lady Gregory an impressive exemplar of the virtues of aristocratic life
when that life was directed to literature, he was similarly influenced
through his friendship with Lord Dunsany – and with Talbot Clifton –
from innate radicalism into detachment. He had, however, managed to
keep his politics and his friendships skilfully apart during times which
were, as Marvell put it in a similarly difficult period, 'something
criticall'.

He took up archery[41] and aviation. When the Irish Aero Club was
formed in 1922 he became a pilot[42] and flew frequently over Dublin
and occasionally to Galway *en route* to Renvyle where his house was
rebuilt partially with the compensation paid by the Irish Government
of about £14,000 – the total cost was about £23,000 – and then converted into a hotel. Accompanied by Lady Heath, a skilled amateur
pilot who was a passenger on this occasion, he crashed at Tullabawn
Strand where they had flown to swim; her sudden emergence in
bathing costume from the plane which was stuck in the sand added to
the d'Annunzio-like legend which collected about Gogarty.[43] Gogarty,

41 Gogarty, *Intimations* (New York, 1950) p. 196.
42 Gogarty, *As I Was Going Down Sackville Street* (1937) pp. 48 ff.
43 Mr Oliver Gogarty's recollection is that Caspar John intended to fly to Renvyle but
had to be content with landing at Galway, while Lady Heath did land at Renvyle but
flew there alone: the minor accident occurred on the return journey.

as well as appearing in the pages of George Moore's *Hail and Farewell*
and Joyce's *Ulysses*, was always inside Dublin's literary life, though his
first-published contributions to it had been made discreetly – in 1905
in *Dana*, the magazine edited by John Eglinton (W. K. Magee); in a
volume celebrating the bicentenary of the School of Physic in Ireland;
and in his first book *The Ship and Other Poems* published in 1918 when
he was forty. Many of his poems appeared the same year in *Secret
Springs of Dublin Song* and while Susan Mitchell's preface to this collection of anonymous poems gives the reason for their anonymity as
not being due to any modesty on the part of the authors, who were
merely wishing 'to avoid each other's jealousy or spite', the com-
parative quiet of Gogarty until his middle age may perhaps also have
been due to his knowledge of the sharp-tongued milieu within which
he lived. He was to bring that knowledge into the light in 1937 – when
he published *As I Was Going Down Sackville Street*.[44] He could be
caustically cruel to his enemies: his desire to be witty often dominated
over kindness, as his set pieces sometimes crushed conversation. It was
not surprising that this lively book set Dublin by the ears and led almost
immediately to a libel action. Disgusted by this, Gogarty, who had
been practising in both Dublin and London (he practised at 20 Gros-
venor Street until 1924) during the twenties and thirties, withdrew to
London, intending from then on to spend most of his time writing.[45]
He finished *I Follow St. Patrick* (1938) and *Tumbling in the Hay* (1939),
two of his best and most original books, then the war found him in
America where he did not practise as a doctor and, having changed his
earlier political views,[46] tried unsuccessfully to get into the Royal Air
Force, then volunteered to join the R.A.M.C., for which he was not
accepted (he was then sixty-one). He stayed in America where he had
originally gone on a lecturing tour and there he wrote more reminiscences, two novels, various journalistic pieces, and more poetry and
only returned on about six or seven brief visits to Ireland before his
death of a heart attack in New York in 1959.

His *Collected Poems* appeared in 1951, the volume containing 184

[44] Neither Moore in *Hail and Farewell* nor Gogarty in this book were inhibited in their
observation and subsequent depiction of the foibles of their fellow men: both were
mockers, and Moore's *Hail and Farewell* must have been a model for Gogarty as well as
Joyce's view of Dublin in *Dubliners, A Portrait of the Artist as a Young Man* and *Ulysses*.
[45] Cf. T. G. Wilson, 'Oliver St John Gogarty, M.D., F.R.C.S.I.: otolaryngologist, statesman, author and poet', *Arch. Otolaryng.* **90** (Aug 1969).
[46] Cf. *A Farewell to the Senate*, anonymous pamphlet in National Library, Dublin,
probably by H. Dixon [1935/1936?], replying to an article by Gogarty in the London
Evening Standard.

poems. Gogarty's revisions, though not on the scale of those of George Moore or Yeats, do present bibliographical problems and so he is best read in this volume containing groupings which differ from the divisions made in earlier books – *Odes and Addresses*, *Earth and Sea*, *Satires and Facetiae*, *Love and Beauty*, *Life and Death*, and *Elegies*.

This would be considered a dangerous spread of subject by some of our contemporary critics, who confuse solemnity with seriousness, and yet memorable poetry does emerge from these apparently disparate *Collected Poems*. It is, perhaps, best not to discuss it here under his different headings, or even chronologically, but to consider it under three other divisions. First of all, there are the poems which we look for in any Irish writer: descriptions of actual places in Ireland. From Goldsmith to Allingham, from Yeats to Patrick Kavanagh this vein runs deeply through Irish poetry. Gogarty knew that this, however, though it be an elemental, innate part of an Irish writer's personal emotional equipment, is but one face of the coin:

> Truth to tell, there are two Irelands. One is a geographical land of beauty, the other is a state of mind. And what is so annoying is that they are for the native inextricably that.[47]

In the second category of his poetry he captures a good deal of that elusive state of mind. It is probably because he writes much of his poetry in order to portray Irish scenery and his own delight in it, and much of it to represent Irish temperament through his own ebullient *persona* that he is, to English eyes, a minor poet of the kind Yeats would have been had he ceased writing in 1899. Up till then Yeats wrote upon Irish scenery and upon beauty as seen through mists of symbolism by a sensitive but self-defeated idealistic lover. Then after 1900 he turned to the opposite extreme: political hatred, the coarse cynicism and bare negativity of a bitterly disappointed lover. But he came into his major strength once he began to combine both sides of his poetic character into the poetry written after 1917 up to his death in 1939. Gogarty, on the contrary, began from a position of balance: he wrote of places he loved, he wrote out of sensitivity or coarseness as he pleased: but like Yeats he wrote in part out of gesture, and, like Yeats, his truth came into focus when he achieved simplicity and knew rather than explored or poetically exploited himself.

Poetry written thus forms the third division of Gogarty's poetry and ultimately it is the most important. It weds a tension in its author. It has the direct speech and economy of classicism, yet it captures

---

[47] Gogarty, *Going Native* (1940) p. 14.

romantic awareness of the immediacy of life. Its basis is the realisation that 'Man is in love and loves what vanishes'. It says this, but does not add 'What more is there to say?': its romantic vocabulary, sometimes carried easily, sometimes very uneasily indeed by its classical syntax, served both the poet's objective mind as well as the emotional impulses and instincts of his human heart.

Poems of the first kind, then, are basic, and they depend, as does so much Irish poetry, upon visualisation. Gogarty recounted an early experience in school which relates to this:

> There was an essay to be written about a country fair during the writing of which I had a vision of sorts: I could see a plain with banners and many coloured pennons waving over white tents; some dim association perhaps with the sign of the Brian Boru [Inn]. I saw, although I did not realize it then, that all writing depends on seeing and then projecting the scene graphically.[48]

This power of visualising informs all his poems of place. Many of them deal with water, they reflect their subject succinctly, they are deceptively easy. Many of them people their places with the Danish invaders who were finally defeated by Brian Boru at Clontarf in 1014. Gogarty had gone to school with Tom Kettle, who regarded himself as a descendant of those Danes, but as one who had come in and stayed. As a boy Gogarty himself imagined the arrival of these invaders along the banks of the Liffey and the Tolka near his home Fairfield, originally Daneswell, at Glasnevin: later in his poetry they become symbolically part of the general corruption of the land which comes with city-dwelling. 'Liffey Bridge' catches this mood graphically:[49]

> I gazed along the waters at the West,
> Watching the low sky colour into flame,
> Until each narrowing steeple I could name
> Grew dark as the far vapours, and my breast
> With silence like a sorrow was possessed.
> And men as moving shadows went and came.
> The smoke that stained the sunset seemed like shame,
> Or lust, or some great evil unexpressed.
> Then with a longing for the taintless air,
> I called that desolation back again,

---

[48] Gogarty, *It Isn't This Time Of Year At All!*, p. 21.
[49] It also appears in 'Just One Glimpse', *Collected Poems*, p. 45, where he wants to see
> The windy oak, the wilding rose,
> Rocks, and the springs that gushed before
> The streets connected slum and store.

Cf. also 'A Double Ballad of Dublin', *Secret Springs of Dublin Song*, p. 4.

> Which reigned when Liffey's widening banks were bare;
> Before Ben Edair gazed upon the Dane,
> Before the Hurdle Ford, and long before
> Finn drowned the young men by its meadowy shore.[50]

Dublin, the town of the Ford of the Hurdles, is well sited for such a poem, for as you look down along the Liffey – away from the city set neatly and colourfully along its grey quays – to the east you see Howth, Ben Edair, the headland stretching away out into the clear distance of the unsullied sea. The connection between Howth and Dublin is stressed again in 'Fog Horns',[51] a poem which moved between contemporary steamers working slowly from the bay into the Liffey mouth and those historic Danes who 'Took a very great prey / Of women from Howth'. In 'High Tide at Malahide' he again casts before his imagination (fed with his reading for his book on St Patrick) the dramatic problem of the identity of the ships entering this estuary north of Howth:

> Oh, look at the ships
> With their sails coming down
> And the wonderful sweeps
> That are steering them still
> To the little grey town
> On the green of the hill!
> Are they Norman or Norse,
> Or descendants of Conn
> Returning in force
> From a lost British town,
> With women and loot now the Roman is gone?
> They are Norse! For the bugles are wild in the woods,
> Alarms to the farms to look after their goods:
> To bury their cauldrons and hide all their herds.
> They are Norse! I can tell by the length of their swords –
> Oh, no; by their spears and the shape of their shields
> They are Normans: the men who stand stiff in the fields
> In hedges of battle that no man may turn;
> The men who build castles that no one may burn;
> The men who give laws to the chief and the kern.
> Salt of the earth,
> Salt of the sea,
> Norman and Norse
> And the wild man in me![52]

His poems of place are often historically peopled, and 'Glenasmole',[53] the Irish name of this valley of the thrushes outside Dublin, moves

[50] Gogarty, *Collected Poems*, p. 52.   [51] Ibid., p. 90.
[52] Ibid., p. 84.   [53] Ibid., p. 70.

from description of the mild bends of the river in the valley to an ancient battle ambush. Again, 'New Bridge'[54] describes a Liffey bridge at Droichead Nua but moves into imaginings of 'The long grey lines of steel' which crossed there long ago, all colours and caparison. This poem links up with 'Portrait with Background' describing Dermot, who brought Strongbow and Henry to Ireland:

> Brought rigid law, the long spear and the horsemen
> Riding in steel; and the rhymed, romantic, high line;
> Built those square keeps on the forts of the Norsemen,
>   Still on our sky-line.[55]

Gogarty, of course, like Yeats some three years before him, had bought his Norman castle in 1920 and described with a similar admiration its limestone and accompanying water:

> The castle by the shallow ford:
>   In ruin, but the upright line
> Above the tangle keeps its word:
>   In death the unbroken discipline!
> And O, what great well-being went
> To build the enduring battlement![56]

This poetry in part is an exercise of digging into his inherited past: each image of the past has gone to his making, and peopling these places is part of a continuous process which probably owed much to Yeats's rediscovery of his own ancestors and Anglo-Irish history. Gogarty, 'the wild man' in him cut off from a fully Anglo-Irish ascendancy background or a fully native tradition, seeks kinship with Norse as well as Norman images of the past.

Within the general category of descriptive poetry Gogarty has

---

[54] Gogarty, *Collected Poems*, p. 68.

[55] Ibid., p. 157. Cf. E. Curtis, *A History of Ireland* (1936) p. 48: The dominant genius of the 'Franks' was feudal, military and romantic. They belonged to the older feudalism, which found its best expression on the borders, but which in England was bridled by the masterful genius of Henry II. In Wales they could conquer as widely as their swords, carry on private war, invade the Welsh mountaineers and divide the spoil among the barons. This was to be their spirit in Ireland. But it was something the Gaels could understand, and such men before long were to become almost as Irish as the Irish. The feudal class lived also in the tradition of the minstrels and the great *chansons de Geste* of Charlemagne, Arthur and Godfrey; it was no great step for them to delight in the music, language and ancient epics of Ireland. Nationalism was scarcely known to these men, who had come over a century ago as Frenchmen and had not yet become English. Adaptability was their genius, and proud as they were of their own blood, speech and traditions, they were ready to treat as equals any race that they could respect and freely to intermarry with it.

[56] Gogarty, *Collected Poems*, p. 73.

range and flexibility. 'Sub Ilice'[57] catches echoes of Browning's talking
aloud; 'Fresh Fields' –

> I gaze and gaze when I behold
> The meadows springing green and gold.
> I gaze until my mind is naught
> But wonderful and wordless thought!
> Till, suddenly, surpassing wit,
> Spontaneous meadows spring in it;
> And I am but a glass between
> Un-walked-in meadows, gold and green.[58]

– gives us the excitement and clarity of Marvell's 'green Thought in a
green Shade' while the mind is equally withdrawn into its happiness.
'The Phoenix' carries exuberantly lyrical Elizabethan echoes; 'The
Waveless Bay'[59] has the sure simplicity of Browning's 'Parting at
Morning':

> A long cape fades beyond the azurite
> Of one calm bay to which the pastures lean.
> The rounded fields are warm, and in between
> The yellow gorse is glaring stiff and bright.
> It matters little what distraction drives,
> Clouds through my mind and breaks the outer day.
> For all I know that distant water strives
> Against the land. I have it all my way:
> Through budding oaks a steadfast sun survives:
> Peace on the fading cape, the waveless bay.[60]

'Between Brielle and Manasquan', a romantic picture of old sea-dogs,
is paralleled by the Australian poet Kenneth Slessor's poems on retired
sailors by the shores of Sydney Harbour, by Dylan Thomas's Captain
Cat in *Under Milk Wood*. And Gogarty cannot resist an applied poem,
'The Isles of Greece':

> Marble was her lovely city
> And so pleasant was its air
> That the Romans had no pity
> For a Roman banished there;
> Lesbos was a singing island
> And a happy home from home
> With the pines about its highland
> And its crescent faint with foam.

---

[57] Ibid., p. 74.   [58] Ibid., p. 84.
[59] Mr Ulick O'Connor has told me of Gogarty's remark to AE during a burst of
sniping in Dublin: 'Don't wave at the Bay window or you may find yourself in the
Waveless Bay'.   [60] Gogarty, *Collected Poems*, p. 89.

> Lady make a nota bene
> That Love's lyric fount of glee
> Rose in marbled Mytilene
> Channelled by the purple sea.
> Sappho sang to her hetairai,
> And each lovely lyricist
> Sappho's singing emulated;
> And this point must not be missed:
> Women were emancipated
> Long before the time of Christ.
> Then not only were they equal
> To their men folk but themselves;
> And the lovely lyric sequel
> Lives on all our learned shelves.
> Yes: we may be fairly certain,
> As results of this release,
> Sappho's was, with all its Girton
> Girls, the fairest Isle of Greece.[61]

Two poems of place bridge the gap between his descriptive poems and poems of attitude, of the Irish state of mind. 'To the Liffey with Swans'[62] commemorates a famous incident in Gogarty's life as a Senator of the Irish Free State during the civil war which followed the signing of the 1922 Treaty between those who accepted the treaty's creation of the twenty-six county Free State and the extreme Republicans. Gogarty was kidnapped from his home at gunpoint in January 1923 and taken to a house by the Liffey near Chapelizod to be shot. He threw his coat over two of his captors in the darkness and hurled himself into the river, emerging lower down on the same side and, thus escaping, dedicated to the Liffey a brace of swans which he afterwards released upon the river.[63] He did his best in the creation of the new state:

> I, who must daily at enactments look
>   To make men happy by legality
> Envy the poet of that baitless hook.[64]

But there were moments, no doubt accelerated by the burning of Renvyle (and with it his books and papers and a portrait of his mother) in the civil war, when he wondered how much had been lost in the change. But the nearest he allows himself this reflection is 'The Dublin–Galway Train'[65] where the towns come sharply into focus across the

---

[61] Gogarty, *Collected Poems*, p. 87.   [62] Ibid., p. 49.
[63] Cf. Gogarty, 'They Carried Caesar', *A Week End in the Middle of the Week* (New York, 1958) pp. 65–73.
[64] Gogarty, 'Anglers', *Collected Poems*, p. 173.   [65] Ibid., p. 40.

central plain, and the train's dignity is contrasted favourably with the change brought by the closer community enforced by a joltingly democratic bus which symbolises levelling change at work in Irish life.

It is time to leave these two descriptive categories and watch Gogarty in his classico-romantic poetry, in particular in his relations to man – and woman. To the latter he is Herrick but, as George Russell suggested, perhaps more than Herrick:

> The Julia of the English poet is a lovely piece of girlhood. That is much, but she will never be more to our imagination. There is some aristocracy of vision in the Irish poet. He sees the lovely girl, but he suggests, however remotely, the psyche within the flesh. In an instant, she might be transfigured in the imagination and become the dream stuff out of which goddesses, naiads and nymphs were fashioned. That is, the images he depicts, however modern in outward fashion, are still in the divine procession and set us travelling with them to
>> 'The Perfect, the Forbidden City,
>> That's built – Ah, God knows where.'[66]

His love poems (he said 'the best poets are they who praised women best')[67] have the ease of Horace and the same amount, perhaps, of sincerity. His Ninde, Lydia, Hermione, and the rest have Horatian identity: but some poems, such as 'Back from the Country',[68] please with an affectionate note of genuine domesticity, others, like 'Golden Stockings',[69] retain the Wordsworthianly pleasure-filled poignancy of a moment's visual experience; and others again catch a deeper note

[66] AE, Preface to Gogarty, *Collected Poems*, p. xii.
[67] Gogarty, *Intimations* (1950) p. 152.   [68] Gogarty, *Collected Poems*, p. 138.
[69] Ibid., p. 160. The poem was written about the poet's daughter, who was playing in long grass at Ticknock (a hill above Dublin), and came back annoyed at the pollen from the buttercups on her shoes:

> Golden stockings you had on
> In the meadow where you ran;
> And your little knees together
> Bobbed like pippins in the weather,
> When the breezes rush and fight
> For those dimples of delight,
> And they dance from the pursuit,
> And the leaf looks like the fruit.
>
> I have many a sight in mind
> That would last if I were blind;
> Many verses I could write
> That would bring me many a sight.
> Now I only see but one
> See you running in the sun,
> And the gold-dust coming up
> From the trampled butter cup.

from Yeats; 'Thinking Long', for instance, echoes 'When You are Old and Grey'.

These two Irish poets offer many interesting parallels. Yeats's superb 'Lullaby', a poem of three stanzas of six lines each, deals with Paris, Tristram, and the Swan: Gogarty's 'Good Luck' deals in its three similar stanzas with Atalanta, Iseult, and the poet himself. The first stanzas of each poem use images of gold and red, the second both deal with the effect of the magic potion, though the third part company.

Such minor resemblances are more than fortuitous: Gogarty and Yeats were, after all, close friends. Gogarty had removed Yeats's tonsils and returned to the nursing home at frequent intervals to suggest suitable dying speeches; Gogarty was responsible for Yeats becoming a Senator; Gogarty lauded Yeats's Nobel Prize, teased 'Yeats, who says that his Castle of Ballylee is his monument'; Gogarty brought Yeats to see *his* tower; even persuaded him to fly with him but not to get on horseback. It was Gogarty who in 1937 arranged with James A. Farrell the munificent American benefaction which removed financial worries from Yeats's last years.[70] Gogarty's vitality and gay outrageous speech struck a responsive chord from the older poet, who saw in him a swash-buckling cavalier, learned in the classics yet a man of action: gay, stoical, and heroic.[71] And from Yeats Gogarty said he had learned something of poetry.

Small wonder, then, that phrases constantly echo between their work in the twenties and thirties. Dublin literary gossip has long held that Yeats rewrote many of Gogarty's poems (Johnson's reputation towered over Goldsmith's in a similar way and it was not at first thought that Goldsmith's poetry was his own), but Professor Giorgio Melchiori is writing a book on Yeats which argues that Gogarty supplied ideas which Yeats developed in several poems.[72]

For instance, Gogarty developed a strong interest in the myth of

[70] Cf. WBY, *Letters on Poetry to Dorothy Wellesley* (1940) p. 140.

[71] Mr Vivian Mercier comments in 'Oliver St John Gogarty', *Poetry*, XCIII i (Oct 1958) p. 35, that Yeats when describing Gogarty's work as 'heroic' seemed 'unaware just how much Gogarty traded in Greek and Roman cliché'. Yeats was content to search through many careless verses for what was excellent because he saw in Gogarty a living and articulate hero. Robert Gregory became a hero in Yeats's private mythology, but by dying abroad on active service; whereas Gogarty succeeded him by, like Horace, escaping to live and talk. Gregory had been 'our Sydney'; Gogarty had equally Elizabethan 'pride and joy'.

[72] Mr Ulick O'Connor thinks that Gogarty returned to classical sources in the twenties; he certainly discussed mythology with Yeats when he was immersed in writing *A Vision*. And a recent thesis on Gogarty, written by Mr D. J. Huxley for an M.A. degree at the University of Sheffield, has drawn on the fact that the contents of the first and second

Leda and the Swan after his dedication of the swans to the Liffey. That dedication – and the poem – had had a touch of d'Annunzio. The poem ended:

> As fair as was that doubled Bird,
> By love of Leda so besotten,
> That she was all with wonder stirred,
> And the Twin Sportsmen were begotten![73]

But Gogarty's 'Leda and the Swan', delicately witty, whimsically ironic, extends this idea:

> When the hyacinthine
> Eggs were in the basket,
> Blue as at the whiteness
> Where a cloud begins;
> Who would dream there lay there
> All that Trojan brightness;
> Agamemnon murdered;
> And the mighty Twins?[74]

According to Professor Melchiori, this is derived from Yeats's 'Leda and the Swan':

> a shudder in the loins engenders there
> The broken wall, the burning roof and tower
> And Agamemnon dead.[75]

But Gogarty's long, tender, yet satiric portrait of an innocently tomboyish 'Europa and the Bull'[76] seems only to have touched off two lines in Yeats: 'Great Europa played the fool / That changed a lover for a bull.'[77] Again, there are links between the last stanza of Gogarty's 'With a Coin from Syracuse'[78] (the whole poem is itself related subtly to Yeats's poem 'Parnell's Funeral'[79] with its Sicilian coin image) and Yeats's 'To a Young Girl', where

> . . . the wild thought
> That she denies
> And has forgot
> Set all her blood astir
> And glittered in her eyes.[80]

---

editions of Gogarty's volume *An Offering of Swans* differ considerably to suggest other links between the poets' work, as well as postulating Gogarty's likely discussion of the Sophocles plays with Yeats before the First World War. (See J. M. Hone, *W. B. Yeats, 1865–1939*, p. 256, and *Letters*, ed. Wade, p. 537, in this connection.) It is to be hoped that Mr Huxley will publish his views on the literary relationships of Gogarty and Yeats in the near future. [73] Gogarty, *Collected Poems*, p. 49. [74] Ibid., p. 144.
[75] WBY, *Collected Poems* (1933) p. 241. [76] Gogarty, *Collected Poems*, p. 112.
[77] WBY, 'Crazy Jane Reproved', *Collected Poems* (1933) p. 291.
[78] Gogarty, *Collected Poems*, p. 153.
[79] WBY, *Collected Poems* (1933) p. 319. [80] Ibid., p. 157.

Gogarty re-creates the idea in

> Straight in the back and bone,
> With head high like her own,
> And blood that, tamed and mild,
> Can suddenly go wild.

'Limestone and Water' achieves the dignity of Yeats's simple yet
majestic descriptions of his own tower; and there are many other verbal
echoes, and images shared. Because the men were friends; because, too,
Dublin had the essential requirement for a literary renaissance. It was a
society small enough for knowledge and skill to be shared among the
elect, where literary personality could prevail within its own right: an
appreciative yet critical audience which knew and was known by its
writers. It appreciated rhetoric used as gesture, and this, ultimately, was
what Gogarty shared with Yeats.

'Myself must I remake', cried the older poet, as an old man. This
malleability of character, arising in part from a desire for privacy of
personality, begot Yeats's theory of the masks about 1909. But it was
no new theory. More than a century earlier Goldsmith had put it to the
test: he chose the mask of laughing at himself, and so others took him
at his own valuation, failing to realise his loneliness, his seriousness of
purpose, and the thwarted and paradoxical fear of being thought to
take himself too seriously. Yeats's greatness lay in his taking himself as
poet entirely seriously[81] and learning to project himself in this role.
Gogarty, however, followed Goldsmith: both men, perhaps because
of their medical education, did not share Yeats's need to strike throughout his life self-encouraging gestures in the face of death. Both lived
perhaps more in the present than Yeats: whose muse was old when he
was young, whose body aged before his desires. Both, moreover, believed in meeting life half-way, and in putting a gay face upon the mask
with which they met it. Gogarty defended such an attitude strongly:

> if you take life too seriously it will make you serious about everything, trivi-
> alities included. Life is plastic: it will assume any shape you choose to put upon
> it. It is in your power to take things cheerfully and be merry and bright even
> though you are surrounded by melancholics who cannot imagine anyone
> being good unless he is unhappy. They equate goodness with unhappiness as
> some ladies in great cities equate culture with seriousness.[82]

---

[81] His comment on Gogarty's poetry in his Introduction to the Cuala Press edition of
Gogarty's *Wild Apples* (1930) indicates the difference he saw between their work, perhaps
that between the professional and the amateur: 'Oliver Gogarty is a careless writer often
writing first drafts of poems rather than poems but often with animation and beauty.'
[82] Gogarty, *It Isn't This Time Of Year At All!*, p. 11.

After Yeats's death in January 1939 Gogarty began his 'Elegy on the Death of the Archpoet' which sums up the worst of death as the loss of friends, places Yeats with his other lost friends and muses on his own coming death:

> Now you are gone beyond the glow
> As muted as a world of snow;
> And I am left amid the scene
> Where April comes new drenched in green,
> To watch the budding trees that grow
> And cast, where quiet waters flow,
> Their hueless patterns below;
> And think upon the clear bright rill
> That lulled your garden on the hill;
> And wonder when shall I be made
> Like you, beyond the stream, a shade.

Gogarty has probably eluded serious critical attention because of this habit of being gay about matters in which he felt deeply. (He was once called 'a lazy body' in the Senate by a Minister, but the Minister wisely did not take up Gogarty's newspaper challenge to a competition in running, swimming and flying an aeroplane.) This paradoxical side of him, perhaps based on a mixture of energy and contemplation, emerged in his epigram 'To Petronius Arbiter':

> Proconsul of Bithynia,
> Who loved to turn the night to day,
> Yet for your ease had more to show
> Than others for their push and go,
> Teach us to save the Spirit's expense,
> And win to Fame through indolence.

Gogarty was not solemn: he hated to run the risk of boring by portentousness. The solution lay for him in a quicksilver mind, in a cavalier attitude: it naturally demanded that he write with ease:

> No wonder Pegasus cast a shoe
> When I succumbed to the English curse
> Of mixing philosophy up with verse.
> I can imagine a poet teaching;
> But who can imagine a poet preaching?[83]

Nothing there to indicate a man who strove for his patients, exercised his ingenuity in providing unusual hospitality for his guests, put his energies into entertaining and amusing his fellows – a role understood by Goldsmith but perhaps not yet generally appreciated as one demand-

---

[83] Gogarty, 'The Forge', *Collected Poems*, p. 35.

ing personal sacrifice on the part of the entertainer and the wit. Nothing to indicate the man who tried incessantly, though without the success he would have liked, to educate what he called the 'mounted-beggar' race of Dublin into the supreme delight of generosity, of recognition of genius. All that is to be taken for granted. Then only will we realise that Gogarty would have wished to operate surgically on his losses when he advised having nothing to do with those to whom you will always seem to be bad:

> and its no use trying to appease them. . . . Have nothing to do with them if you
> want to lead a good life that is a merry one: 'For only the good are merry.'[84]

This attitude may sometimes have concealed only too successfully the very real generosity in the man who writes with Elizabethan ease and appreciation 'To A.E. Going to America':

> Dublin transmits you, famous, to the West.
>   America shall welcome you, and we,
>   Reflected in that mighty glass, shall see,
> In full proportion, power at which we guessed:
> We live too near the eagle and the nest
>   To know the pinion's wide supremacy:
>   But yours, of all the wings that crossed the sea,
> Carries the wisest heart and gentlest.
>   It is not multitudes, the Man's idea
> Makes a place famous. Though you now digress,
>   Remember to return as, back from Rome,
>   Du Bellay journeyed to his Lyrè home;
> And Plutarch, willingly, to Chæronea
> Returned, and stayed, lest the poor town be less.[85]

It is an attitude which permits much flexibility, which allows him to write with metaphysical casualness 'To the Fixed Stars':

> Even the primordial Dark that once
>   Engendered light, nor growth debars,
> Is phosphorescent with dead suns,
>   And pregnant with the dust of stars.[86]

It is an attitude, too, which encouraged him to construct strong lines:

> Then do not shudder at the knife
>   That Death's indifferent hand drives home,
> But with the Strivers leave the Strife,
>   Nor, after Caesar, skulk in Rome.[87]

---

[84] Gogarty, *It Isn't This Time Of Year At All!*, p. 11.
[85] Gogarty, *Collected Poems*, p. 25.   [86] Ibid., p. 12.   [87] Ibid., p. 192.

He had learned to write English in classical metres, sapphics and anapaests particularly; his classical training had taught him to watch his endings; his cadences are often superb; his architectonic skill can be forced into giving scope for discursive playing with his subject in longer poems like 'Leda and the Swan', 'Europa and the Bull',[88] and 'The Mill at Naul'. This wit can successfully adopt the tone of earlier poets, as in the seventeenth-century wit of 'Begone, sweet Ghost, O get you gone! / Or haunt me with your body on.'[89] And all because he saw his poetry as a gesture. Count Mirabel in Disraeli's *Sybil* was equally careless of the dullards with his gay *Vive la Bagatelle*, his advice to take care of the circulation. Mr Ulick O'Connor's sympathetic biography[90] has shown Gogarty walking the wards as well as Sackville Street and in this admirable book his serious outlook on life emerges. This is the real justification for taking his poetry equally seriously, with all the virtues which can emerge when this kind of versatile renaissance man speaks directly out of sentiment, not sentimentality. The proper parallel is with Goldsmith's realisation in *The Deserted Village* that he would never achieve his desire of returning home to Ireland; for this poem allows the essential Goldsmith to speak out of heartfelt sentiment. Yeats achieved this kind of clarity in the last few poems he wrote in which he simply saw the actions and ideas of his life clearly and finally before him, asked himself the point of it all, and said he knew no answer to what lay beyond his approaching death. What is interesting in Gogarty is that this, the testing kind of clarity, has an innate gentleness. This is what he would have wished as epitaph, to be considered as his intimates described him: 'A gentle man on Earth / And gentle 'mid the Shades.'[91] This quality emerges very clearly in the poem 'Death May be Very Gentle':

> Death may be very gentle after all:
> He turns his face away from arrogant knights
> Who fling themselves against him in their fights;
> But to the loveliest he loves to call.
> And he has with him those whose ways were mild
> And beautiful; and many a little child.[92]

It is not altogether unexpected, if we concede that ultimately, beneath the persiflage, and permitting its airy heights, there was, and had to be,

---

[88] Mr Ulick O'Connor considers the Leda poem derived from Ovid, the Europa poem from Moschus.   [89] Gogarty, *Collected Poems*, p. 137.
[90] *Oliver St John Gogarty: A Poet and His Times* (1965). The sub-title is appropriate.
[91] Gogarty, 'Palinode', *Collected Poems*, p. 186.
[92] Gogarty, 'Death May be Very Gentle', *Collected Poems*, p. 192.

as basis, a bedrock of belief. This is what causes Gogarty to rise above
mere cliché when he advances the equable acceptance of death; it en-
courages him to applaud and appreciate, and in so doing to seem (even
in an angry age) a very memorable minor poet indeed:

> I, as the Wise Ones held of old,
>   Hold there's an Underworld to this;
> And do not fear to be enrolled
>   In Death's kind metamorphosis.
>
> More wonderful than China's halls
>   To Polo; more than all the West
> That shone through the confining walls
>   When great Magellan made the quest.
>
> Enlarged and free, the wings of Rhyme
>   Cannot outreach its purple air;
> The generations of all Time
>   And all the lovely Dead are there.[93]

[93] Gogarty, 'Sunt apud infernos tot milia formosarum', *Collected Poems*, p. 190.

Index